Righteous Content

PRE

RELIGION, RACE, AND ETHNICITY
General Editor: Peter J. Paris

Righteous Content

Black Women's Perspectives of Church and Faith

Daphne C. Wiggins

NEW YORK UNIVERSITY PRESS
New York and London

NEW YORK UNIVERSITY PRESS
New York and London
www.nyupress.org

Library of Congress Cataloging-in-Publication Data
Wiggins, Daphne C.
Righteous content : Black women's perspectives of
church and faith / Daphne C. Wiggins.
p. cm.
Includes bibliographical references and index.
ISBN 0–8147–9391–6 (cloth : alk. paper)
1. African American women—Religion.
2. African American women—Religious life.   I. Title.
BR563.N4W493   2004
277.3'0082—dc22   2004015441

New York University Press books are printed on acid-free paper,
and their binding materials are chosen for strength and durability.

Manufactured in the United States of America

10 9 8 7 6 5 4 3 2

*I dedicate this book
to two very gracious women of God:
my mother, Mrs. Thelma G. Wiggins,
and the Reverend Mildred L. Stanford,
a dedicated minister and dear friend,
who departed this life before she
could see this work in print.*

Contents

Acknowledgments

My deepest appreciation is extended to all persons and institutions that assisted me in bringing this book to completion. In its earlier stages, I received support from the Fund for Theological Education, American Baptist Churches, USA, and from the Louisville Institute for the Study of Protestantism and American Culture. The Junior Scholars Grant of the Southwest Commission on Religious Studies and the Wabash Summer Grant provided more resources so that I could complete a second round of interviews and research the impact of women's ministries on the church. These institutions also provided opportunities for sharing of research, mentoring of junior scholars, and career networking. I am especially grateful to Jim Lewis, of the Louisville Institute, and Lucinda Huffaker, of the Wabash Center, for the consultations and mentoring events that these agencies provide.

I owe a debt of gratitude to my former colleagues in the Religion Department at Texas Christian University and at the Divinity School at Duke. My colleagues at TCU were unmatched for their collegiality. The rigorous scholarship of my Duke colleagues enhanced my own grasp of the power of scholarship to impact spiritual formation and its importance for theological education.

There are many other friends, beyond colleagues in those departments, who impacted the text by impacting my life. The members of the yearlong Mining the Mother Lode Workshop taught me in various ways what it means to come into one's own voice in teaching and scholarship. The 2001 class of Wabash Summer Teaching Fellows demonstrated high levels of creativity in their teaching and how to integrate scholarship into the classroom. Both colloquiums also were occasions for many coffee-cup conversations about teaching, scholarship, the academy, and professional development.

I must acknowledge separately a few colleagues: Nancy Ammerman, who provided me my first opportunity as a researcher; Cheryl Townsend Gilkes, whose expertise on women in the Black Church spurs me on; and the Womanist Approaches to the Study of Religion and Culture Consultation, where I sat with and learned with the scholars who are defining womanist scholarship. I have had some exceptional friends whom I could call at odd times. They encouraged and prayed for me, finetuned some of my ideas, and kept nudging me by asking for the first autographed copy. Thanks to Jim Hunt, Cheryl Gooden, Debra King, Marsha Woodard, Robert Russell, Florence Simmons, and Harry Williams for their friendship. With these professors, ministers, and friends I often talked less about the actual manuscript, but they were invaluable in assisting me to assess the impact of the process of writing on my life.

This book would never have happened without the support of my family and my church home, Union Baptist Church. I have learned anew the truth that we all rest on someone else's shoulders. I must acknowledge the thirty-eight women who let me enter their lives for a time and who unashamedly shared their love of God and regard for the church. When I doubted whether this volume would ever be completed, their words compelled me to tell their story and taught me what an honor it is to be trusted with the interior spaces of others' lives.

I would also like to thank Dana Povonavich, for her meticulous editing of the manuscript, and Jennifer Hammer, my editor at New York University Press, for her guidance and persistence in this process.

Introduction

Hearing from the Sisters

Enter most African American congregations and you are likely to see male pastors standing before predominantly female audiences. This pattern has been characteristic of the Black Church since the late nineteenth century.[1] Female-majority congregations in America were evident among New England Puritans even earlier, beginning in the midseventeenth century.[2] Throughout the eighteenth century, the increase in female membership was so pronounced in "mainline" Protestantism that American Christianity became characterized as sentimentalized, feminized, and domesticated.[3] The historian Ann Douglas attributes this change to the disestablishment of Protestantism in the colonies. With the tie between church and state legally severed, Christianity's influence on the public was diminished. Markedly fewer men entered the clergy, financial support for the church decreased, women's role in the economic and intellectual spheres declined, theology responded more to domestic issues than public matters, and men became increasingly absent from church participation. This trend, which began in the pre-Revolution era, was a fixture of American Protestant liberalism by the end of the nineteenth century. The Black Church would manifest the same phenomenon of male absenteeism throughout the twentieth century, albeit for different reasons.

The Black Church of the twenty-first century is similar to, yet distinct from, white Protestantism in regard to gender participation. Like its white counterpart, it attracts a large female constituency, depends upon voluntary female labor, has a male-dominated clergy, and affirms traditional sex roles as biblically sanctioned in much of its preaching. It also shares common theological elements, denominationally specific liturgical styles, and a range of polity structures with mainline denominations. The uniqueness of the Black Church can be found in its social origins and in its commitment to a liberating theology that seeks to transform individuals spiritually and to respond to the existential and material conditions of African Americans and the larger society. While a few black congregations were in existence prior to the Revolutionary War, African Americans established their first denominations in the early nineteenth century. These first ecclesiastical bodies, the African Methodist Episcopal Church and the African Methodist Episcopal Zion Church, grew steadily and were augmented by the founding of state and national Baptist conventions in the latter part of the century.

The Black Church is often discussed as if it's a singular institution or a monolithic gathering of faceless people. In reality, its story is in fact that of the many denominations and female-dominated fellowships dedicated to the construction and maintenance of a sacred world for African Americans. Whether in their roles as soloists, ushers, nurses, church mothers, Sunday school teachers, missionaries, pastor's aides, deaconesses, stewardesses, or prayer warriors, women are at the core of the Black Church, which could not exist without them. This reality is often eclipsed by the emphasis on the preaching and visionary tasks that define the pastoral office, which males have dominated.

How do we explain the dedication of African American women to the church, particularly when it seems that men dominate the formal clergy leadership roles? Historians locate their answers in the social, political, and economic antecedents that propelled the church into its position as an institution uniquely situated to attract female loyalty. As an interdisciplinarian and a sociologist, I approach female participation by analyzing contemporary cultural values, religious sensibilities, and behaviors. My starting presupposition is that institutions extract loyalty from their members because they satisfactorily meet the primary needs of their constituency. These needs may be verbalized or unarticulated. One may ask, what cultural and spiritual needs are met for women within these institutions? How have women created and participated in this multidimensional sacred world? How do we explain the esteem church women have for the church? These questions led me to examine the faithfulness of these church women.

This book explores the religiosity of black women. It chronicles and interprets aspects of their religious lives, bringing to the fore the behaviors and beliefs of the female membership of black churches as few texts have done. Let me offer a word about the term "religiosity." This term has been used synonymously with "religious involvement," "religious commitment," and "religiousness" in scholarly literature. It is sometimes used interchangeably with "spirituality" in popular trade books. Sociologists have not agreed upon a unitary definition for this concept, although the interest in religiosity has steadily increased since Joseph Fitcher, in 1951, provided one of the first schemas for categorizing the ways people practice their faith in a study that examined Catholics.[4] Those dimensions have been expanded and more definitive models developed. Today, the study of religiosity has developed from doctrinal and unifocal measures to ones that are more complex. Scholars no longer presume a normative religious loyalty of Americans. They attend to the particularity of populations and use multidimensional measures in their quantitative analyses.[5] Qualitative studies of religiosity have also increased, using methods such as interviews and participant observation. Our increasing awareness of living in a religiously plural nation and postmodern society has directed attention to the religiosity of baby boomers, generation Xers, and adherents of Native American, Eastern, and New Age religions, as well as the enduring mainline denominations.

I define "religiosity" as *an individual's beliefs and behaviors in relation to/on behalf of the supernatural, as well as the consequences of these aspects upon that individual.* Religiosity does not have to be confined to persons who participate in an institutional context, but, in this study, I limit myself to persons active in congregational life. Moreover, all the women in this study would define "the supernatural" as God. I utilize the term "religiosity" over the more popular term "spirituality" because the latter has come to denote a religious quest by those who have defected from or resist institutionalized religion, traditional rituals, or theological positions of established denominations.

The population for this study was not national. I focused on women in two of the largest denominations that make up the Black Church. These women provide us with a slice of black religion and a lens through which to understand the Black Church at the turn of the twenty-first century. They give us a glimpse of devout congregants in their diversity and unity.

I intentionally studied a small sample, as to garner qualitative depth in my data gathering, rather than mere volume. All of the participants lived in Georgia at the time of the research, although some were not born in the South. They have been Christians and in their respective congregations for various lengths of time. Some began attending "in their mother's womb," while others had been at their current church only a few months when I interviewed them. They are women who allowed me to share their personal and religious lives through worship, meetings, and semistructured interviews. I worshipped with these women and absorbed the religious culture of their congregations. Pastors granted me interviews and access to worship services, Bible studies, auxiliary meetings, church records, and, most important, church members. With unusual candor and little hesitation, these women opened their lives and spiritual worldviews to me, inviting me into their homes for protracted interviews and sometimes confiding to me personal experiences and religious perspectives of the church they had kept to themselves.

These women are our entry into the world of the Black Church and their own religious worlds, particularly the theological, psychological, ethical, and ritual dimensions. Some of my conclusions about African American female religiosity and the church are not surprising. For instance, these women constituted the majority of the volunteer labor, supported the church financially, and were the inspiration and creative force behind many programs and ministries in the church. The majority of the women were also actively involved in the church beyond Sunday morning attendance, whether or not they held formal positions of leadership. For all of them, their relationship with Jesus was central to their self-understanding and their religiosity, and the primary medium of this Christ-centered faith was the preaching moment during worship.

Along with these expected findings, I discovered important, less-acknowledged aspects of female piety and women's relationship to the church. I found that the ethical dimension of their faith required care for their families, church members, themselves, and their racial and geographic communities. There was also some consensus among them about which ritual aspects of the service were paramount for their own growth and which aspects were dispensable. On the issue of pastors, it became clear that these women were not blind followers of male clerics, as they have sometimes been stereotyped, but maintained malleable expectations of pastoral leadership in tension with theological understandings of human frailty. Furthermore, in spite of its limitations and fallibility, the church was the place from which these women drew spiritual sustenance for handling personal and societal challenges such as marital strife, racism, infertility, and health concerns.

A Necessary Text

Why write a book centered on the lives of black church women? The quick answer is because it's long overdue. What can we expect to mine from the analysis of women's actions and views of the church? We can expect a realistic portrait and analysis of what lived religion is among black women and within the Black Church. This text helps us interpret the significance of faith in God and church participation at a time when many are turning to more individualistic pursuits of spirituality. The interior experience of religion is a real, yet intangible force that forms and transforms individual lives and affects entire communities. Pastors, lay workers, scholars who theorize about the salient qualities of religious faith, students of feminist and womanist approaches to religion, and Christian women will find this text useful for their own analyses of the Black Church. It will also be a resource for understanding gender dimensions of faith and one's own religious experiences and for assessing American religion in the new millennium.

This book is the result of many different motivations coming together. One impetus emerged from my review, during graduate study, of the social-scientific literature on female church participation. Three interpretive frameworks have dominated the explanations for female participation: psychological theories, socialization theories, and structural location theories.[6] Each helps clarify the motivations and behaviors of female adherents on a macrolevel, but each also tends to treat women as a monolithic group. Differences between white and black Christians—in participation rates and political activism, for example—have been established in several studies, as have contrasts between male and female religiosity.[7] The explanations for racial as well as gender differences still need further refinement and attention. One cannot preemptively assume that black women's religious practices and experiences parallel those of white females or carry the same import for them. We need to look more closely at the impact of social, economic, and cultural contexts on the shape of women's religiosity. Failure to do so reinforces the presumption of a universal women's experience.

Another impetus for this study was the fact that the history of American Protestantism has given only limited attention to the Black Church and its contributions. The history of American religion has been an imbalanced study of the trends, contributions, and theologies of mainline (white) denominations. This dominance in religious scholarship creates the perception that white religious experience is the normative standard for evaluating religion's impact on American culture, society, politics, and values, as well as the regard devotees have for the church. Black religious culture should not be regarded as marginal to the religious landscape or as a simple replication of white Protestantism. There are many research areas that could be enriched by regarding black church women as resources for interpreting the state of American Protestantism. Individual quests for spirituality, increases and declines in church attendance, the church's support of "family values," the role of women in pulpits, and the impact of feminist and womanist rhetoric upon parishioners are a few of these areas.

A third reason for my attraction to the study of the faith and faithfulness of this cohort was my desire to bring to the fore the voices of black women in the growing corpus of historical and sociological studies on the Black Church. In some ways, this text asserts the obvious—that religion is important to black women. However, we do not know much about the reasons for this centrality. There is a paucity of scholarship about the significance of faith practices among African American church women. Major studies of the Black Church conspicuously disregard these women's religious contributions and experience. Scholars have relied upon male clerics to interpret the contributions, activities, and ministry of the church. The pastor's role on behalf of others and the community and the societal impact of specific congregations has been the focus of congregational studies, not the church women's perspectives or contributions.[8] Such works have made valuable contributions to our understanding of the institutional, ideological, theological, and cultural parameters of the Black Church. However, reliance on male pastors and documentary evidence increases the probability that certain problems will occur, such as omitting women's contributions from the official records of churches and equating the pastor's assessments of church life and mission with the membership's perspectives. The denial of the role of lay women as religious agents, cultural carriers, transmitters, and interpreters of the Black Church is another potential problem.

These problems can be diminished when we expand our conception of who can speak on behalf of the church and regard the oral histories and narratives of church members as texts that have merit and authenticity alongside written sources. Laity in general, and women in particular, have been treated as passive followers, rather than as creative agents who think and act independent of the pastor or as persons who contribute to the genius of the church. By acknowledging women's perspectives and actions on behalf of the church, we gain not only data that help us interrogate or expand established conclusions about the Black Church but also a different lens through which to see the salience of religion for American women.

This research project emerges out of observations and changes I have experienced in black Baptist churches. For the past decade, there has been an intensified interest in many Baptist congregations (as well as other denominations) in the economic and social oppression of African American men. Rather than giving equal attention to the plight of black men and black women, resources and discourses often focus on men. I have had repeated conversations with black male clerics who have expressed significant concern about the paucity of black men among their members. Some have responded programmatically in their churches with an intentional evangelistic outreach toward unaffiliated black men. Their comments imply a belief that more is required to attract and keep men in the church than is required for women. In addition, the church assumes women's continued presence and support; thus, no parallel outreach is needed.

Male clergy assume that women's participation suggests their concerns are satisfactorily addressed and that the church is faring well by this constituency. This perception, however, might be only part of the truth. The present emphasis in many black congregations on why men aren't in the church makes it too easy to fail to ask why women are. The inattention to why women attend church presumes that women will always be present and the backbone of the church. With the constant stream of new female replacements, insufficient attention is given to this dominant constituency. At a time when thousands of women fill stadiums to hear Bishop T. D. Jakes's message of spiritual and emotional healing, it is too easy to perpetuate the myth that black women are an undifferentiated and uncritical faithful mass.[9] This book provides contemporary data to evaluate that depiction of female religiosity. It also gives us an "ordinary" woman's perspective of recent changes in black churches, such as the increasing number of female ministers.

Lay women have rarely been given the opportunity to discuss their commitment to and perceptions of the church. Admittedly, a sample of thirty-eight persons does not capture all there is to learn about church women; yet, we can learn from this diverse group of women. Their narratives expand our existing knowledge concerning female attendance and about why women demonstrate great loyalty to the church in the midst of increasing secularization.[10] Their stories recount the resources the church provides for parishioners, spiritually and instrumentally. They also reveal the dimensions of the church that are most life-enhancing and vital for them. In addition, they reveal their understanding of and their hopes for the Black Church.

Righteous Discontent

The religiosity of black women has been the subject of some recent notable texts. Cheryl Townsend Gilkes's *If It Wasn't for the Women*, Kesho Yvonne Scott's *The Habit of Surviving*, Marcia Riggs's *Can I Get a Witness?*, Emilie Townes's *Embracing the Spirit*, Gloria Wade-Gayles's *My Soul Is a Witness*, Delores Williams's *Sisters in the Wilderness*, N. Lynne Westfield's *Dear Sisters*, and Marla Frederick's *Between Sundays: Black Women and Everyday Struggles of Faith* are just some of the notable works.[11] These texts, along with an increasing corpus of essays, have laid a foundation for this study in many ways. They give visibility to women's historic roles as cocreators of the institutional and religious culture of the church. They also challenge scholars and practitioners to examine anew what is regarded as religious work, how women invoke the presence of God in worship and how spiritual formation has been a central resource for the survival of African American women and their communities. I build upon this foundation, analyzing recent data to affirm, critique, and expand existing interpretations of female religiosity. This text contributes the perspectives of women who continue to live the intersections of race, gender, and religion everyday, while seeking to respond with integrity and faith.

One work in particular merits discussion as a foundation for the present book. It has been a decade since Evelyn Brooks Higginbotham's *Righteous Discontent: The Women's Movement in the Black Baptist Church, 1880–1920*, was released. It received critical acclaim from the scholarly community. The book provides a thorough historical analysis of black women's power within the Baptist church and their impact on the discourse within the National Baptist Convention, USA. Higginbotham filled a gap in Black Church and women's studies scholarship by documenting the work and the theological commitments of church women at the turn of the twentieth century. She demonstrates persuasively how the

Baptist church functioned as a public space and the breadth of the discourses that have taken place therein. We also learn about the intersection of class and race among church women. As these women worked for the alleviation of dire poverty and social conditions, they also practiced a "politics of respectability."[12]

Higginbotham narrates a story of a formidable group of women, ones who were not subservient to the men who held office in the parent body. Rather, they were a distinguished group of women, many formally educated, who had proven their commitment to the well-being of women and to African Americans. Through their service in state mission associations, they fought against injustice within the church and in society. They worked with twentieth-century feminists and reformers but did not develop alliances with every cause; they carefully assessed which causes, religious or secular, would further the struggle for full enfranchisement and economic and social equality for African Americans.

These women defined their own brand of feminist theology, although twenty-first-century sensibilities might judge it as not very revolutionary. They did not endorse the publication of the Women's Bible, in 1895.[13] They were not as strident as later feminists and womanists voices would be concerning female clergy and ordination. Members of the National Baptist Women's Convention believed that women had the capacity to influence men and that they must use that power of persuasiveness positively. While they emphasized that women needed to be of high moral stature to exert their influence and embraced some aspects of Victorian womanhood, they did not install the black woman on a pedestal. Motherhood was honorable but clearly not every woman's destiny, a point supported by biblical women who were loyal to Jesus and the early church. In their eyes, women were not innately weak or subject to temptation. Just as men and women were linked in the downfall of humanity, so are they partners in the salvation of humanity. Men are charged by God not to dominate women but to work with them. Women are capable of work in the public sphere.

Higginbotham also documents the breadth of women's work. Efforts were not confined to the church; rather, women were committed personally and as an auxiliary to charitable philanthropic work and to advocacy for women's opportunities for training and employment. This was no small feat at a time when an overwhelming number of black women were domestic workers or still engaged in sharecropping. They were agents of critique and change; yet, they also accepted contemporary ideas that women and men are inherently different and possess unique traits. Living at the intersections of racial and gender oppression, women regarded themselves, and African Americans in general, as having a special role to play in America's future. They were moral exemplars to the nation. To counter negative stereotypes and to demonstrate the industriousness of women, they created training opportunities to prove the desire for improvement and the industriousness of blacks.

Notwithstanding the labor and direction they contributed on behalf of blacks, these women had to strive to be heard within their own denomination and as part of a larger gender discourse; they had to compete with the attention suffragists were garnering for women's voting rights. Women fought for a separate domain where they could exercise authority and control finances. Yet, deference to male authority was inherent in many of their actions and proposals for racial uplift. *Righteous Discontent* shows us the agency and impact of black church women's work. It also reveals the tensions and opposition women encountered in negotiating multiple oppressions. Higginbotham argues that, while these women never altered the hierarchical structure of the church, they refused to accept sexism; they created other spheres of influence, rather than restructure the existent ones.

Righteous Content examines the religious lives, perspectives, and involvement of African American women today. It is not a replication of Higginbotham's study. Rather, I suggest that the two texts may be seen as a pair of bookends. The first text reveals women's religious commitments and agency at the beginning of the twentieth century. The current one engages black women's religiosity at the turn of the next century. A century has passed since the formative years of the National Baptist Women's Convention. Then, women such as S. Willie Layten, Virginia W. Broughton, Mary V. Cook, Lucy Wilmot Smith, Susie C. Foster, and Nannie Helen Burroughs articulated the need for a theology that responded to the concerns of African Americans more inclusively. What differences in the Black Church and black women's roles might we identify a century later? Higginbotham focuses on one denomination. My curiosity was piqued, and I determined to identify the aspects of women's religiosity that traverse denominational boundaries. The church is presented by Higginbotham as a domain for social change, a space where women had a keen awareness of the critical role it could play in racial uplift. My interest is in whether that same awareness and passion are the determinants of women's ongoing loyalty to the Black Church. Black Baptist women did not advocate for the denomination to include women in the ranks of the clergy. Has the situation changed significantly within the Black Church, and what part have lay women accepted in that struggle? Higginbotham focuses on the official leaders and persons of influence within the denomination. I provide a contrast by conversing with lay women whose names might not ever be called at a church convention. Finally, *Righteous Discontent* argues that women were unsettled about the state of affairs in their denomination and churches. As I collected and analyzed the *Righteous Content* of these women, I found evidence of a different resolve.

Design of the Book

This book is composed of the results of semistructured interviews and field research I completed within two Protestant congregations in a metropolitan area of Georgia. One congregation was dually aligned with the National Baptist Convention, USA, Inc., and the Southern Baptist Convention. The other was a member of the Church of God in Christ (COGIC). I selected congregations within historically black denominations, since African American Christians overwhelmingly hold membership in these religious bodies. My selection of congregations was also based upon the satisfaction of several parameters characteristic of a "typical" Black Church and their congruence with the cultural norms of African American churches. The primary criterion was a multigenerational, female-dominated membership of approximately two hundred to five hundred persons. The size range reflected the average size of black religious congregations nationally.[14] It also increased the possibility that the church would have a greater offering of ministry options that met members' needs across the different stages of the life cycle. I sought multigenerational congregations to increase the probability that I would be able to locate women with faith commitments and church experience of different lengths. Organizationally, I looked for consistency in the offering of worship services and teaching opportunities. Each church had Sunday services and at least one other weekly scheduled teaching or worship event.

I considered several other factors, as well. I selected congregations where the pastor had a tenure of four years or more and was involved in the community on behalf of the church, reflecting the historic role of the black preacher as community advocate and activist.[15] I decided upon congregations that had manifested stability in their leadership, ruling out those that had an interim pastor, those in which the pastor had recently departed, or those in which a pastoral search process was under way. Admittedly, longevity does not necessarily reflect a socially engaged ministry or an effective pastorate; it could indicate sheer tenacity and perseverance. However, choosing churches with pastors of considerable tenure allowed me to be sure that the churches had the stability necessary to enable me to assess the qualities women seek in a pastor.

The clear demarcation and teaching of gender role ideology in the church was given less significance. Every church explicitly and implicitly socializes its members into gender roles, constructing and reinforcing them through the church's rhetoric, symbols, and structure (what it says and does and how). It was my assumption that, in churches with clearly defined gender roles and expectations, I would find greater conformity to these roles. Where the gender constructions for men and women were less pronounced or more liberally defined, I expected to encounter greater flexibility of roles.

I recorded and transcribed the interviews with women from both churches and administered a survey to both congregations. The interviews focused on women's religious socialization and degree of involvement, the function and mission of the church, the division of labor, concepts of God and church, and the rewards of church affiliation. There were subthemes related to these areas, and other topics were probed as they emerged in our interviews and worship times. These pages do not contain all of their responses; neither are all the women's responses to any one question included. The quotations cited throughout the text have been chosen for their representation of the whole group or to illustrate the diversity of perceptions and faith experiences within this population.

This book is divided into seven chapters. Chapter 1 introduces the women and describes how they became participants in church during their formative years. I examine aspects of their religious socialization such as the role of family, community norms, and peer pressure. I discuss several cultural forces at work in religious socialization: the assumption of church as female space, the gender bias in socialization of male and female siblings, and the role of maternal influence. I also engage the question of choice in religious participation and examine whether the women could have refused participation. I conclude the chapter by shifting from the women's past to the present by introducing the congregations of which they are currently members.

In each subsequent chapter, a particular aspect of Black Church life is addressed. Chapter 2 examines the ritual life of the church, exploring the dimensions of a religious institution that women intentionally seek in worship. Prayer, praise, preaching, and communal associations are the ritual components at the center of the discussion. In addition, the quality of pastoral leadership is essential to a spiritually vital congregation. How do women assess good preaching? How ought church members respond to each other and engage with one another? What is significant about the praise portion? Is the pastor an "icon" of spiritual perfection or a leader with clay feet? Do pastors need to be active in community and civic activities on behalf of the church? These are some of the queries women responded to during the interviews. Chapter 3 engages the topic of the types of assistance women have received from the church. Some of it is tangible; most of it is not. The most common kinds of assistance identified pertain to religious knowledge and spiritual and personal transformation. Instrumental assistance (help in practical everyday tasks) was rare.

The mission of the church is the focus of chapter 4. Here we see that women indeed have and are guided by a historical awareness of the centrality of the Black Church to the African American community. They revealed their commitment to the broader "community" and the church's response to these needs. I examine several issues: What are the limits of the church's work? Does evangelism take precedence over social ministries? What does it mean to be church? Is there evidence of valuing the priestly aspects of ministry above the prophetic aspects?

Chapter 5 turns our attention to the division of labor within the church. In each church, there were designated tasks for men and women. Coupling those observations with the women's perspectives on who can serve as church leaders, I examine the women's acceptance of the predominantly male clergy and female membership in the church. I present evidence to challenge the cultural mythology that women are more ardent opposers of female clergy than men are and suggest institutional and theological determinants for their ambivalence on this issue.

The Black Church has functioned as a surrogate world for its members and the community. In this world, one can enjoy cultural comfort, common social experiences, a shared theological vision, and similar religious commitments. Part of that shared commitment has focused on the eradication of racism and amelioration of its effects. In chapter 6, I discuss the intersections of racial awareness and religion at the beginning of the twenty-first century. The existence of racism, even in the midst of a metropolitan area distinguished by its large African American population, culture, and leadership, does not escape these women. The church provides a respite from the complexities of being a racial minority in America. It is a renewing space where persons can escape the gaze of white America, while simultaneously wrestling with the biblical mandate for a racially and ethnically diverse Christian church.

Aspects of religious life and experience are never as one-dimensional or discrete as researchers would like. These events, beliefs, and behaviors do not stand alone, although my use of separate chapters might imply that such a separation is possible. We should, however, be mindful of their interrelatedness. I have written each chapter as a self-contained unit more to aid the reader than to maintain rigid demarcations between aspects of female religiosity.

The respondents' words are included in the text as much as possible. While interpretation is involved even in the selection of which data to include or exclude, I have tried to maintain the distinction between what I was told or observed and my interpretation of what it contributes to our understanding of female religiosity and the Black Church. In the process of making invisible woman visible, I have exercised caution. I have tried to respect and protect the identities of these women and their congregations, which graciously shared their religious lives and faith journeys with me, by reporting their words with and without names. Those quotations that have names attached may also include brief descriptors. In addition to names, I have included ages, vocations, marital status, and other identifying data in a very limited manner. All names of persons and congregations are pseudonyms.

1

We Always Went to Church
Women and Religious Socialization

Church attendance among African Americans is proportionately higher than attendance among white Protestant Americans. Attendance rates are one indication that the church has not lost its stature among black Americans to the extent it has among whites. The high regard for the Black Church has been predicated on its institutional centrality to the cultural, social, familial, and economic well-being of African Americans. Its autonomy and leadership in these areas have also been persuasive features that promote and extract loyalty from its membership. This loyal membership is predominantly female. Why are women the dominant membership in an institution committed to the welfare of the entire black community? Why do women participate in the church so consistently? Did they start attending as children and never stop?

"Going to church" was a constant in the lives of the majority of the women I studied. They were church members at the time of the study; in addition, prior to joining their current congregations, they had been in other churches, either voluntarily or by mandate. The sociologist Hart M. Nelsen has found a correlation among the importance of religion, maternal church attendance, and the religious participation of African Americans.[1] The effects of maternal religiosity upon male and female youth were the same, suggesting that the enduring effect of maternal devotion is supplanted or finds another expression among males as they mature past adolescence. It also suggests that the social, cultural, and psychological factors that anchor women in the church merit a closer look. It may also point to the effect of the larger community and societal values upon parental and familial efforts to provide religious training.

The family unit has been the primary context for religious socialization; however, it does not have a monopoly on teaching religious values. The values and norms of the neighborhood, as well as the availability and types of churches in the community, influence whether members attend. These women's stories revealed household practices and community norms that transcended regional and class boundaries. The nonattendance of adult males occurred in families from every economic status and geographic region.

In the following pages, we examine these women's early religious socialization and church involvement. I didn't know these women in their early years, so I am dependent upon their own recollections of these events. Since memory is selective, some important facts may have been forgotten or replaced with events that are more contemporary. It was beyond my ability to authenticate these memories. However, since the significance of the data lies more in what the women actually regard as important than in the empirical nature of the facts, I consider these retrievals to be accurate. I am less interested in the exactness of the women's memories than with what the memories reveal about the women's religious development, what types of events they recount, the impact of social forces, and the meanings the women have assigned to them.

Let me say a word about the definition of "community" in this study before we turn our attention to the women's lives. There are two standard sociological definitions of "community," one territorial, the other "relational" or "sociopsychological."[2] When community is defined as territory, community is equated to a spatial dimension or a physical area; community is seen as a synonym for approximate neighborhoods. However, persons who share a bond of common identity develop and share a community, as well. This meaning emphasizes the relational aspect of community. Marcia Riggs asserts that this connection is aptly applied to African Americans because of their shared identity of collective oppression and continued discrimination. Many times this common oppression took place in the confines of black residential enclaves (slave or free) or a segregated labor market. Being a part of the community establishes the expectation and warrant for blacks to make "special claims on each other."[3] This common identity has as its counterpart cultural norms and practices that have been born out of a history of oppression. I define "community" as inclusive of both dimensions; both meanings were reflected in the questions I asked, as well as suggested by the women's responses.

Profile of the Women

The women in this sample were aligned either with Calvary Baptist Church or Layton Temple Church of God in Christ. There were twenty-five from Calvary Baptist and thirteen from Layton Temple. They covered a spectrum of ages, occupations, and marital statuses. They also varied in their length and history of church participation. All were regular in their attendance at the time of the interviews.

Twelve persons were native to the state, and twenty-six were migrants. Ten of the transplants had relocated in the last eight years. All of the women were African Americans except two, who were natives of Jamaica. Their ages ranged from twenty-four to seventy-seven, with a median age of forty-five. Nearly a third were in their thirties, and another third were in their forties. Fourteen women were married, and twenty-four were single. Of the single women, four were divorced, two were widowed, fifteen had never been married, two were separated, and one was in a common-law marriage. Just over half were mothers.

Educationally, two had not completed high school, ten had some college or vocational school training, ten had earned a college degree, and fifteen had completed advanced work beyond the bachelor's degree. Thirty-three were employed, while five were either retired or disabled. Their median annual income was between $20,000 and $34,999, which situated them as a group in the ranks of the middle class. They had belonged to their present church on average about three and a half years. All but five had at least one other family member attending the same church. In most instances, this person was a spouse or a child. Just under half had been members of other denominations.

Compulsory Childhood Attendance

In many contemporary churches, Sunday attendance looks like a gathering of adults and senior citizens. Children often constitute a minute portion of the worshippers in the sanctuary. In some congregations, children's church, Sunday school, and the nursery are the contexts in which youth are introduced to the faith. However, there still is often a lapse in children's participation as they get older. Pastors express frustration about the lack of youth involvement, the loss of a spiritual and moral compass among teenagers and young adults, and increased levels of biblical illiteracy among adult members. It seems that the past practice of taking children to church in black communities is waning. With the lessened participation of youth, church leaders find that transmitting the faith to the younger generation is an exasperating task.

The place of the church in the community and the religious socialization of the women in our sample points to a different era. Almost without exception, these women were expected to go to church as youth and grew up in communities where attendance was normative. Jerri was raised in her formative years by an aunt. Church was not an option.

> We couldn't tell our mama or ask mama "can we go to church" or [say] we didn't want to go to church. We had to go to church. I was raised by my aunt. I had to go because my aunt made us go to church regardless of whether we wanted to go to church. . . . That is why now when I hear children telling their parent that "I don't want to go to church" and the parents say "stay home"; deep down that hurts because I know [back] then we didn't have a choice unless [we] were dying [laughs]. When we couldn't get to the Anglican Church, which was further away, there was another little Church of God close by, that we'd go to Sunday school and Bible study. It didn't matter what church we went to as long as we left the house that Sunday and [went] to church.

Many other women echoed these sentiments and experiences. The expectation of their participation was often present whether or not both parents attended. More than half of the sample went to church with only one parent or primary caretaker. A few women were sent to church in the custody of other relatives or adults. For example, Denise and her sister were given permission by their mom (her biological aunt) to go to church in the care of the local school bus driver and his wife. Her mom did not go to church.

Regardless of who took them to church, attendance was a common feature of these women's lives. All the women had participated in church by the age of ten. Most had started earlier and continued to go until they left their parents' home and gained independence.

Theresa summed up her church attendance in a few words. I asked when she started attending church. She responded, "I guess since I was born, I mean, I've been going since I've known myself." Joyce also frequented church since childhood. As a preacher's child, she found that her early years revolved around church services.

We went to church every time the doors were opened eventually. We went to church every Sunday, three times for the day, because we had morning worship, then we'd have Sunday school about 4 p.m. Then we had gospel service in the night. We lived right behind the church, so it was like what would be offices was where we lived. So even if we weren't physically present in church, we heard everything that was going on in church. We heard all the hymns lined and everything.

The most consistent religious practices women reported during their childhood were attending Sunday school and morning worship service and participating in youth activities. Opportunities for participation beyond Sunday worship varied according to the denomination to which they belonged. Some of the most common offerings were choirs, Sunshine Band, Purity Class, Junior Church, Baptist Training Union, Girl Scouts, and Youth Day. Michelle was exposed to church life and its youth activities at an early age, and church has been a consistent part of her life. She started church "right after I started breathing. Honey, I don't ever remember not going to church, I'll put it like that." As we continued to talk about her early years in church, she gave a rich description of the ethos of her initial church home.

The church that I grew up in was a small, kind of close-knit family congregation. Lots of, not lots of, several large family groups, generations and generations of a family attending this particular church. Both my mother and father were always very active in church and in auxiliaries, and my father was a trustee. My mother did some different roles around the church. [She was] very active. My grandmother was a member of the church, she was very active, and she was a deaconess. My grandfather was a minister, but he did not pastor at that church. He was the pastor of a couple of smaller little country churches that were a couple of hours away. They weren't weekly meeting churches. That's why he pastored a couple of them. They met alternating Sundays. I was always active in the church. We went to Sunday school, youth groups, and choir. The church itself was, I won't say completely opposite of Calvary, but it was very different. Well, there were some similarities and some differences. It was a traditional Baptist church, real quiet, no hooping, no hollering, no screaming or jumping, no clapping. You know none of that kind of carrying on [laughs].

Church participation did not feel like a conscious choice to Michelle. It became such a part of her lifestyle that she rarely questioned it. As we talked about whether she was made to go, she responded.

> No, I mean yes and no. It was so repetitive after a point. It was not even a conscious decision. It was not like "oh, I wonder if I'll get up and go to church today." It's not that kind of thought. It's like "I'm going to church every Sunday unless there's a reason not to like death, some major illness, something out of the ordinary." You don't just get up and decide you're not going to church today.

Choice was not an option for most women in relation to church. Attendance was mandatory for nearly two-thirds of them. Often, women originally from the northern states were sent "down South" during school breaks or to spend the summer with relatives. Their southern relatives in rural areas required attendance while visiting, so the visitors would make sure to pack their "church clothes." While most said that they had to go to church, only four said they felt forced to go. It seems that choice was neither interpreted as oppressive or met with much resistance. As children, the women went to church to be obedient to parental rules, to exhibit the proper respect due elders, or as a requirement that was necessary to get other privileges in the home. Sharon remembered that one of the house rules was that if you went out on Saturday night, you had to get up and go to church on Sunday. However, Sharon did not need to be coerced to go to church.

> We went to Sunday school, morning service, we stayed for dinner, and we'd stay for afternoon service. So we'd get to church about 9 or 9:30 in the morning for Sunday school and wouldn't get home until 7 or 8 p.m. at night. That was every Sunday, and we did it because we wanted to. My mother didn't make us do it. I remember one time, I did something, I don't recall what I did, and my punishment was I couldn't go to church that evening. . . . I guess it bothered me because I wanted to go to church. My mother knew it was something I was really looking forward to going to. It was an anniversary of some type. She just wouldn't let me go.

Rosalind and her siblings realized that church attendance got them more than just spiritual sustenance:

If we went to Sunday school and church, then we could go to the movies on Sunday afternoon. They [her parents] weren't very strict. They tried to make it strict for a little [while] and make us go to BTU [Baptist Training Union] and we used to say, "Now, mom, you know this is a little much."

Among the twenty-two who described themselves as "having to go," a third admitted that they enjoyed going to church. There were positive benefits of church participation—seeing neighbors, playing with classmates, and getting answers to their religious curiosity. As they got older, these women learned to negotiate absences from afternoon services or midweek programs. Parents allowed some concessions so that they might participate in school- and church-sponsored activities.

To say they "attended church" does not fully capture the positive regard for church conveyed by this group. Beyond attending the primary worship services on a regular basis, they perceived their congregations as welcoming. Church provided an outlet for individual expression of talents, encouraged social relationships, and provided spiritual sustenance. Church was also regarded as meaningful because it was an activity undertaken with a parent; in some cases, going to church with a parent not only reinforced religious values but also had a favorable impact on the parent-child relationship.

During their youth, few women challenged their parents on the issue of attending church, believing that there was no room for debate or change. While some admitted not being converted to Christianity during these years, the stress upon participating communicated their parents' genuine concern for their spiritual foundations. Kelly spoke of her mother's concern in this regard. Her mother was more concerned with her having some type of religious grounding than with her being a member of a particular faith tradition. Kelly was introduced to Christianity while being reared by her southern grandmother, who was Baptist. Later, she was suddenly thrust into the Islamic faith when she was sent north to live with her mother, who was Muslim. In her later teen years, she was drawn toward the Presbyterian church; this was the denomination of an aunt with whom she spent summer vacations. Throughout this period of experimentation, her mother was nonjudgmental and continually encouraged her to become committed to God and a fellowship somewhere. It was only when she took a hiatus from participating in church altogether that her mom became directive. In the most succinct fashion, her mom told her, "I went somewhere; you're going somewhere. I don't care where you go as long as you believe in something."

Family Devotions

Religious instruction for the women I studied took place largely in the church, but family devotions were a secondary, although not consistent, source for introducing the women to God. Using collective Bible reading, instruction, and family prayer as measurements of a family's devotional practices, I identified four women as products of families that had regular devotional periods. An additional three were from families that occasionally had collective devotional periods. The most structured devotional times occurred in one of the households where the father was a pastor. This family had a period of prayer and Bible study daily. In other families, it was the custom to offer a prayer at dinnertime or to read the Bible on Sunday, a task usually fulfilled by a parent. Gail shared how talking about the Bible was a nightly event in her household.

> Yeah, we did Bible, we didn't pray together that much as a family. We would read the Bible, we would discuss it. . . . See, the way we grew up, we had family hour when my father came home. Like I told you, my mother was always at home, so mamma cooked dinner, had dinner cooked every night at 5 o'clock. Daddy would come home; we'd eat dinner, and after we ate dinner we would always sit around the table and talk. You know we would talk about the Bible. We'd talk about God [and] about what happened in our day.

Parents were also active in assisting children with learning a recitation for church or memorizing a Bible verse for Sunday school. It was the rare occasion when children actually saw or heard their parents pray together or when they were given the responsibility to lead the family prayers.

Postadolescent Attendance

Following their early years of participation, many women experienced a lapse during their late teen years. More than three-quarters stopped going to church at least once after having started attending as youngsters, though they returned to church during their twenties and thirties. They were recruited back into a congregation by a friend or through a strong recommendation of the church or its pastor. Most of the explanations for these lapses were related to life transitions, such as gaining independence, rebelling, having children, or changing marital status. Twenty-nine women in the sample had attended or completed college or a trade school, and half of those who had received advanced training had a period of sporadic attendance or stopped attending altogether during their college years. Religious choice and independence were related to economic independence, professional development, the establishment of a separate domicile, and the expansion of social options. With their newfound independence came a shift in church participation. It is important to note that only rarely was the decreased participation due to distrust of religious institutions or doubt about the dogma of the church.

Karen converted to Catholicism at the age of twelve, influenced by her attendance with her aunt. She attended a Catholic high school, a Catholic university, and a Catholic church from her early teens until she started college. However, she started questioning some of Catholic theology in high school. She stopped going when she was in college and didn't seriously start looking for a church until she was thirty-four and had relocated to Georgia.

> I was in college. I might have gone my freshman year. I was really falling out with it in high school, with Catholicism. And I might have gone my freshman year. I'd go to mass, a Jesuit church, but after that, I just stopped going. I mean I probably didn't go the rest of college until when I got married and stuff, cause my ex-husband, he was raised Catholic. . . . So I would say, all, most of my college [years] I did not attend any organized church.

Karen didn't consider herself a total spiritual dropout however.

> I took a lot of theology [in college], and by then I was sort of bitter, moving away from the Catholic church, but theology and spiritual ideology interested me. I remember taking a world religions course or something like that and how man looks at God, like, you know, Buddhism and Hinduism and Confucianism, Judaism, all those. I'm just intrigued with that. The Jesuits make you take so much theology that if you take two more courses you have a minor [laughs], but I liked it. I took a lot

of philosophy and a lot of theology because it interested me the way that people view God. I might not have been a consistent churchgoer, but I have always felt a great curiosity about God and [how] He feels about me and how people looked at Him. So I've had spiritual leanings, if not the practice.

Among these women, earlier periods of inactivity were almost regarded as a rite of passage. The women found that being away from the watchful eyes of parents, having adult responsibility for their time management, and feeling a desire to experience college life to its fullest impeded participation and competed with their religious upbringing. The women who continued to attend church during college did so for spiritual as well as other reasons. Some had a formal responsibility to fulfill, such as being the church pianist. Other women were drawn to the church because it was the common practice on campus, because it was a requirement of sorority pledging, or because it offered a proven conduit for establishing ties with a surrogate family that would provide respite from the pressures of college life. Linda never completely stopped going to church. "I mean, in college I was on campus, so I didn't have to go as often when I was sleepy. But other than that [I went]. I still felt bad when I didn't go." Marilyn occasionally lapsed in her attendance, but not frequently. She went a few times a month while at school.

> We had a chapel on campus that I would go to from time to time. I did not have a car, nor did any of my friends, so we couldn't get out to go to other churches in the community. When I was pledging a sorority, we went to church every Sunday, either on campus or off campus; that was interesting . . . we went to different churches in the community, different faith churches, and different denominations.

She never thought about not going to church. Her attendance on campus was augmented by her trips home.

> I came home a lot, not a lot, but they were only two and a half hours away. Every time I could get a ride home, I would go home, and if I were home, I'd go to church, so I never really thought about it. I'd probably get home every six weeks or less. Probably every six weeks, so I was going to my regular service at home, and then these other ones, so I never really thought about I wasn't churched.

Male Religiosity and Participation

The women in this study were reared in congregations where the majority of members were females. They also were reared in homes where male family members went to church less frequently than female members. Nearly half reported that a different enforcement of church attendance applied to their male counterparts. Twenty-five women grew up in households where male siblings or cousins of similar ages lived with them; half reported that boys attended with the same regularity that they did. Ten said the boys either were shown more lenience about regular attendance or did not have to go at all. Some noted that this dismissive attitude toward male attendance started as early as when the boys were only sixteen years old. Two did not recall their male siblings ever going to church. Theresa spoke of the expectation to attend church that she grew up with. The boys needed more coercion than the girls did to attend.

> Well, attending church played a very big role in our upbringing. The boys, my mother, it was like she had to make them go to church, "get up and go to church," and they were like "I don't want to go." "Get up and go" [she'd say]. I mean she really had to make them go, but for the girls it was something [else]. When it was time to go to church, it was time to go to church, you know. We had to go, that was just it; we had to go to church. . . . The girls and the boys, everyone had to go to church.

How did they explain male recalcitrance or account for the leniency shown to the men in the household? Some pointed to concessions to male rebellion and to the time demands of part-time jobs and extracurricular school activities. It was the way things were. Other women attributed the leniency toward boys to a larger pattern of latitude given to men in general, as evidenced by their later curfews and greater independence in selecting friends. Overall, the women accepted the difference and were minimally troubled by it.

Women did recall one factor that had a positive impact on their male sibling's participation—paternal participation. In households where the male parent was in a church leadership role, women reported that little distinction was made between boys' and girls' attendance requirements. Twenty-seven women were reared with fathers or surrogate father figures. These men were church attendees (fifteen), nonattendees (ten), or occasional attendees (two). Among the attendees, there were three pastors, four deacons, one trustee, and three choir members. They exhibited regularity in participation and commitment of time and perhaps required more of their sons because of their own involvement. However, these fathers rarely were as involved in the church as mothers were, and greater piety was attributed to mothers than fathers. Maternal religiosity was still the standard for evaluating church commitment and abiding faith. Men were described as attending "not as much as mom," and sporadic attendance was explained by comments such as "when he wasn't drinking."

Women from the female-headed households were less knowledgeable about the religious habits of their dads, although they interacted with them in other ways. Three knew that their father had gone, or still went, to church. Two were taken to church by their dad even after their parents divorced. Unlike for their male siblings' nonattendance, the women could not identify reasons for their fathers' lack of participation. They did reject several explanations, including their fathers' work schedules, political engagements, responsibilities to service organizations, and physical limitations. The women ultimately concluded that men's nonparticipation largely reflected a lack of interest.

Not only were these women's male family members absent from church, but also other men from the community did not attend church as regularly as women did. The churches of these women's adolescent years consisted predominantly of women. Very few recalled a "home" congregation that had nearly equal proportions of men and women. The dominant family configuration included women and children. The men who were present often functioned in official capacities in the worship service or held offices in the church. The women also consistently noted that men were not as expressive as females in the worship service. Women's sentiments about the low number of male participants are exemplified in this refrain: "I just thought that was how it was supposed to be." Furthermore, it seems that the paucity of men who attended church could not be accounted for by an absence of black men in the community. Although some of the women were not living with their biological fathers, their neighborhoods were not devoid of male relatives or significant male friends of the family who were part of the women's lives (e.g., a mother's boyfriend).

Role Models

To be a good role model, an individual must have positively impacted another person's life or have qualities or character worthy of emulation. To learn who functioned as religious role models for these church women, I asked them to identify one or more persons who impressed them as extremely "religious" or devoted to church during their childhood and preteen years. Most named two or three persons. The most frequent responses were mothers, grandmothers, aunts, other women, or people in the role of preacher or deacon; those who were preachers or deacons were overwhelmingly male. With the exception of the pastor, male role models named were usually family members. Grandfathers were mentioned more frequently than fathers or other male figures. A brother, a national figure, and a cousin were each only mentioned once as a religious role model.

Overwhelmingly, these women saw other women as their spiritual models and mentors. Fifty-seven women were identified, by name or function, as role models. By contrast, only twenty male figures were so identified. Mothers were referenced four times as often as fathers. Women could cite both behaviors and attitudes that indicated religious commitment. They pointed to actions such as reading the Bible or other devotional literature, praying, attending church regularly, and treating other people in an overall respectful or gracious manner. The dispositions cited were strong beliefs, faith in God, a loving, and giving character, and evangelical zeal. To a lesser degree, filling an official role in the church was a qualification that identified one as a role model.

The Communities

Women participants lived their formative years in the North and the South. Twenty-six grew up in bustling urban areas of the North, including Chicago and Detroit. Ten were from rural communities. One participant from a rural area described her small farm community as a place with "two churches and a lot of fields." Two women came to the United States as adults from Jamaica; both had lived abroad and been raised in military families. Geographic stability was a feature in most of their lives during childhood. The majority of respondents lived in one location until they completed high school and were, along with their siblings, reared by at least one biological parent.

Denominations and access to churches varied across communities. Some recalled the churches available to them in the immediate neighborhood by names and denominations, although they could not remember specific denominational affiliations (e.g., Lott Carey Convention, Missionary Baptist). Estimates of the size or average Sunday attendance in previous congregations were often gauged relative to those of their present church.

The majority of the women attended Sunday worship service regularly as children. Once in church, they found their participation buttressed by positive encounters with peers and teachers who attended. Distaste for church was undercut by the knowledge that many of their schoolmates also attended churches somewhere. Most spoke positively about fellowship and the sense of belonging they experienced. Church provided access and opportunity to see friends or other family members. Others associated church with warding off social ostracism; attendance was the "price" of maintaining high regard among one's neighbors. One woman remembered that the practice and expectation of attending church was so pervasive that you would be talked about if you did not attend. Eva, who described her neighborhood as "conservative," said of her community, "You went to church on Sundays and worked in the yard on Saturdays."

Although attending church was a community value in many of the respondents' formative neighborhoods, there were exceptions. In communities where church involvement was not the norm, women perceived themselves as being engaged in a deviant practice. They were the "odd family," getting up and going off to church. These particular women expressed feelings of being marginalized by the community because they attended church when their neighbors did not. Other women realized that they were distinct because they attended a church out of the immediate community, attended on an "irregular" day (Saturdays), participated in church activities when their peers were engaging in recreational ones, or went to a church other than the "premier" congregation in their community.

Women raised in rural areas and in the South were involved more consistently in the church than were those reared in the North. In addition, women reared in the South depicted the communities of their youth as locales where church was indeed a regular part of one's social and cultural life. As youngsters, they sometimes spent the entire day in church, often because they went to rural churches that met only once or twice a month. This pattern was more common in the South than the North. Meals would be prepared to take to church, and members took time for dinner between services. The length of Sabbath observances was impacted by the existence of few alternatives for collective gathering, the church's role in the dissemination of important information, and the social and religious importance of revivals and homecomings. In the northern urban centers, congregations were more likely to meet weekly. I noted that there was a slightly more relaxed enforcement of attendance among those reared in the North, a practice possibly influenced by the greater frequency of worship times and competing options for youth involvement.

Discussion

The majority of the women in this study were reared attending church with mothers or other significant female relatives who were active in local congregations. They were socialized at a young age into religious life, sensing women's importance to and familiarity with the church. They learned that attending church was both a desirable and a mandatory practice for girls. We might initially conclude that their present attendance reflects in part a continuation of a habit established during childhood. The disparity in participation levels between men and women lends some plausibility to this interpretation. Yet, since all youth are likely to avoid the church for an extended period, other variables most likely impact women's adult religious participation.

A national study of black clergy reported by Lincoln and Mamiya in *The Black Church in the African American Experience* demonstrates that contemporary clergy are aware of the uphill battle they face in trying to attract and retain youth in the church.[4] The most difficult years to hold youth and young adults are between ages seventeen and thirty-five. Clergy attributed the disappearance of this cohort primarily to boredom, lack of relevant programs, the bias toward adults in congregations, and the exclusionary nature of church programs. A smaller percentage considered youthful dissociation to be a normal stage for teenagers. They felt that "young people in late adolescence and young adulthood were in a stage of life, a time to become independent, to search and test things out for themselves. In other words, it was natural for them to rebel against adult authority, express doubt, and not attend church."[5] As I talked with women, they cited many of these reasons. Many of them had interrupted their church attendance as they gained autonomy from home. Only one attributed her disaffiliation to hypocrisy in the church, secularization, and outgrowing her childhood faith. Still, this doesn't explain why women pass through the stage and return, while many men disaffiliate for much longer.

I am persuaded that exposure to an institutional context where the sacred space and experience are constituted primarily by women fosters an allegiance to the church. In addition to the church's being a female enclave, women's experience of being trained in the faith by women and their observing women responding to each other's needs as well as those of the larger community foster an additional level of loyalty. It is not hard to establish that most black churches are predominately sacred spaces for women. The absence of fathers in attendance, the small numbers of men in the congregations, the programming within congregations, the volunteer labor and leadership that women give to maintain the church all support such a designation. In this context, church becomes a safe public space, unlike any other, where women can engage and negotiate the realities of their own lives and of African Americans.[6] The only black institutions that can garner similar loyalty and address women's social concerns on a national scope are sororities and civic groups such as the National Association for Colored Women.

Education of various kinds is an integral part of the programs of black congregations. Women are the majority of the teachers in most church settings. Additionally, fellowship times, homecomings, and church suppers become festive moments and opportunities where the culinary donations of women (and some men) can be praised and enjoyed. Bible studies for women are held. The consistent reference to raising children and the dominance of women in the congregation, choirs, usher boards, and prayer meetings indicate that the Black Church is an institution structurally and culturally maintained by women and largely for women.

That the Black Church is a female assembly does not suggest that churches have intentionally discriminated against men or that they have been oblivious to men's lack of participation. Women note their absence but do not assume responsibility for their male counterparts' absence or fault the church. The sociologist Cheryl Townsend Gilkes has offered some explanations for men's absence from the church (and the family). She attributes it to significant social demographics and cultural dynamics within our society. There is a smaller population of black men nationally than of black women. The death of black men as a result of poverty, malnutrition, and racism and the higher rates of incarceration and homicide among black men have reduced men's availability to participate in church. High black unemployment affects men's inclination to participate in congregational life because of the expectation of financial support and self-doubts about their own manhood. Young urban men are often socialized into a culture that dissuades them from participation in any mainstream social institution or activities, especially churches, "which are usually identified in street culture as the province of older black women or straight types."[7] In addition, cultural forces that impact men in general are at work: Sunday sports and recreational opportunities, the need for extended rest in preparation for the upcoming workweek, and the perception of heavy church involvement as a sign of weakness. These forces, while not offering a conclusive explanation for the gender disparity, remind us of the complexity of the cultural norms that have to be overcome for men to participate as fully as women in the church.

At the beginning of a new millennium, we see continued interest in and response to the absence of men in American Christianity on a national level. Religious movements such as the Promise Keepers[8] and Manpower Conventions[9] and numerous independent initiatives by local congregations have attempted to increase male participation and to make Christianity more attractive to men. These appeals are often linked to a belief in the duty and ability of men to successfully head households, families, and the church. These organized efforts reveal not only the widespread perception that church has been a preserve of women but also the perception that it should not be. Thus, these initiatives become the rallying point for men to reclaim lost territory in the church and their homes.

Certainly, the women in our study were concerned with the lack of a strong male presence in the church. It is one aspect of congregational life that could be better addressed. More than the void, the initiatives their churches were taking to reach out to men were central to the women's thoughts. Many of the efforts appeared to target the most "downtrodden" of men, such as the homeless. This was just one signal to me that the women were active on this matter. Ministry to the homeless was one of the initiatives that was implemented by both men and women.

Another finding that supports the perception of the church as female-friendly is the imperative for women to be exposed to it. In households where there were both boys and girls of the same age, there was not only a different level of urgency regarding boys' attendance but also a greater freedom for boys to engage in other types of social activities. Girls were allowed to participate in church as much as desired, but they experienced rigid restrictions on other recreational activities, such as attending movies and dances, dating, going to town, or being in settings where they were unsupervised by a responsible adult. Whether these rules were due to real or perceived community dangers or to Christian morality, the consequences were a sanctioning of religious space as female-friendly. The idea that society is dangerous was also transmitted. Therefore, church attendance among girls was promoted both as a means to Christian faith and as an acceptable alternative to less desirable social experiences and activities. The church is an institutional buffer against social and physical threats to girls. While boys face different social dangers, the less rigid parameters they face imply that they are better equipped to negotiate and protect themselves from these threats.[10]

Present Congregational Contexts

Calvary Baptist Church

Calvary Baptist Church[11] is a middle-class African American Baptist congregation, founded in 1990 and pastored by Reverend Melvin King. He has a Master of Divinity degree and was pursuing his doctorate in ministry while I worshipped with this congregation. The church has affiliations with the Southern Baptist and National Baptist Conventions. During the time of my observation, the congregation purchased and relocated to a new edifice. I spent approximately two-thirds of my time in the older location and one-third at the new site. This church was the third congregation Reverend King had pastored. The majority of the founding members of Calvary Baptist Church were persons who had followed his leadership in the other two churches.

When I began attending Calvary, the church was housed in a one-story brick edifice, located on six acres of land and set about one hundred feet from the street. On the left side of the property was a trailer that provided additional classroom space and a space for choir rehearsals. The sanctuary was not very ornate. It had two sections of seating separated by a middle aisle. The seats were stackable chairs. On the left was an alcove that could be closed off by partitions. It served as a library or a Sunday school classroom and could be used for overflow seating. The pastor's office was to the left of the pulpit, and the secretary's office was situated in the hall behind the pulpit. The interior was white with wood paneling. Some minor renovations had been made to the building when the church first moved in, but no major changes had been undertaken. The church realized that it would quickly outgrow this building.

Calvary had two morning services on Sunday, Sunday school, children's church, midweek prayer, and Bible study. Sunday attendance (combining both services) ranged from 250 to 300 persons. The eleven o'clock service has a greater number of attendees. Besides Reverend King, there are two other ministers considered staff; during my attendance, one was male and one female. Both associates assist with the liturgy during the morning worship services and communion services. Neither assistant earns a salary from the church. The male assistant has been with Reverend King since the founding of Calvary Baptist. The female associate minister had arrived within the past year. When she joined this ministry, she was already licensed to preach. She was not the first woman preacher to unite with Calvary. Another female preacher had preceded her. However, she too must have joined already licensed, for Reverend King informed me he had not yet licensed or ordained a female minister.

The official decision-making units of the church are the Deacon's Board, the Coordinating Council, the Advisory Council, and the Trustee Board. The Deacon's Board has only male members, while the others included women. Calvary does not use the words "auxiliary" or "club" to describe the specialized initiatives in the church; it prefers the designation "ministry." There are many ministries in the church—a little something for everybody. These include the birth month ministry, deacon's wives ministry, political action ministry, couples ministry, praise ministry, prayer ministry, mentoring program, hospitality ministry, membership ministry, children's church ministry, and newsletter ministry. The music ministry includes three choirs. With the exception of the deacon's wives group, all ministries are open to men and women. Calvary is a church that buzzes with constant activity. Activities at the church are regularly scheduled on at least three nights each week. Members are constantly coming and going to their various teaching and programmatic groups.

A unit in this church that I had not encountered in other Baptist churches is the Coordinating Council. Leaders of every ministry, along with the deacons, meet monthly to report on their ministries' activities and needs. Coordinating Council meetings are open to the entire membership, although few non-Council members actually attend. In addition to this leadership group, Calvary has an Advisory Council. This is a more select group of members with whom the pastor discusses the vision for the church and the implementation of any new initiatives. This body has the power to veto suggestions that the pastor or members present. Appointment to the Advisory Council and to the Deacon's Board are at the pastor's discretion; however, current deacons are consulted about persons under consideration for that board.

Officially, there is a Trustee Board, but it is neither very active nor very distinct from the other boards in terms of membership (according to several women). It consists of the Deacon's Board and a couple of other members. Unlike many Baptist churches, Calvary Baptist has no clear line between the responsibilities of trustees and those of deacons. The deacons are intimately involved in decisions about the use of the building and purchases and are fiscally responsible for the legal matters of the church. Normally, this is the work only of the trustees in Baptist churches.

In this congregation, men and women share responsibilities for morning worship. Both are involved in leading the congregation in praise songs, ushering, and delivering the announcements. Women constitute the majority of the choir members; men (not ushers) lift the offerings and dominate the preaching and praying in the life of the church. Each service is audiotaped and available for purchase at the conclusion of the service.

The new location for Calvary Baptist Church is alongside a four-lane thoroughfare about twenty minutes east of the former site. The new building was purchased from a white Southern Baptist congregation (which shared the building for a brief period). In the new location, there are more parking spaces, an entire classroom building, and an eight-hundred–seat sanctuary with a balcony. To add to the already existing ministries, the church started a Christian school, from preschool through the sixth grade, and expanded its staff, hiring a Minister of Christian Education and a director of the school.

The rate of growth that Calvary had experienced prior to the move has rapidly increased since the relocation. I found that most members had been attending about two or three years. Slightly more than a quarter had been there for a year or less. Overall, half of the congregation had joined in the past four years. Clearly, this was a burgeoning congregation. Family members did not come to church alone; nearly three-quarters came with at least one other family member, usually their child or spouse. Calvary is a black church in its commitments and its population. It includes African Americans and blacks of other nationalities. The gender ratio was three women to one man in attendance, a figure consistent with the average African American church.[12] The median age of members fell between thirty and thirty-nine. Nearly a quarter of the congregation were in their twenties, and another quarter were in their forties. In other words, four out of five people in the church were between the ages of twenty and forty-nine.

Layton Temple Church of God in Christ

Layton Temple Church of God in Christ (COGIC) is housed at the crest of a hill, in a small, stucco-type building in the heart of an urban residential neighborhood. As one travels east or west, one can see the cross-shaped marquee, which carries the church name and a new religious slogan weekly, from hundreds of feet away. Set on a corner plot with no trees and surrounded by parking spaces, this edifice is ten years old. The congregation relocated to this site from the southeast section of the city. This is the third location the church has occupied. Elder and Mrs. Blue are the founders of the church. Layton Temple started as a mission church in a tent twenty-two years ago. Officially, the church has more than 350 members, 200 of whom can be counted on for support, according to Mrs. Blue. Attendance on a Sunday morning was much smaller than this figure. The average adult attendance was between 85 and 105 on any given Sunday.

Layton Temple sits close to the sidewalk curb. Yet, when you step over the threshold, it is as if you are entering another dimension of space and time. Through the double glass doors that open onto the street, you enter a small foyer, where you are warmly greeted by a member of the hospitality auxiliary. If you are a visitor, your contact information and church affiliation are recorded in the church guest book. Next, you are ushered into a T-shaped sanctuary that has two main sections of seating on either side of the central aisle. The pulpit area is raised, with a central chancery, and flanked in the rear with six chairs for clergy. Flowers are placed on either side of the pulpit, and the choir loft is located behind the clergy. On the floor to the left of the pulpit is a section of seats for men only (the left side of the T-shape). Visiting male clergy, associate ministers, members of the men's fellowship, and young boys accompanying their dads sit in this section (although the boys are not supposed to). Drums, an organ, and a piano are in the adjacent area, raised to the level of the pulpit. Opposite this section, on the right side of the pulpit, is the seating for the Mothers Board, an official auxiliary of the church.[13] A small podium, where announcements are read, is on the floor adjacent to this seating section. In the case of an overflowing crowd, worshippers fill in the back pews of the seating reserved for the Mothers Board. The interior décor of Layton Temple is not very ornate. It has wood-stained pews, nondescript burgundy carpet, and interior, thick, double-plated windows. Burglar bars protect the lower section of the windows. The walls hold several banners displaying local attendance awards earned at state meetings.

The average length of attendance among members in this congregation—three to four years—is slightly longer than that for Calvary Baptist. Nearly two-thirds of the membership have been there for five years or less. During my study, a fifth of the congregation had joined in the past year. For the most part, Layton Temple is constituted of a few interrelated families and their extended members. Persons come to church as families; more than half of the members have one or more household members who also attend. Fourteen percent have no other relatives in the church. Like Calvary Baptist, Layton Temple COGIC consists of African Americans or people of African descent. Two or three white persons attend with some regularity. They don't appear to be strangers to the congregation. I discovered that one of them was the daughter-in-law of one of my respondents.[14] The four-to-one ratio of women to men was slightly higher than at Calvary Baptist.

Clearly there are some differences between these two congregations. Yet the similarities in their commitments to preaching the gospel and enhancing the welfare of African Americans and those in the surrounding community reveal the underlying unity they share as well as their anchoring in the Black Church religious culture. Furthermore, they maintain a continuity with the ritualistic elements—preaching, praying, demonstrative worship, fellowship—which have defined African American worship and sustained generations of the faithful, the majority of whom have been women. We turn our attention now to the sustenance derived from these liturgical elements for this group of church women.

2

Where Somebody
Knows My Name
The Culture of the Black Church

We are concerned for one another; if you miss somebody, you
might say, oh, they may be on vacation or [she] may not be feeling
well, but if you keep missing them you get on the phone and say, "I
ain't seen you, dear friend, is everything okay?" [If they say] "Yeah,
I'm okay," [I] just take a little breather and say, "Okay, just check-
ing on you [to] make sure you're okay," that kind of thing.

—Denise

Consider the aspects of worship services in the black church
tradition, and many images come to mind. Music, preaching, responsive
lessons, ushers in uniformed attire, prayer, welcoming of visitors—these
are some of the more pervasive ones. These elements of black religious
culture vary by locale and denomination, but, whatever the mixture of
these liturgical elements, the worship service provides meaningful occasions for participants to encounter God, find spiritual instruction, relief,
renewal, and build community with one another. Congregations that do
this well are able to garner loyalty and commitment from their members.
In addition, the worship services in the Black Church have enabled
African Americans to construct and maintain a socioreligious worldview
that has empowered and sustained them through years of oppression and
racial and economic discrimination.

The church is also a place where networks are established that demonstrate care and concern. Denise demonstrates her commitment to maintaining the community by contacting absentee members; she expects others to value and share this responsibility to reach out to absent or lapsed

members. This informal practice of noting who is not present and seeking to find out why is one way women create a congregational culture in which everyone is regarded as extended family members.

Members expect this care from one another. It is not expected from the pastor to the same degree. The pastor should be accessible to the congregation and sufficiently involved in the lives of members so that persons do not regard themselves as insignificant to their pastor. The pastor's primary task is to proclaim the gospel with wisdom and power and to provide astute leadership. The ability to do these tasks well can be the distinction between a thriving church and a stagnant or dying one. This ability can also cultivate loyalty in members, a loyalty that sustains a pastorate when it is threatened by scandal. Thus, the religiosity of black women is not only anchored in the aforementioned liturgical elements but is also defined by two additional elements, communal associations and pastoral leadership.

The discussion of this group's expectations and experience of church is organized around five dimensions of congregational life: prayer, praise, personal associations, preaching, and pastoral leadership. These are the aspects that women consistently cited as the indispensable features of church and the ones that have had a positive impact on their commitment to God and their congregations. The features they seek include the three central features of black worship—preaching, music, and the frenzy—identified by W. E. B. Du Bois in *The Souls of Black Folk* nearly a century ago.[1] These elements have changed in content and form over the century, but not enough to have lost their power to draw worshippers into the presence of the Holy. All five dimensions provide the necessary bridges for these women to cross from the mundane world into the sacred realm.

Prayer

Corporate prayer was a significant component of worship services in both congregations. In Layton Temple, before the call to worship is extended, members are invited to the front of the church for altar prayer. The minister of the hour stands looming over them from the raised pulpit. Members grasp hands or wave their arms in acts of praise. These moments are for spiritual refocusing, diminishing the mind's preoccupation with the cares of the world. They prepare persons for worship. The assistant minister offers the invocation, praying for the worshippers and for the worship that is about to begin. The organist's melody can be heard softly in the background. The minister's prayer is punctuated with outbursts of "thank you, Jesus," "praise God," and "have your way, Lord," as persons spontaneously respond to the preacher's petitions. At the completion of prayer, words of adoration continue as members return to their seats, some still with upraised hands.

Collective prayer at Calvary Baptist occurs midway through the order of worship, rather than at the beginning. Members are invited to the altar, but movement is not mandatory. Many more individuals stay in their seats than move forward to the altar. Prayer counselors greet persons who gather at the altar. Some members clasp hands with fellow members. One of the pulpit associates, either male or female, offers the morning prayer as the prayer counselors walk among the parishioners, praying for particular needs and laying hands on individuals as a gesture to convey God's grace and consolation. Sometimes oil is used in this moment. At other times, a prayer counselor just touches a person's shoulder as he or she passes by. There is no rushing through prayer time. Members in the pews are allowed to sit down if they become weary. At the conclusion of prayer time, worshippers are exhorted to return to their seats, claiming an answer to their prayers and rejoicing.

Many of the women ranked prayer time as their favorite part of the service. It was considered their time to seek God, to unload burdens. One woman spoke of how prayer time is the most sacred time of the service in her estimation. Although it is a corporate ritual, to her it is a very individual experience. She remarked, "That's the time when you can just talk to God and, you know, whatever it is you want to say, [you can] . . . that's my time, and I know there's a minister up there who prays during that time. Sometimes I hear their [i.e., the ministers'] prayers, sometimes I don't, but I'm praying at that time."

Praise

Both Layton Temple and Calvary Baptist created a ritual space where members could experience the power of God and where God's presence seemed to move like electricity from person to person. During a typical service, one is likely to observe shouting, lively gospel singing, note taking, people spontaneously rising to their feet in affirmation of the message or "running."[2] Services incorporate spontaneous testimony and dialogical preaching. Members answer the preacher's pronouncements (call) with their heartfelt amens (response). The pastor is both mediator and celebrant in the worship service. Members and clergy can be observed fully rejoicing in the visitation of the Spirit.[3]

Praise was a designated portion of the services in both congregations. In each church, there are designated persons responsible for leading the worshippers in the adoration of God. These are churches where God has to be felt, not just talked about. For the celebration to occur, time is given to ushering in the Spirit and preparing those present to receive the proclaimed word. Calvary Baptist has a Praise Team that leads the congregation in song. Increasingly, these singing ensembles are replacing the traditional devotional periods led by deacons or missionaries. At Calvary, the Praise Team ministers prior to the formal beginning of the service and the entrance of the pastor. The church members stand or sit during the songs, while the members of the team (four to five persons, mostly women) introduce and then sing the words of the songs. Hymnbooks are not used during this segment of worship. It is common to see people enraptured in their worship of God through either verbal praise or physical movement and gestures. Such moments indicating an individual's spiritual release and God's presence in the sanctuary are welcomed. Once the minister who is serving as worship leader enters the sanctuary, the group ends its ministry. However, a selection can be prolonged if the minister elects to do so. Prolonging a musical selection can also occur during the course of the service, or the pastor may elect to initiate a praise chorus when he feels moved by the Spirit.

The praise segments in worship differ in the two churches. Layton Temple has a more traditional team of a few devotional leaders, usually persons in official positions such as deacons, mothers, or missionaries. Two designated persons walk to the front of the congregation after members have returned to their seats from altar prayer and the choir has processed in. The persons might be two men, two women, or one of each. Missionary Brown, a stately woman of fifty-plus years with a strong alto voice, regularly leads the devotional period. She can be counted on to fill in at a moment's notice. Her repertoire of songs seems endless. The devotional segment lasts from fifteen to thirty-five minutes, depending upon "the move of the Spirit." In addition, anyone can initiate a song just by beginning to sing or by standing up in his or her pew.

Another distinction is that this portion of the service is not just for turning one's focus upon God. It also facilitates corporate encouragement of the faithful through testimonies. Sandwiched in between a song and shouting, a testimony may suddenly be offered. Members quickly quiet themselves as they listen reverently to the person's account of the activity of God being attested to. The narrative can be an answer to prayer, an unexpected blessing, an affirmation of faith in the midst of trials, or a need for the prayer of the saints. Responses vary from immediately praying for the person to erupting into another extended period of praise and rejoicing.

The stereotypical images of the time-bound, staid Baptist church or the never-ending Pentecostal church do not apply to these congregations. Time is the servant of the churches, not their master. The regard for time is conveyed by the worship structure; every moment is ordered to keep the rapt attention of worshippers on God, not on the ordinary. At Calvary Baptist, bulletins carry extensive announcements but only a very select number are read during the morning service. Distractions such as walking during the service, chewing gum, and crying children are discouraged. Layton Temple's services last longer than Calvary's as a rule, but Elder Blue defies the stereotype of a long-winded Pentecostal preacher who has little regard for time.

In Layton Temple, some women who are senior citizens have physical limitations that keep them from standing for long periods during the singing or praise. These women are less physically demonstrative than younger members. Nonetheless, all like the infusion of "spirit" and emotional release evident in the praise portion of their services. They talk about it as a drawing out of the self (away from problems) and a transforming context. Its effect allows the worshipper to momentarily transcend his or her mundane problems and to focus on God. That experience has consequences far beyond the limits of the service.

Even with their limitations, this group of elderly women in both churches is exuberant. They wave their hands in the congregation, stand to their feet to "encourage the preacher," or otherwise express joy in their seats. A member of the Mothers Board at the Baptist church was enthusiastic about the liveliness of the worship services, although she is physically limited by the condition of her legs. The importance of a lively service is captured in her words: "If I can't feel nothing, ain't no need of me going to church. I want to feel the Spirit." Younger members echoed her sentiments. Anita, a choir member, who described herself as "one of those whooping and hollering people," talked about how she loved the excitement, particularly as it accompanied the increasing, climactic momentum of the message. She recalled being asked, "Why do you have to be so loud?" She responded,

> God is not nervous, He's not nervous, you know. We can shout and scream, he's not nervous. The Lord, he enjoys it, and the louder we give it. He [God] says, as long as you are praising me and not just making sounds. You know, really and truly, [God] enjoys it. And I can appreciate it because I know it doesn't take all that for a lot of people, but it take that for me and I enjoy [it]. I guess coming from a background of being laid back and [rules], "we can't do this" and "you can't do that." All these "can't do," "can't do" . . . I enjoy it, and I believe what it [the Bible] says when it says make a joyful noise unto the Lord. I enjoy being drugged; I enjoy being high on Christ. I get a kick out of that.

Everyone was not as expressive as Anita was, but the character of worship impacted those with quieter dispositions, as well. A member's euphoria communicates an authentic visitation of God's presence, which is enriching even to the observer. Linda, a self-proclaimed "nonshouter," gave voice to the sense of authenticity such a moment conveyed to her by contrasting her present joyous worship context with the staid congregation she once was a part of:

> I mean, at my mom's church, you know, you might see somebody tapping their foot but you're like, is there anything really going on in there [within the person]? Are you feeling anything? And I kinda feel like I'm still in that mode [of being quiet]. I'm not into shouting cause that's how I was raised, too, but I like seeing people [shout]—you can tell that something's going on, that they're feeling something and it's not fake.

Personal Associations

Church is meaningful not only because it connects one to God but also because it provides opportunities to build relationships and to establish familial and extended networks. The desire for a fellowship that feels like a family, an "extended" or "surrogate" community, was quite prominent among the women. Their choice of words signifies relatedness and function. The church is the place they turn to and depend upon for assistance when necessary. It serves to connect women to communication, service, and support networks. Church is valued for its ability to foster interpersonal relationships and to replace the impersonal engagements of the larger society. The desirable context is a church where one can be recognized by name or by face. It is somewhere you're likely to be missed when you're absent.

Size affects members' opportunities for fellowship and building alliances. Layton Temple's Sunday service attendance averages 100 persons. Calvary Baptist's average attendance began around 250; attendance more than doubled after the church relocated to the larger building. Denise wanted the church to grow but expressed concerns about the impact of constant growth on the worship services and on the sense of closeness she had come to value. "I love my church family. . . . I like the closeness. I hope because we're moving over to a larger building that we don't get so [quiet] . . . we are a jubilant people; we really enjoy praising and lifting up the name of Jesus, and I hope we keep that, don't lose that." She also noted that visitors sometimes comment on the friendliness of members.

> They say, "Oh, y'all so friendly." I move toward the visitors, [saying,] "Oh, hi, so glad you came, please come back again," all this kind of stuff like I [had] been knowing [them] for years. [There's] a lot [of people] at Calvary who say that's what brought them to us, they may visit twice and somebody say, "Oh, you back again" and make them feel good that the people remembered that they had been [there]. "Oh, it's so nice to see you." They say they just loved that. And I hope we keep that warmness because when you get into big churches as I said you just kind of lose it cause it just get so B-I-G, so big and [sighs] . . . I know, I don't want to put no limit on God. I want us to get big, but I want us to keep the same momentum of being a close-knit family.

Overall, these women did not see their church's size as prohibitive to building intimate relations, but several admitted they had experienced feelings of detachment, aloneness, and insignificance in other congregations. A married graduate student in her late twenties spoke of the self-affirmation she received in her church. She liked "just knowing that people look for you and you're not a number. They know your name, or at least they know your face. . . . They will at least know you weren't at church last Sunday. [They ask], where were you?" Yvette echoed a similar sentiment. Twenty-four and a recent addition to Calvary Baptist, she found the camaraderie, care, and implicit pledge of assistance appealing and compelling:

> Everybody in the church seems to be committed to each [other]. No one seems to be out on his or her own, [no] personal endeavors. I'm not saying they're going to be there, but nobody there seems to portray that [they won't]. I like an environment where everyone is unselfish, and no one is not good enough to be around.

In both churches, the older women were revered as wise elders and served on the Mothers Board. The younger women had each identified a special woman whom they regarded as an "adopted parent." Family was a common metaphor for the church. One woman seemed to take the metaphor literally. She regarded the pastor or the deacons as the patriarchs, and the Mothers Board fills the matriarch's role. As in a nuclear family, emotional expressions found within families—intimacy, warmth, recognition, hugs, and smiles—were also expected from the church family. Mother Williams recalled how she found her fellow members to be loving and accepting soon after she joined the church. At the onset of her visits, she was going through some "rough times."

> Every Sunday when I went to church, [I was] just getting hugged and shaking hands and feeling just as much a part as if I'd been there all the time, and I said, "Well, I ain't got to start at the bottom here." I don't think there's any place that I can go that will make me feel more like I can contribute something. I'm not much of a bench warmer. If I'm in something, I want to contribute. If you ain't doing nothing, I don't need to get on that bandwagon with you.

Initiating visits to those in the hospital or calling because someone missed a service or a meeting is another expected demonstration of care. These women sought and found church communities where fellow Christians were approachable and where pretentiousness was in small supply. Gail expressed the ethos of her church in these words:

> [The people are] just friendly and loving, a little phoniness in there every now and then, but you can get by that [laughs]. They're just loving people. I come from a very loving family. We kiss, we hug all the time. We see each other every day, but everyday we kiss, we hug. Everyday I tell

my mother, "I love you," you know. And so that's what goes on at Calvary, and when you're not there, you know you're missed because people will always say, "I missed you last Sunday" or "I didn't see you in church today"—that kind of thing, and it's not just when they see you. I've had people call [me]. I had some surgery a couple of years ago, and I mean, you would have thought my room was a floral shop. They just show love, and I like that.

Most women spoke lovingly of their churches. People were warm and inviting and made them feel accepted. Many metaphors and images were offered to connote the significance of the church. The adjective "safe" was one descriptor of church. It is "a safe place" and "a safe haven." I probed the meaning of safety with Rosalind. She elaborated,

> When I say "safe," you know that when you come to church, you can come and just pour your heart out to God. You [are] able to come and talk to someone about your problems, knowing that no one is going to go and put [it] all over the news, you see? [It's] someplace that you know you can go and feel like "I know I have a friend there." I know I can go and talk. It's somebody who's not going to compromise with you; they're going to set you straight and let you know if you're wrong [and] you've got to change, but without telling everybody, unless you feel comfortable with telling everybody.

Intimate relationships and a surrogate family were central concepts in women's assessment of the church. The nature of social relationships was given careful consideration when they were determining where to worship. Most of the women in this sample were active participants in the liturgical and missionary aspects of the church. They did more than appear on Sunday for the central worship service; they also volunteered time in two or three ministries in their churches.

Although intimate relationships were highly valued, some women in both churches appeared to separate their need for social relationships from the people and functions of the church. In other words, not everyone relied on the church for her social well-being to the same extent. For some, church is there to meet their spiritual needs; other needs could be fulfilled elsewhere. I found this sentiment among respondents who came to church alone. The phrases "I do not go to church to socialize" and "I'm a loner" were articulated more than once. Members of this smaller cohort found most of their friends outside the church. There were no uniform reasons for this compartmentalization. A member of Layton Temple was standoffish because she liked to have fun and relax and regarded the church members as "too sanctified." Others had alternate networks of friends they relied upon. They maintained close relations with friends in other churches, family members, and lifetime friends from days when they were not as active in a church. Offering a somewhat distinctive perspective from the others, Ellen admitted shying away from close attachments to church members. At age fifty-six, she doesn't go to church looking for understanding or acceptance.

> No, I don't go [for that] because I feel that I can praise the Lord and walk out of there and be on my way . . . and the reason [why]? I guess my background helps me with that. We were in a small church, and a small school, [they were] all black . . . growing up I thought people talked about me. I use to cry and come home, and my mom said, "They talked about Jesus Christ, so who are you?" so I got over that. So, I don't look for acceptance. I just go for one purpose, to praise the Lord, and then I get on out of there, because I've never been a person with a lot of friends. I've never been surrounded by a lot of people.

The women's comments were supported by their survey responses. On the average, women had two of their closest friends in their church, but one-third had no close friends in their church. Regardless of the degree of detachment from, or connection with, fellow church members, the women's positive regard for the church was sustained. They did not, nor do I, interpret this lack of close friends as meaning that they felt lonely or outside the religious community. Joyce held herself responsible for not developing relationships with people.

> I feel like I know the faces, even if I don't know the names, which I guess is the thing that I kind of want, to know people there. Nothing has really happened. I know people there superficially in a way. I like the deacons a lot. I feel like I know them real well. I feel like they provide a real good ministry, and [also] my pastor. But in terms of just other people, I don't really feel that close to other people in the church. When I go to church, I say "hi" and everything, "hi" and whatever, but I don't really feel like I'm that connected. But I know why that is. I'm going to take responsibility for a big part of that. I know from experience that one of the ways

that you get to know people is to get more involved in stuff that's going on and get involved in the different ministries, and you get to know people in those smaller pockets. You can develop more meaningful relationships, but right now, it's kind of hard to really get to know people, [with] just that little contact.

Joyce's involvement has been primarily Sunday morning worship over the past year and a half. It is her intention to begin attending Sunday school; however, a hectic work schedule has impeded her ability to participate in the classes, as well as to mingle and develop relationships with church members. Both she and her husband have jobs in medical fields that require long hours. Additionally, because she recently moved to Georgia, most of her friends live elsewhere.

> In the past, most of my friends were connected to the church. I don't have that many friends here. Most of my friends are not part of the church here. Most of my friends are out of state. And part of it, too, is that we [have] such frantic lives, we just don't have any time for [making friends at church]. We just work and come home and you're beat, and it's night. I get here at nine o'clock in the night; what time do I have to do anything?

Unlike Joyce, who faces time constraints, a member of the same church acknowledged that previously established networks had lessened her desire for more intimate relations with church members. The emotional and psychological support of family members she had relied on continued to be available to her. This member had been divorced while a member of another church but had sought no assistance from its members. When she joined Calvary, she had already emotionally detached from her husband. At the time of our interview, she had begun to develop relationships with other members, but the new attachments did not supplant her family's vital contribution to her sense of well-being. Her close relations with female family members are reflected in these words:

> We're [her sisters, her mom, and herself] extremely close, sometimes close to the point that I think it's detrimental. Because if anything were to ever happen to my mother, I think I'd probably crack up. Well, I know I wouldn't, because God wouldn't let me. But I'm extremely close to my mother and my sisters. You know, they're the persons I talk to.

Whereas women would usually talk to their girlfriends, I talk to my sisters. Yeah, we're kind of like that. I mean I have a girlfriend that I'm close with [in Calvary]. She's a support base for me now, but I didn't know her when I was going through my divorce. At the time of my divorce, my girlfriend who I consider my buddy was in [another state], and she had always told me that my marriage wouldn't last, anyway. So my mother and my sisters are my support.

Biblically Centered Preaching

Among the many accolades given to the Black Church is the high regard for the rhetorical skills of its preachers. Effective preaching can be the pivotal factor in church growth and in members' satisfaction. A preacher's expertise in proclaiming the gospel can also be an important determinant of his or her vocational mobility. Expertise is sometimes assessed by the preacher's skill in delivering of the message. At other times, content and contemporary relevance may be the elements on which the assessment of the preacher is based. The women referenced both execution and content as they revealed what constituted good preaching and its centrality to their lives.

In worship services, the overall rhythm, pace, greetings, music, and other elements of the service were important, but all were eclipsed in importance by the sermon. More than anything else, these women came to church for "the Word." The quality of the preaching was foremost in their consideration of which church to join. A few women went so far as to suggest that they could have a church service without music (or with very little), since the preaching was what they came for. Betty, now in her fifties, has spent all of her life in the Church of God in Christ. She described her love for the preached word this way:

> Now, see, I'm strange about music now. I don't care for it. I like to hear the choir sing. I support the choirs, as long as they're singing two songs, but don't try to give no concert. I don't like musicals. I'll go to them, but I'm bored stiff. I have gone and listened to different preachers all night long, but when it comes to music and stuff, I cannot sit there and listen to songs all night long. Never have done it. I don't listen to the radio unless I'm in my car. I had the radio on the other day, and some preacher was on and then they started some music. It's not that important to me

[music], like I said. I like praise service and all, but I don't like for it to go on forever. But I can listen to that preaching, yes, I can. I sit down some Saturday nights and watch TV; I think it's channel 52. Preacher after preacher, after preacher, after preacher comes on. I could listen to every last one of them till they go off.

I asked what she gained from listening to sermon after sermon.

I get the Word [chuckles]. I guess my spirit is hungry for more of it, and I think it's because every time you hear the same scriptures read and the same scriptures preached on, it's a different message, most of the time. Just to show you how the Lord operates, he gives one this measure to their understanding, and he gives another [a different] one, and then you get a deeper understanding of some of it. I just enjoy it.

In both Layton Temple and Calvary Baptist, the preaching was the apex of the worship service and commanded the rapt attention of worshippers. On my visits to Calvary Baptist Church, I observed worshippers jotting down notes during Reverend King's messages. In fact, he periodically reminded members to bring their own Bibles and to mark a significant text as he cited it. He also encouraged them to learn the Bible for themselves so that they would be able to evaluate whether someone was really preaching the Word with accuracy.

The women focused largely on the sermon's content and delivery. They desired clear expositions of the Bible and messages that were particularly relevant to present-day circumstances and challenges. They listened for sermons that were uplifting, addressed daily living, equipped them to handle crises, provided them with skills to share the Christian message, and strengthened their resolve to live the Christian life. Lori emphasized how relevance and applicability are very important aspects of preaching for her. She told me what she appreciated about Reverend King's sermons:

It's always something I can take with me throughout the week. I can reflect on it. I can think of when it ties into everyday living. I've heard a lot of preachers and . . . sometimes I don't know what they are talking about. It's nothing I can relate to, nothing that applies to my life, and therefore I find myself looking around the church, leaving church, and just not paying attention. That doesn't happen in church with me [now].

I'm really focused, because he brings the Word, and he brings it where it applies.

"The Word" should be delivered with conviction, clear illustrations, and not too much extraneous information attached to the message. Michelle regarded biblical exposition as primary in what she looked for in a church. I asked her, "If you were to prioritize what you go to church for, what would it be?" She quickly responded,

> The message. Because of the way that Reverend King relates the Bible and his teachings to day-to-day things that we all go through, deal with. [He] kind of gives you a different outlook and perspective and something to actually think about and hopefully make some changes, positive changes as a result of it. And the next would be music.

Deborah looks for the healing aspects of the gospel. It was part of what attracted her to the church. I asked her to reflect upon what she expects to get out of her church and how those needs are met at her church. She gave this answer:

> It is the liberation of the gospel when it is given in its raw form and not camouflaged. I think it would be liberation. . . . Most of his [Reverend King's] messages are very uplifting, very inspiring. He does not do a lot of fire-and-brimstone messages, so they're very healing. He has a very healing ministry, I think, and I think that's why the Lord has sent me there, I really do, for the healing. So, that's what I really get from his messages.

Sermon structures and delivery styles varied between the preachers and the two congregations. Some messages were structured with three-point outlines that meticulously interpreted five well-chosen verses. The sermon at Layton Temple was a complex interweaving of biblical citations and allusions, lessons of morality, admonitions to those who were causing strife, and counsel to married couples, all loosely held together by a text announced as the sermonic text but not thoroughly expounded upon. One of the sermons I heard at Calvary could be described as a well-crafted narrative with a constant movement between the biblical past and the present, punctuated with illustrations and scriptures aimed at pushing members toward spiritual growth and practical life changes. Despite the differences in delivery, the preaching slowly built toward a crescendo, erupting in a challenge to individuals to bring their lives more in line with the teachings of the Word or to commit their lives to God. Neither preaching style was preferred by women. Whooping, the climatic moment in traditional black preaching, marked by rhythmic tones, cadences, and testimonial fervor, was more a feature of Reverend King's preaching than of Elder Blue's. However, it was not a requirement for a sermon to be considered palatable.

Both pastors called down the spirit upon the people and called the people up to glimpse a new vision of God and God's purposes. In other words, the preaching was the bridge to creating a religious ethos through which one could experience oneself as loved by God. The climax of the preaching was regularly followed by periods of praise and shouting by the laity. While this occurred with a bit more consistency in Layton Temple than it did at Calvary, each congregation had its unique way of affirming the proclamation that had just gone forth.

As women talked about the centrality of preaching, they made a distinction between preaching and teaching (although there was not a rigid demarcation). Eva described preaching as "yelling" and "shoving stuff at people." She was not against the preacher's obvious enthusiasm as he preached but thought that "you could be excited and not raise your voice." Her description of teaching reflected the sentiments of several others:

> Teaching is when he takes his time, and he's not necessarily trying to get your attention with his volume, but he's trying to get attention by the relevance of what's in the Word and how it deals with you on a day-to-day basis and how we apply the Word to how we live. That's teaching, 'cause from that I've learned ways to handle life, to handle problems.

Many women favored this didactic approach. They recalled other churches they had attended where traditional preaching that ended with a whoop was not meaningful to them. Thelma, a woman in her late fifties, talked at length about her attraction to a teaching style rather than to preaching. She maintained a delicate balance between honoring the churches, which had nurtured her in the faith, and critiquing where they had fallen short in equipping the people of God.

> Back in the old days, the church was, like, that rock, that solid place and you went there, you went to service . . . it was something that we did.

We knew God, we believed in God and . . . [then] everything was based on right, wrong, and respect. You knew what was right, you knew what was wrong and you knew respect. You knew the church was a place of respect. You knew you had to respect the church. You knew certain things you didn't do in the church. . . . Your parents taught you those values, but [once] you got into the church, the things that the church should teach you, long years ago they just didn't teach you how to cope, I guess that's what I'm trying to say. The old church didn't teach you, didn't give you how to cope, [didn't tell you] where it is in the Bible. They preached and they called it . . . I have a cousin who's a preacher and he calls it, what is it when they [whoop], yeah, he calls it whooping, and you know that's what they did [makes noises imitating whooping], and sometimes you didn't even know what he was saying cause he was going through all these whooping phrases and stuff, and I remember, we still talk about it sometimes now, that you went to church and people said, "Yes, we had a good time, we had a good time, oh, he preached today." Then you ask[ed] him what did he preach about. "I don't know, honey, but he sure preached," you know, doing that sort of thing, so I got discouraged 'cause I wanted more than that.

Now she appreciates well-organized, thoughtful, and biblically based sermons. She feels that she is in a church where the Bible is primary; the emotional response and heightened sermonic ending (when it occurs) have a solid anchoring. Others were not as tolerant in their tastes as Thelma was. They looked for churches where they would not get a steady diet of whooping.

Just as there was variation in preferred preaching style, there was diverse opinions about what the content of the sermon should be. Betty noted that Elder Blue could address many topics in one sermon. Some of those seemed to be chosen according to what the membership was telling him in private about their lives.

You know, pastor's a preacher that skips around a lot. He'll start over here. He'll jump to here. He'll jump to there. I have no problem with that; a lot of people do. He'll preach on three, four, or five things in one sermon. He tries to go back to his main theme, but sometimes he does and sometimes he doesn't. That doesn't bother me, it really doesn't. Ask your question again?

I repeated my inquiry about the repetitive and major themes she hears in his sermons.

> I think sometimes he gets on the homosexuals a lot because people keep going to him and he says [pejorative words to describe them]. I said, "Pastor, you using some words, and every time you use them I cringe." He says "bulldagger," oh, I hate that word, and I just go, "Oh" and then he says, "sissies." The way he says it, you know? He was hitting on that pretty hard one time. But, then, I know a lot of people don't understand, but I know people are going to him and telling him stuff, so that he just had to do it. If he had not done it, then they would say he don't care, he just letting it go by and all that kind of stuff. He talks about . . . he was talking about sin the other day, just [says] sin is sin basically. That's what stands out in my mind, that he talks about. . . . The messages that he preaches . . . he's really talking to the men a lot of times, and I found out that some of these women [are] going to him about their husbands and stuff and so that's when I find him really preaching on that. That's when we know that somebody [has] been to him, and they might not want to call their husband in, see (that's what I think he should do). But then I guess he [the pastor] figures the wife would have to pay for it later.

Concerning sermon content, some women thought that too many references to social and political events could take away from the biblical instruction. Others thought that too many race-specific statements were a detriment to solid preaching, since the Bible and God's message were universally applicable. For everyone who was turned off by political commentary and race consciousness in the sermons, others welcomed this multilayered content. Gail, for instance, welcomed the inclusion (in moderation) of racial concerns in sermons. She can engage the issues of African Americans and racism and still affirm a racially inclusive church.

> I welcome hearing how to deal with [racism] at church, but I don't want it to be a constant thing. I don't blame everything that happens to me in life or in the workplace on the fact that I'm black. I guess I'm more or less accepting . . . to me it's like, "Okay, you're black, accept it. Things are not the same for you, they are not ever going to be the same for you, but then again if they were the same for you, you'd not be a stronger person." We're [Black people] actually more survivors because of the

way we've been treated. If we were treated any less, or any other way, I don't think we would be as good as we are in a lot of other things. So I look at that, and I don't think we should make an issue of our being black. I mean I have no problems with going to church with someone white.

In addition to preaching, which was an important element of worship, the Bible held a very authoritative position in the women's lives. A third of the group described the Bible in terms that indicated a literalist posture of interpreting Scripture. This subgroup regarded the Bible as "the inspired Word of God, without error not only in matters of faith, but also in historical, scientific, geographic, and other secular matters." An almost equal proportion regarded the Bible as inerrant with regard to faith and morals and as "the Word of God, and its stories and teachings [as] providing a powerful motivation as we work toward God's reign in the world." These two perspectives of Scripture suggest more liberal interpretation. The centrality of Scripture was also reflected in their devotional practices. Nearly two-thirds reported having some form of daily private prayer and meditation ritual. Slightly more than a quarter engaged in devotional practices at least weekly. Along with reading the Bible, they relied on other study aids for greater understanding of Scripture.

The first four dimensions of church discussed in this chapter pertain to the worship service. These elements—prayer, praise, communal associations, and preaching—point to the fundamental ritual elements and ethos that ground and sustain these church women's spiritual lives. A dimension of church life that impacts all the others is the fifth element—pastoral leadership.

Pastoral Leadership

Reverend King and Elder Blue are much-loved pastors in their congregations. They are held in high regard and exhibit the qualities that were identified as desirable in a pastor. These include integrity, ability to preach and teach, a pleasant personality, accessibility, and approachability. Political involvement in the community was of lesser significance. The church needs to be led by a pastor with conviction, but not one who is an autocrat or a dictator. A pastor must be someone who can cast a vision and motivate congregants to support it. A member of Layton Temple spoke in this vein:

> Basically, I look for a pastor that I've never heard anything about, you know [nothing] wrong, and one that preaches the Word. See, I'm gonna tell you, he ain't got to be a great preacher, he does not have to be the greatest preacher in the world, just preach me the truth. I'll deal with the rest of it. So I look for a saved pastor. See, I can deal with the sinners around me [laughs heartily], but you give me a saved pastor because I want my leaders to be saved, but the rest of it, I don't care. . . . I believe in being committed to the church as a whole, as a body. I believe in being committed to the pastor and his wife. If I can't be committed to them, you know, I don't need to be there. I believe in the pastor's program. If he has a vision from God, I believe in helping him to carry it out as best as I can. I don't believe in bucking against the pastor. I don't believe in talking about the pastor. I don't believe in talking about his wife, but sometimes I might be a little guilty of it. But she's sweet, and, you know, we tell her to her face [she's sweet]. . . . You know, that's how I look at them. My son would often see Elder Blue out in public, in the grocery store, at the gas station. He never would say anything to him, he'd just stand back and watch him. He'd say [to me], "Ma, he's always the same. He never changes; you don't ever hear him getting loud, laughing loud, acting common, you know, you never see that in Elder Blue." And that's why he joined our church, although he don't go there [now].

The pastor is the chief interpreter of the Word. His word is to be given respect and followed, but it is not totally definitive even in interpreting Scripture. Women submitted to pastoral leadership without relinquishing confidence in their own abilities to decipher the Bible for themselves. Mother Williams, confident in her hermeneutic skills, recalled being under the leadership of a nationally prominent television evangelist when she lived in another state. That preacher was known in part for his teaching of a "prosperity" gospel.[4] According to her, he was sometimes boastful about his possessions and implied that material acquisition was linked to one's spiritual condition. "He would tell you if you weren't doing certain things that's why you don't have a Cadillac or, you know, that kind of thing. . . . I didn't believe that and some of the other things that he said, but I knew that the man was ordained."

While she listened to his preaching with skepticism sometimes, she was still confident in his pastoral leadership and regarded him highly. She said, "Nobody would go through what you have to go through and build a ministry like he built and all if they're not sincere. The pastorate especially is very difficult." Perseverance and sincerity were qualities that endeared him to her. They seem to function as a sort of litmus test as to whether the preacher was really authentic and committed. She had no tolerance for persons who spoke negatively of pastors or tried to sanction them. The accountability and correction of the pastor is not the laity's duty but God's:

> Some people think that their duty is to monitor and direct the pastor. I hear people say, "I told him so and so," and I look at them and say, "You don't know how dangerous that is." God doesn't need me to monitor his ordained. He didn't put no halo around my head and tell me, "You check out this new pastor I've ordained." You know what I'm saying? So, I tell people that all the time when they, especially when they start running their pastor down to me, I will tell them how I feel, and if they want to continue, I just walk off.

Other women regarded the pastor's pronouncements as worthy advice but not always binding, especially in the areas of marriage and child rearing. Betty is married, and her husband is not a Christian. She gave her pastor's sermons a positive evaluation; however, she didn't give equal endorsement to him (and his wife) as counseling resources.

> I wouldn't dare go to my pastor with stuff like that [referring to marital strife] unless it was something I really needed counseling with. You know if it's not, if it hasn't, it's according to what it is. I wouldn't go to him . . . maybe something like that [communication issue], but I wouldn't go to him about my husband's adultery or stuff like that, 'cause, see, they could advise you, but if they haven't been through it, it makes a difference, even if you've heard about it a whole lot and [not been through it]. But they've never experienced that kind of thing, so what they're telling me may not even [be appropriate].

It was pointed out "there's a fine line between advice and telling someone what to do." While they expected the pastor to give instruction in these areas, they believed that the words of the pastor were not to be treated as universally applicable or binding. Concerning the church and the pastor's role in a member's life, Linda provided this perspective: "I think they can offer guidance. They can offer counseling. But each marriage is different because each person is different, so I think all they can do is set the guidelines and tell you, 'This is what the Bible says' or 'This is what experts say' or whatever, but they can't actually tell you what to do."

The entire group of women held their pastors in high esteem and expected that they would lead by example. However, their high regard and their expectation of exemplary leadership did not blind them to human failure. Several women had previously changed churches on the heels of scandals involving clergy accused of various ethical violations. Now, years after the fact, some of the women were still reluctant to talk about those situations in any depth. Others had remained members of congregations through those tumultuous times. The decision to leave or remain was not predicated solely on knowledge of an indiscretion or misconduct. The congregation's (and the official board's) responses, the pastor's reaction to the charges, and the overall impact on the congregation influenced their decisions, as well.

Early in my time at Calvary Baptist, I learned that Reverend King had been accused of misconduct at one of his former pastorates.[5] The charge of misconduct (although unconfirmed) was a pivotal reason for his leaving that congregation and founding a new one. I pursued inquiry into this area cautiously since the women were reluctant to talk about it. Some of their fears that they were revealing a secret or "talking about the pastor" seemed to dissipate when they realized I had knowledge of the circumstances before speaking to them. How aware were they of these past events? Had the accusation influenced their decision to join the church? What was its impact upon their decision whether to retain membership in this congregation? I sought answers to these questions and was more interested in the impact of the charges of impropriety than in the events themselves. The women's responses to my probes demonstrated both practical and theological considerations. The pastor's humanity, the demonstration of Christian forgiveness, and their awareness of their own imperfections and failures intersected to counter any hasty judgments.

Previously an active member of a Pentecostal denomination, Susan was totally dismayed by what she had learned about church members and Baptist polity through the period of accusations. The process of charging a pastor and members' making allegations against their pastor was a shock to her. She thought that the charges were ludicrous and was more bothered by the suspicious way in which the "evidence" was gathered and how members reacted than by the accusation itself. She observed a lot of confusion and harassment of the pastor. She ultimately relied on her ability to "try the spirit by the spirit" to sort it all out. In her estimation, he had demonstrated more Christlike behavior than the parishioners accusing him had, so when the church divided she followed Reverend King to the new church plant. Other women of Calvary expressed confidence in Reverend King's leadership, notwithstanding the past events. Having already regarded him as their spiritual mentor, they had decided to remain loyal to his leadership. They believed that the sanctioning of clergy was God's responsibility. God would be the judge of everyone's sins, and it wasn't their job to expose another person's human frailties.

One of the women in this group has been under Reverend King's pastoral leadership in three churches. Now in her senior years and a member of the Mothers Board, she talked about coming to terms with the allegations.[6]

> And I thought, whatever he done, long as he carrying the Word of God, I'm listening [to] the Word of God, not what they saying about him. . . . I'm trying to work out my own soul's salvation, and whatever he doing, he got to give an account of it himself. I don't have to give an account of what he's doing. I got to work and see God for myself. Rumors, I guess they will always be floating.

Anne had been a member of this same congregation about a year before the split occurred in the second congregation. She spoke of what she looked for in a church and how that related to her processing the conflict surrounding the pastor. "I look for a pastor who . . . is God-sent, and that I can sort of feel that in his presentation of the Word, and I also look for encouragement, support, reassurance, that kind of stuff coming from the church body as well as from the pastor." Like others who had no clear evidence to support the claims, she eventually dismissed the charges as mere rumor and malicious slander.

> Ministers are called of God, and if there is a character defect, that's not for me to judge, and I felt like as long as he was doing his job as a minister, you know, I was okay with that. And I guess probably the fact that it was just rumored as far as I knew; [I was okay] cause I didn't know of any of it to be fact.

She was not ignorantly closing her eyes to what she did not want to confront. She had already recounted to me a prior "church scandal" that she had experienced at another church, which involved a prominent church leader who had impregnated a teenager in their congregation. The issue of proof seemed critical to her judgment of the situation. Her decision might have been different if she had had facts, rather than rumors.

Rosalind, who joined the church aware of the past controversy surrounding the pastor, spoke of its impact on her as very slight, but she had not dismissed it altogether. "I wasn't there. I was aware of it, but I didn't get involved in it. I mean, [name of friend] is very close to Reverend King, so, uh, she kept me informed about what had happened and all that kind of stuff, but I don't get involved in politics in church." As I inquired as to whether she had been at all hesitant to join the church once she had this information, she quickly replied, "Nope, it was about the message, it was about what I felt at that church as a whole. So that never bothered me." She not only made her peace with these revelations; she had also reconciled knowledge of two other incidents of clergy misconduct. One concerned a pastor accused of mismanagement of funds and an extramarital relationship; the other concerned her encounter with a pastor during her teenage years. In this latter situation, she had fended off his sexual advances as he chased her around his office. The pastor was the individual who allocated the church's scholarship funds to high school students, and, in her estimation, she was later denied a scholarship because she had not given in to his sexual advances. Rosalind, who spoke matter-of-factly about these past incidents, could be called a realist. She stated, "I don't get involved so much [in the politics of the church]. I'm not surprised at stuff that goes on in church, among human beings. We are still human beings." She never stopped going to church because of these incidents. She even spoke of extending forgiveness to those pastors.

> I pray for them. I pray for Reverend King. The way he ministers to me, I almost felt that, whatever it was, it was gonna be made all right. That whatever happens, God, you know, none of us are perfect. Heaven knows I'm not perfect. Why should I expect him to be? But to see somebody be molded and changed, that's a blessing to me.

Only one woman spoke of a church scandal so distasteful that she had abandoned church for several years. The majority, however, believed that the durability and power of the church was greater than the moral failure of its leadership or a scandal. Their institutional loyalty was rooted in their practical and theological understandings of self and community. A professional woman in her mid-forties was shocked one night when a church officer shared gossip and slanderous remarks about a member with her. She eventually came to regard the incident as a test of her faith, rather than as an incident that would cause her to leave the church. She is resolved to look beyond human frailty to God in times of church conflict.

> I'm going to be there anyway because I'm not there for the people; I'm there for me. I just had to realize that you [couldn't] put your faith in people; they're human. You know that just because somebody is a deacon or a deacon's wife, that doesn't make [him or her] any less human or any less capable of wrongdoing than it does me. That goes for the pastor, too, because if I had listened to rumors about the pastor, I would've been long gone.

Discussion

One of the more obvious conclusions to draw from these data is that the worship practices and ethics of the Black Church maintain continuity with the constitutive elements upon which African American have rested their faith for generations. The preaching, praying, praise, and fellowship may change in their length and form, but they still anchor the black Protestant religious experience. Rather than deacons lining hymns, now praise teams initiate this corporate celebration of God's presence. While persons commute longer distances to church and have greater choices of ministries to which to channel their unique gifts and talents, their regard for a church can turn on whether "somebody knows my name." Preaching has to be an experience beyond cognitive appeal. Women want all of their senses engaged in service; their hearts and their heads must be appealed to equally.

These devotees do not take preaching lightly. While they depend on their pastors to rightly divide the scriptures, they don't relinquish their interpretive skills entirely to the pastor. These women were confident that they could hear God for themselves even while they admitted some limitations in their biblical knowledge. Confidence in their own interpretive skills fostered independent thinking and subverted an uncritical dependency upon pastoral leadership or teachings.

In the act of preaching, the minister fulfills the priestly function of mediating an encounter with the Holy. It is the preacher's task to create a liminal space through rhetorical performance, to enable persons to move from the profane into the realm of the sacred. Preaching becomes the occasion for instruction, proclamation, rebuke, and, most of all, transcendence. The quality of preaching is assessed by how intensely one can make an unseen God visible or make the intangible truths about the Divine appear more compelling than present realities. African American preaching has not traditionally been a one-way communication. It is dialogical, engaging the heart and the head, the pulpit and the pew, and eliciting spontaneous responses of affirmation. In some denominations, the call-response character of congregational expressiveness may be minimal or discouraged, but the expectation of the climatic preaching moment remains constant. Robert Franklin summarizes the expectation this way: "Black people expect the sermon, as a word inspired by God and located within the community, to be spiritually profound, politically relevant, socially prophetic, artistically polished, and reverently delivered."[7]

While traditional black preaching still holds sway in many African American congregations across the country, church women give witness to the increasing appeal of a more expository style of proclamation. The attraction need not indicate a disdain for the former style as much as the desire for more of the best of black preaching—anchoring a sermon in the Bible with practical relevance and application, clearly articulated. As if listening to a self-help guru or a motivational speaker, women want practical steps for change. They want stages for implementation of their faith, not just inspiration to remain faithful. Jubilant climaxes layered on a skeleton of a message are hollow. On the other hand, hearing a preacher "going to Calvary" at the conclusion of an instructive and inspiring sermon is uplifting.

These women did not have a uniform regard for the Bible. Their survey responses indicated their view of the Bible aligns with the conservative end of the spectrum. For them, the Bible is inerrant, infallible, and true in fact as well as in theological significance. However, this may simply reflect the "official" teaching they have ingested regarding the Bible, rather than how they are actually utilizing and reading Scripture. African Americans have affirmed a high view of Scripture while simultaneously functioning as if there's a canon within a canon.

This reading strategy renders some parts of the Bible more authoritative than others. Because of the oppressive way in which the Bible was used among slaves, slaves did not appropriate the use of the Bible without proving it by their own experiences and liberation paradigm.[8] The theologian Howard Thurman recounts this hermeneutic strategy at work. His grandmother, a former slave, always forbade him to read to her from the letters of Paul.

> With a feeling of great temerity, I asked her one day why it was she would not let me read any of the Pauline letters. What she told me I shall never forget. "During the days of slavery," she said, "the master's minister would occasionally hold services for the slaves. Old man McGhee was so mean that he would not let a Negro minister preach to his slaves. Always the white minister used as his text something from Paul. At least three or four times a year he used as a text 'Slaves, be obedient to them that are your masters as unto Christ.' Then he would go on to show how it was God's will that we were slaves and how, if we were good and happy slaves, God would bless us. I promised my Maker that if I ever learned to read and if freedom ever came, I would not read that part of the Bible."[9]

Thurman's grandmother depicts how some African Americans, recognizing the manipulation of the biblical text, claimed the right to interpret Scripture and to wrestle with its meanings in light of their existential knowledge of God. Confident that she knew "her master," she rejected the imposition of the slave master's Christianity. I am not suggesting that contemporary church women reject entire books of the Bible categorically. They have, however, learned to claim their authority to interpret it and believe they can distinguish what is God's voice and what is a biased pastoral interpretation or misplaced emphasis.

The biblical scholar Renita Weems has offered one explanation for why black women continue to be attracted to the Bible and find solace in it, even as an increasing number of scholars articulate "eloquent and impassioned charges against the Bible as an instrument of the dominant culture." She rejects the idea that African American women's love of the Bible indicates a "lack of sophistication" or a "slavish dogmatic devotion to the Bible."[10] Its attraction is not predicated on blind allegiance, but the Bible is central in black women's lives because the portrait of human relations it presents "reflects a distinctive way of living that African American women have valued and continue to advocate with great energy."[11]

Weems provides a compelling argument that what may sometimes appear to be biblical literalism is actually a critical appropriation of the Bible informed by the experience of oppression in America. Oppression has taught black women to "resist those things within the culture and the bible that one finds obnoxious or antagonistic to one's innate sense of identity and to one's basic instincts for survival."[12] I do not have sufficient data to determine whether these women's regard for Scripture is a thin veil for a more subversive reading of the Bible. However, Mother Williams's critique of the prosperity gospel suggests a reading strategy through which she aligned herself with the oppressed rather than the privileged. We need to know much more about the social locations and theological commitments of the women in this group to assess how black women read the Bible. Weems's analysis tempers any quick conclusions that black women are fundamentalists or that their public theology and regard for the Bible necessarily tells us how they read it.

The Black Church has functioned as a surrogate family during the postemancipation period, the northern migrations of the twentieth century, and even the destabilization of urban families in the post–civil rights era. The practices of creating fictive kin, establishing extended family networks, providing economic and social assistance, and transmitting moral teachings for those experiencing hardships has been one of the legacies of the Black Church. The assumption of responsibility for one another occurs within the confines of the Black Church as worshippers interact. Through fellowship, or sometimes through formal channels through which they seek assistance, members establish new networks that bring persons from the periphery of a new community into the flow of resources and new associations. The importance of church relationships may also be heightened for recent migrants to the state or for single persons in the church.

Among the group of church women that I studied, twelve were native Georgians. The rest had relocated from other parts of the country and had only their immediate household family members to rely on. The associations forged through collective worship and church involvement ameliorate feelings of displacement, establish new relationships, and provide access to the local African American community for interpersonal as well as business purposes.

Many women regard the church first and foremost as a family. Given the prevalence of this image, an unexpected finding was the dual orientations toward developing intimate relationships. One orientation was to be engaged; the other was to have arm's-length interactions. The first orientation needs little elaboration. Engaged women attended worship and participated in other aspects of the church's life. They valued establishing emotional and spiritual ties with fellow members, not just instrumental ones. On the other hand, the arm's-length group neither desired nor maintained close friendships with other church members. They took satisfaction in getting their explicitly spiritual needs met through worship but depended upon nonchurch members for their larger support system. Demographics cannot account for this distinction. In both groups, there was a nearly equal division between married and single persons; half had children, and their positions ranged from student to full-time employed. The women's length of time in their congregation was not a distinguishing factor.

That individual needs for church friendships among women vary should not be surprising. In the absence of a definitive explanation, I suggest that one or more of the following reasons may be at work. The arm's-length stance of some women toward church peers suggests that they compartmentalize church from other dimensions of their life. It may also be that the trust, mutuality, time, personal vulnerability, and intimacy that are intrinsic to sustaining friendships were in limited supply for these women at that time. A third possibility is that the church has become only one of many spheres where they find meaning and sustenance. Given their ability to negotiate and direct their work, family, social lives, and other dimensions of their lives with greater freedom than was once accorded blacks, these women may believe that the relatedness found in the Black Church is not as central to the maintenance of their cohesive family system or church association as it once was. Women turn to the church for explicitly religious education and fortification, rather than for the ancillary social benefits. Thus, the arm's-length and engaged postures are not opposing orientations as much as two positions on a fellowship continuum. The church may still be the unrivaled institutional center of the black community, but, in some women's lives, it has competition.

In the Black Church, the preacher is expected to be a role model, head and shoulders above the rest of the congregation. The women's decisions to submit to pastoral authority are related to their assessment of the pastor as a spiritually rooted leader with integrity. Church has to be a safe context, and the pastor's demeanor and skill are fundamental to creating a sense of community. Scandals, therefore, can destroy the sanctity of this institution. Here we find one of the many tensions that church women in these congregations and beyond have faced—how to respond to misconduct by clergy without ruining the communities that they cherish so dearly. There was no unified response to this challenge. My conversations with these women occurred before the national exposure, indictment, and conviction of the Reverend Henry Lyons, in 2000. The attention given to the improprieties of the former president of the National Baptist Convention, USA, Inc., incited various debates and commentary in both the Black and the national media about clergy ethics.[13] However, these women considered the ethics of the accused as well as the accusers, as was done in the public discourse surrounding Reverend Lyons's improprieties. They also reflected upon their own human fragility and on Christian teachings on judgment and forgiveness. Often, this combination led them either to extend forgiveness to the clergyman or to postpone judgment. This stance raises concerns about female complicity in maintaining a moral double standard, one for members and another for the clergy.

Women's alleged acceptance of clergy misconduct points to a larger pattern of silence in black churches. I am not suggesting that these women should have responded to knowledge of alleged clergy misconduct any differently than they did. It is clear, however, that acceptance (not to be construed as approval) of clergy misconduct is one of the impediments to open discourse about clergy ethics, sexuality, and sexual ethics in the Black Church. This complicity may be manifested in different ways. First, members are willing to offer forgiveness and to put the past behind them. Second, women may shy away from ensuring that sexual ethics is included on the agendas of Christian education conferences or gatherings of ministers' wives and clergy. Third, women may regard misconduct as a temporary moral failure, rather than examine it as an abuse of power that has larger ramifications for the entire congregation's health.

Several women either lived through, or were aware of, the accusations made against their pastor in Calvary Baptist. They regarded him as a good, solid spiritual mentor for themselves. Thus, it seems that when the spiritual worship is especially meaningful, people can separate the messenger from the message. Additionally, while they revere the clerical role, none of the women expected perfection. They acknowledged clergy's humanity and all the temptations that exist and concluded that a minister's moral failure need not necessarily result in outrage or distrust of the minister's usefulness as God's instrument.

To a significant degree, African American clergy still attract followers by the power of their charismatic leadership. In contrast to mainline denominations, which embed ecclesiastical authority in the office and the hierarchy of the church, a unique effervescence, effective leadership, and charisma are the attributes that maintain clerics in African American pulpits. The independent organizational structures of many black denominations mean that there is no formal process or extracongregational authority to appeal to when one encounters accusations against a pastor. This leaves the responsibility for investigation and adjudication to the laity.

Clergy misconduct impacts the Black Church long after the event or accusation, for the oral tradition keeps these stories alive and even generates embellished versions that continue to circulate. Most religious communities expect a more stringent code of moral behavior from the clergy than from the membership. In reality, however, it seems that a lower standard of behavior for clergy is all too easily accepted. This has been particularly frustrating for men who are concerned that the clergy are forgiven for behaviors that are unacceptable for other men inside or outside the church. Men are disconcerted by what appears to be a double standard that allows male pastors to violate the norms by carousing, womanizing, drinking, or gambling. They also believe the shortcomings of male ministers are forgiven by a largely female audience, while other men's indiscretions and "failures" are not and are not taken in equal stride.[14] The church stands under indictment by some black men for its reluctance to admonish, correct, and restore those within its own ranks. Consequently, the folklore of clergy misconduct quietly undermines and diminishes the church's symbolic role as a haven, a locus of spiritual sustenance, and a standard bearer for those outside (and inside) its walls. While the public perception may suggest that women are the lenient ones, there is reason to challenge this view. At the congregational and denominational levels, it is usually male-dominated boards that have the official power to determine whether to investigate a pastor's conduct and to oversee the process of adjudication and censure in the case of clergy misconduct. Nonetheless, in the face of an occasional public scandal, the Black Church continues to endure, attracting new persons to the Christian faith through its effervescent worship, its powerful proclamations, its promises of extended family, and its extension of God's grace and human compassion to those who stumble.

3

The Fuel That Keeps Me Going
Practical and Spiritual Assistance

I can't imagine not going to church. It's a place I can just be me. If I want to cry, if I want to be happy or if I just want to sit there, I'm very comfortable. It lets me reflect on what last week was about and pray this week is going to be a better week. When I don't go to church, I notice the difference. When I don't go to church, maybe it's just psychological, but I just feel like I'm lost. My week, I don't know what to expect, because I haven't been in church, I haven't prayed. I haven't started my week off right.   —Lori

Church is a very important aspect of Lori's life. It contributes stability and structure to her week. It is a place where she can express a range of emotions and be herself. When she doesn't attend on a Sunday, she perceives a difference in how the week unfolds. Church and her belief in God are the glue that holds life's experiences together. Without church, a sense of listlessness emerges. Since she has such a strong reaction to not attending, we must ask what it is that makes church such a significant element of her well-being.

Sociologists have provided us with several explanations of religious attendance among church women. Labor force participation, women's role as the primary child care provider, the focus in church upon matters germane to "women's work," and the existence of specialized enclaves where women can exercise power and address their specific concerns are some of the more plausible theories for women's church attendance.[1] These theories provide useful information for understanding women's church attendance at the macro level; yet they are limited in accounting for variation between individuals or groups of women who have had different rates and types of workforce participation. They also don't account for the effect of different cultural norms and practices.

Along with sociologists, several womanist scholars have given attention to the centrality of the church in the lives of black women.[2] Less concerned than sociologists with the trends in church participation, womanist scholars have emerged primarily in the disciplines of theology, ethics and religiocultural practices of congregational life.[3] Womanists affirm and document the agency and contribution of past and present women in the establishment and work of the church. These scholars also lead the way in critiquing the oppressive practices of the Black Church. They have criticized the use of gender-exclusive language, the symbolism of the divine, formulations of suffering, the lack of leadership roles for women, and the use and abuse of power within the church. The most strident voices imply that the Black Church is not a place of equality and liberation for women. Theologian Delores Williams cites numerous violations of the African American Denominational Churches against black women and its membership at large. On her list of infractions she includes sexism that denies women equal opportunity in the church's leadership roles; the collusion between some black male preachers and the political powers in America; the indoctrination of black women to self-sacrifice and emotional dependence at the expense of self-love and healthy self-esteem; and the failure to adequately pool resources to combat poverty rather than to build new edifices. She also cites the church's rejection of the preaching and pastoral call of women, its silence in the midst of the AIDS epidemic, its incitement of homophobia, and its otherworldly focus and lack of concrete responses to immediate hardships.[4]

Critiques of the Black Church's treatment of women cannot be lightly dismissed. Sister Lori is finding inspiration and hope in the very institution some womanists portray as failing to address women's realities. To explore this inconsistency, I begin from the premise that congregations are vital contexts that often fulfill multiple needs of women adequately enough to garner their loyalty. To deny women's positive regard for the church is to regard them as passive vessels without the critical skills to evaluate the churches in which they participate and to underestimate black women's abilities to live in places of paradox.

In exploring the types of assistance the church provides and the needs it meets for this group of black women, I assume that whatever frustrations do exist are not overwhelming. I explore the central concerns of black women's lives that the Black Church does address sufficiently. How do women gain access to resources of the church, and which type of assistance is most pertinent to them? A word about what constitutes assistance is appropriate here.

In their research on the range and access of services to elderly African Americans provided by the church, Robert J. Taylor and Linda M. Chatters identified three primary categories of assistance—instrumental, emotional, and appraisal—and the patterns of delivery related to them. The instrumental category includes direct services and material aid. Emotional assistance relates to empathy and caring, and the appraisal dimension refers to the information and benefits provided to the recipient regarding personal issues.[5]

The types of assistance I identified were not as discreet as those in Taylor and Chatters's study; the forms of assistance often overlapped. For instance, a visit made by church members to a congregant who is recuperating from an illness has elements of all three. There is the direct giving of money and food (instrumental), the emotional uplift of feeling cared for (emotional), and the reinforcement of one's importance and value as a member of the community (appraisal). Because of the overlapping nature of the types of assistance, some situations were easier to delineate as belonging to one category more than another. I discuss these aspects as discrete types of assistance as much as possible. However, it is clear from the women's descriptions that the support they receive from their church and members overlaps categories.

Taylor and Chatters do not give particular attention to religious education and fellowship as services the church provides. However, I included them in the appraisal category because they are two additional opportunities for the individual to enhance or reassess her identity and life direction. I give attention to the range of services received and the meaning that women give to them. In some of my questions, I used the term "benefits," as well as "services", "aid," and "help," when referring to types of assistance. These terms are used interchangeably throughout the chapter.

In these women's lives, the types of assistance most received were not evenly distributed across the categories. Instrumental assistance was the least often cited. Emotional and appraisal assistance were discussed to a greater degree. In the emotional and appraisal categories I have included several dimensions that emerged from these women's lives but were not items that Taylor and Chatters included. These are supply of role models, spiritual fortification, empowerment for work, and reconstituted identity and enhanced self-esteem.

Instrumental Assistance

The group of women I studied received two primary forms of instrumental assistance: help with household tasks and help in taking care of family members. Church members had come to their aid when they needed furniture moved, transportation to church, groceries purchased, and yardwork completed. Visitation by the pastor or church members during illness was repeatedly cited as a form of care. Often, prayers, food donations, monetary gifts, and telephone calls accompanied these visits and continued afterward.

One recipient of instrumental aid was a sixty-seven-year-old widow. She had worked as a live-in babysitter for much of her life and had been on public assistance several times over the course of her life. She received assistance from members getting to and from her work locations and was picked up for services on Sunday. As she recounted times when her church family had been there for her, she strung together numerous examples.

> Now if I need something from people in the church, they respond. I have a good church family. They respond right quick. I can call on the deacons' wives and any of them will come to my rescue. . . . [Can you give me an example?] Gosh, I have so many of them. I needed some money to get one of my grandsons some shoes one year when school was fixing to start. Well, one of the members pulled out $35 and gives it to me to get my [grand]son some shoes, and I didn't have to pay it back. And then I had some more members, this was before they left here, I could ask Barbara for some money; I asked Barbara, "Could I get $100 from you and I'll pay it back to you later?" I ain't never paid that money back, but I got $100 from her and her husband went and bought me groceries once, just bought me a big, big bag of white potatoes, 'bout like that [indicating size], and bought me flour, meal, and blackeyed peas, and pinto beans. They just, my church people been real good to me, . . . and just about a month ago, well, one of the church members give me money for Christmas, and they give me Christmas baskets and stuff for Christmas turkeys. Yeah, I have some good church members.

Another woman, also a senior citizen, received help in acquiring furniture she needed.

> I've never had to go to the church for anything. I'm trying to think, never, never. . . . But I think they would be there. They know that I am a devoted member, and I'm sure they know my financial situation with the church . . . in fact, I have another table and new chairs. I was like, I needed a table and chairs for Christmas, and the deacon couldn't get it over here fast enough. They come and do things around my house for me because they know I'm single. They clean my gutters and don't want to take any money, just different things like that.

Overall, direct assistance to church members was minimal and infrequent, although it did exist. Most of the women had never asked for any practical aid. This may be indicative of the median income of the group and the large proportion of them that fell in the middle-class economic brackets. Direct assistance most often was offered to those in lower economic brackets. The median range of household income of Layton Temple members was $20,000 to 34,999. Eighteen percent had household incomes between $50,000 and 79,999. The median household income for Calvary Baptist was between $35,000 and 49,999. Both churches had nearly the same percentage (19 percent) earning between $50,000 and 79,999. Seven percent of the Baptist church members reported household incomes of $80,000 or more. Overall, Layton Temple members appear to have slightly lower incomes.

Emotional Assistance

Role Models

Single mothers identified the provision of role models for young children as a notable form of emotional assistance. In each congregation, there were educational classes for toddlers through youth where children were introduced to the Christian faith. There was also a cohort of adult males who functioned as adoptive fathers, big brothers, or models of upstanding Christian persons. The role the men fulfilled was not economic in nature but a symbolic and surrogate one. A thirty-four-year-old member of Calvary had her son several years before she got married. She joined during her pregnancy. She looked for and found a church that would function as an extended family. Members have been accessible to her and helpful in rearing her son.

> At the time in which I left [my former church], I was pregnant with Bobby, and I knew that I wanted him to grow up in a church where he could have a similar church experience as I did . . . developing friendships and being, you know, feeling like he's a part of [it], and if he felt like he needed to go to somebody, somebody he could talk to who was not family. . . . 'Cause I don't, we don't have no other family here, [that is,] biological family. It's just the three of us. I wanted him to be able to have that as a support mechanism.

Tony, a single parent, spoke of the aid she received from a church official in guiding her son when he was having trouble at school.

> We've never been sick or anything, but a couple of times my son was acting up in school a couple of years ago. I asked the children's chapel coordinator and his Sunday school teacher to talk to him, and they did. I don't know if it made any difference. I'm probably the one that made a difference, beating his behind or restricting him, or whatever I did [laughs]. They talked to him; they love my son.

Support through Illness and Family Crises

Another common source of aid was emotional support prior to and after being hospitalized. This support came primarily in the form of visits and prayer support. A respondent spoke of the host of visitors she had after surgery.

> Well, I had surgery, had a hysterectomy, and the deacons came to pray with me and visited me. The minister of music [came also]; not Reverend King, then we had Reverend Bell. I don't know if you remember Deacon Jones, he came to be with me during my surgery. He came to see me while I was in the hospital to be with me. The deacon's wife, she came back to visit with me. They called me to check on me, to see if I needed anybody to do anything for me, to pray with me. When I was out another time for my back, I was out the month of September last year with my back. I had a pinched nerve in my back, and again the deacons called

me. Reverend called me. Choir members called me to check on me to see how I was doing, if I needed anything and they prayed with me.

Another woman recalled the immediate response of members when her aunt died. "When my mother's sister died, the deacons were right there. I mean, that same night they were there. I feel like if there's anything I needed that I could call the church and they would be there."

The majority of participants were largely pleased with the services rendered by church members and the pastor. A few expressions of discontent about the fulfillment of these tasks did surface. One participant stated that a select group of members appear to command more of the pastor's attention than others do. One time, her name had been listed in the bulletin announcing she was home recovering from illness, but no one came to visit. Once recuperated, she made a point of informing the pastor of her concerns. She believes it was influential in putting some new protocols in place for deacons and membership committee members to keep abreast of persons assigned to them. Although the system still does not work smoothly, she saw improvement and was pleased with the response of the congregation the next time she was sick.

> I don't know if the prayer counselors or someone else had picked it up. . . . I do know the next time I got sick I got flowers and a card [laughs]. . . . But you know my thing was I shouldn't [have to] come to you to point this out . . . and it's happened to other people too . . . I'm not doing this, saying it just for myself. I'm saying it for others too. . . . You count up my tithes [laughs] . . . and I don't miss a beat with the tithes [which she sent even while convalescing at home].

While the amount of discontent was minor, it should not be dismissed. It reveals a conflict between the minister's style of pastoral care and the members' expectations of their pastor and congregation. Reverend King, the pastor of Calvary, stresses members' connections to one another and is pleased with the pastoral care that the membership provides to each other.

> I'm usually the last one to know [if someone is sick]. Really, this is no lie. If someone gets ill, is hospitalized or homebound, by the time I get to see them, members and deacons have been to see them before I even get there. When I get there, they'll say, "Oh, the deacons were here last

Sunday" or "The deacons were here last week." They [the deacons] have a list of persons that they visit from time to time and I might not even be aware of it, but by the time I get there, some members have called or come by. I really thank God for that because I really think that's what really keeps people engaged in the church. I used to think it was the prominence or the dynamism of the preacher, but I've gotten mature, and you realize there are some connections going on, that people feel connected.

The concerns about pastoral care seemed more heightened at Calvary Baptist Church than at Layton Temple. At Calvary Baptist, women are experiencing the changes of a fast-paced growing church, some of which disrupt the religious expectations developed in the smaller, more intimate building. The rapid growth in this congregation may be affecting how quickly information about illness and hospitalization is disseminated. Furthermore, indicators of dissatisfaction point to the strong desire for a pastor who is accessible and personable, and for a church that treats all members the same.

Appraisal Assistance

Spiritual Fortification

Spiritual fortification is one benefit of church participation. By spiritual fortification I mean the individual's attestation of having a spiritual anchor, of relying upon his or her faith for courage to face challenges. It means the ability to utilize one's Christian worldview as the sphere for defining, interpreting, and resolving life experiences. It is a sense of groundedness against life's ups and downs, and the manifestation of Christian-based moral sensibilities. In the vernacular of African Americans, it might be described as having a sense of "somebodiness." It's exuding the confidence that comes from knowing "who I am" and "whose I am." Repeatedly, these women emphasized the spiritual power they had received, which helped reconstruct their own lives, and its consequences for how they understood themselves or felt about their lives.

With the fervor of evangelical conversion narratives, a woman recounted how God had been present as a restrainer in a moment when she needed to "hold her tongue." It is God who releases individuals from destructive lifestyles or who enables them to feel love and acceptance. Women spoke of faith as a source of constant strength. The church provides the context for self-confidence to grow, offers interpretation and integration of pleasant and disruptive experiences, and grants peace to replace inner turmoil. What became apparent in this study is that this empowerment is mediated by the church but separate from it. There was both confluence and separation of the roles of church and God.

This sense of spiritual empowerment was poignantly conveyed by Ellen, who talked about the medicinal effects of church. To use metaphorical language, church becomes the aspirin one takes for a headache. She said:

> When you have a headache, you can take an aspirin, and you can get relief, but when you are feeling sluggish spiritually, you can go to the church, pray, listen to the Word, and then have a renewal, a spiritual renewal. You'll feel better, you're uplifted . . . like you can go on another day, that's what I mean. 'Cause with a headache, you just can't kind of do the things you want to do. I mean you just don't feel like it . . . from being in fellowship with others you feel better, you feel like you can go on.

Rosalind echoed the benefits of church participation, using the analogy of the delayed effect of a vitamin regime. Church is like vitamins:

> In the sense that you go on a regular basis, and you take vitamins on a regular basis. You don't always see the results at first, but if you keep doing it then you'll see the results of it. Like when you go to church and don't immediately feel uplifted, but then it comes back later.

Spiritual empowerment can mean a resolve to shift directions or to give up a destructive practice. Susan, whose faith has made her more committed to staying away from the wrong crowd, attributed her steadfastness to the religious instruction she receives. When I asked, "Why do you go to church?" she responded,

> [I go] because I don't know everything, and there are a lot of things that I do not [know]. That's my spiritual food to keep going. I mean, there

are some decisions that I make at work that are technically based on my beliefs, you know, "Do unto others as you'd have them [do to you]." I mean that is just so simple, but that came out of the Bible. That didn't come out of Hans Christian Andersen, you know.

Tony, who has been going to church continually since childhood, spoke of how her church participation anchors her week. She is uncomfortable if she stays home on a Sunday morning.

[Church] gives me a way to get through the week in a sense, but it's kind of, it's like there are certain things that are part of how you operate and how you run your life and that is one. That is a central piece of it. So, if I pull that piece out, there would be some fragmentation in terms of how my life is working. In the past, I think church has meant a lot to me socially; now it still does, but I don't think to the same degree.

Anita described her psychological state without church in these words:

I think my week is not complete; I think I haven't learned anything new for that week. I feel depressed. I feel like that because when I praise the Lord at home and in my car and everywhere, it's not the same. I praise the Lord. But I feel like when you're together with other saints praising the Lord, you know, it makes you feel real good.

Appraisal Assistance

Empowerment for Work

Some participants credited their relationship with the church and God with enhancing their socioeconomic status or professional options. In an indirect way, they attributed "success" in their occupation, as well as their overall achievements in life, to their relationship with God or to strength they received in church. Some linked the two whether or not they considered themselves committed Christians at the time they entered their professions. Some went farther than giving God credit for their present achievement; they also credited God with their chosen employment or career direction. Ellen went to graduate school many years ago. She sees God's hand in how things worked out.

Well, I just think about my getting in an internship, my getting into graduate school. You know, because when you look at them [schools] on the surface you don't know how that's gonna happen, but he provided the way, and the other thing, when I went to grad school, my parents drove me, but I didn't know where we were going to stay that night.

While she was in the registration office, a woman inquired about her, took her home, and found a place for her that night and for her parents. Veronica, a woman in her forties, recounted how God had impacted her employment through an opportunity for advancement she received. She was working as a medical technician at the time.

I mean, it was a job that I know that the Lord had to bless me with, 'cause when I went into this particular job I had no training. I was doing surgery, helping with surgery, and I had no training whatsoever. They showed me. They pulled me off my floor, showed me one time; after that point on, I was working in the position, as far as moneywise and everything, and I knew it wasn't nothing but a blessing of God.

She had this conviction about the source of the job even after she lost it. Just as she credited God for receiving the promotion, she also credited spiritual forces for losing the job. The paradox of her faith is seen in how she regards "the devil" as destroying some good and God as simultaneously producing growth in her.

Things had started happening in my life that I didn't quite understand. I lost my job, and I know it wasn't nothing but the devil. I was taught if you pay your tithes, the Lord will take care of you and you'll have a job . . . and that was what I was doing and some things [weren't working]. In other words, I was being taught, being taught [to] use my faith—who I am in Christ and where I am in Christ—you know? I was being chastened. That's the best thing I can say, and I got upset. I got mad. I said, I'm not going to church. I said look at this, all my friends [who were doing wrong were prospering] . . . It was an attack. Everything that was good for me [was gone], I mean I was at a new level in my job, [had a] brand new car, everything I ever wanted, I was just getting it. And then, everything, even my love life, was just snatched away.

God has been a resource for charting life's major decisions. God is also the one to turn to for assistance in dealing with stressful job situations. Delia, a middle-aged woman who is unemployed, provides another example of the intersections between work and God. Going to church did not direct her into a specific profession, but the church and her faith have been invaluable sources of sustenance during this period. Her faith in God has buttressed her self-esteem, increased her trust that her financial needs would be met, and taught her "what her faith is made of."

God and work interfaced for Mother Williams in a different way. A woman with a strong evangelical zeal, she was quite skilled at moving a conversation to the matter of personal salvation. She spoke at length about the people she encounters in her work with senior citizens. She is eager to share her faith with anyone if the opportunity arises. Her initiatives at proselytizing and offering to pray with clients have resulted in reprimands from her supervisor.

> I was challenged [before this director came]; the last director told me that she had a complaint. "I'm embarrassed to say this, but one or two of the ladies, your coworkers, said you're always talking about God and Jesus Christ and they don't feel that is proper for you to do."

Despite the possibility of being fired, she minced no words about continuing to share her faith.

> I said, "I see that whoever complained is a person with a small mind who thinks they are smarter than they are—a person who doesn't know that everything that is made belongs to God and that but for the grace of Jesus Christ, they wouldn't be here on the job." And I went on pointing out the blessings, and I said, "Someone downtown didn't do that for me. [Company name] didn't do that for me. It's the grace of God that they have the qualifications and were in a place where they were accepted in this job. I speak to those who want a lift." . . . She said, "But I would prefer it if you didn't do it." I said, "Well, I'll tell you something. . . . I don't intend to work nowhere I can't present Jesus Christ when I know somebody needs him! If I can't talk about God somehow, I'm not going to work [here]. . . . You see, I haven't done it so much that you had to speak to me, you are participating, doing what somebody else on the job wants you to do." . . . So I said, "I won't run it in the ground, but I can't promise you I won't speak about the Lord." . . . I said to myself, "Now

next time she say something to me, I'm gonna go. I'm going to cut out." But I was producing [snapping her fingers] so fast, that I doubted that anybody was going to ask me to leave, you know.

I wondered if there was a correlation between her convictions and her present economic security. Mother Williams is in her seventies, has a steady income, and is a retiree who "chooses to work." It's possible that her economic stability and ability to decide whether to work fuel her evangelical zeal. Nevertheless, her position demonstrates a faith that cannot be undermined by an employer's threats. She is willing to bear the consequences of her convictions and gives priority to God above approval from her employers.

Rosalind, a nurse, describes the empowerment she gathers from church and God. She applies the label "spiritual" to herself, rather than "religious." The effect of attending church carries over beyond Sunday and helps her handle stress. She has relied upon her faith to help her maintain her composure. "It gives me groundedness. I mean I don't get upset at stuff that everybody else is [upset about]. It gives me a calmness; I'm more grounded and able to see through the muck."

She recounted an incident at her job the previous day when one of her coworkers was episodic (exhibited physically erratic behavior) because he had not taken his medication: "He went off on me, cussed me out, I mean to the point of threatening me." When coworkers who came to her aid were ready to beat him up, she was calm and just concerned that he receive the proper assistance at that moment. I asked her whether her ability to handle this situation could be attributed to her training and mediation skills, rather than to God. She did not deny her skills but explained, "It's only through my spirituality and my closeness with God [that] gives me that confidence. I feel confident when I'm at work, even with all the chaos going on."

Appraisal Assistance

Reconstituted Identities and Personal Transformation

The God whom these women encounter in church is not a fragile, meek, and mild deity. They believe in a God who is immanent, always present, full of power, and dependable. God is never a man, although usually referenced with the male pronoun and described with personal and anthropomorphic attributes. They referred to God with a host of metaphors, some indicating function, others God's being. God was referred to as "my center," "the creator," "sustainer," "judge," and "mystical entity." God is acknowledged as beyond confinement to a human body and as incomprehensible to the human mind. Most of these women have a "faith in God" that is experientially based, tried, and proven. Each could say, "I know God for myself."

The strong emphasis on experiencing God, however, should not be interpreted as to suggest the absence of a more critical reflection on the nature of God. For instance, Gail shared some of the questions she's pondered about the reality of God. "God to me is this mystical entity that I often think about. I wonder how He looks. I wonder if He's really in heaven. I wonder if there really is a God." Standing by itself, the statement might suggest she is a skeptic, a person of little faith, or a budding agnostic. However, even as she ponders out loud about the existence of God, in the next breath she affirms a strong belief in God. She is a nurse by profession; her reflections demonstrate how her work and life experiences contribute to her theological musings. She commented,

> I know that there is someone, and I have to believe it is God who gives me life and breath because I know it's not man. . . . I know about anatomy and physiology, so I know that it's not man that makes our heart beat or the blood run through our veins or our arteries. I know that. I know that there's something greater than man that makes me touch this table [banging the table with her fist], and I know instantly that it is hard, because that has been transferred to my brain. I know that. I know there is something more powerful than man is. And I know that there is someone who has gotten me to this point in my life, because like they say, "If it hadn't been for the Lord on my side, where would I be?" I know that I should've been dead, and I'm serious about that, you know. So I know that there is some great force that keeps me living and gives me the strength to make it from day to day.

Transformation of the self was a theme repeated by many of these church women in this sample. Some have become more positive since they have been in the church. Kelly, who initially went to church out of habit and to socialize, described herself as someone who used to see things as "half-empty rather than half-full." She states, "I go more so now 'cause I've been getting, been being more positive and inspirational. That's why I go."

Sheila, another respondent, told of losing her shyness, something that used to limit her even in worship services. She spoke of the freedom she now feels to be expressive in worship. Everything in church gives her a new sense of gratitude for her life, and she doesn't mind letting others know it.

> I'm just so thankful for everything I have. I'm ready to let the Lord know "thank you Lord." . . . I remember the time I wouldn't even put my hand up to thank the Lord in Church. I wouldn't put my hands up or anything like that or openly praise the Lord. The Lord has been real good to me. I have to let him know every chance I get, and I do. The Lord has been real good to me.

There were numerous personality changes or behavioral traits that women pointed to as a consequence of being in the church. They spoke of not taking things too personally, shifting from dependence on self to dependence on God, willingness to trust others, refraining from sexual activity, and losing the desire for marijuana. Rene appeared to make the distinction between what the church has done and what God has done: the church has been of assistance in fine tuning the strong sense of self she already had.

> I believe the churches that I have been in let me know who I am. I'm not gonna say that it's given me a black identity. I've never had an identity problem, anyway. I'm a child of God. What I put down as my color is irrelevant. I don't consider myself a black Christian. I consider myself a child of God. That's how I look at myself, and because I don't put that stigma on it [my identity], I can go anywhere. What happens is sometimes when we label ourselves black Christians, white Christians, we only go in the avenues of where that color line is.

Rene is a confident in her ability to move with ease among persons of different races. She also manages several roles and responsibilities in and outside the church. This confidence comes from her relationship with God, a relationship defined by protection from straying rather than acceptance after straying.

God has guided my footsteps and watched out for me, and He showed me that without Him, I couldn't do anything. Without Him in my life, without His protection, without that shielding in my life, a lot of things that happened to everybody else, it could have happened to me. But because of His grace and because of the purpose that He had for me, [they didn't]. My husband would have never married me if I had a child. That was one prejudice that he had. He didn't want a premade family. If that [had] happened, my whole life would've been changed.

Sandra acknowledged a distinctive shift in three areas—social habits, internal religious life, and material aspirations. We get a sense of this transformation in the following commentary.

I don't like hanging out anymore. Even though sometimes I go to a social function, or I might even go to a club, but when I'm there, it's just that. The fun I used to get out of it, I don't get out of it anymore. I still like entertaining, but it's a different type. I like helping people more. I think I've always liked helping people. It's just that what I used to do and what I'm doing now is different. When I sing, I sing with a difference. It's just a different feeling that I get now when I sing. When I pray now, there's a difference in my prayer. My prayers are, not that they weren't sincere then, but they're so deep [now]. Words cannot express how deep my feelings are for the Lord. Where as I used to, for example, want this big fabulous house . . . now I've learned how to deal with the smallest house and realize that it can be small, but if you got a whole lot of love in that house, and harmony and peace there, that's all that matters. I have calmness about me now. I tell people about the love of Christ more.

The appraisal dimension is also inclusive of the acts, strategies, and conversations that increased self-esteem. Several women spoke of the church (and its members) helping them to learn to love themselves again after failed marriages and to triumph over depression and low self-regard. Karen talked about a new awareness of God's provision when she was lonely. She reflected on the loneliness she had felt when she broke up with her husband soon after having a baby.

I think I turned to the Lord like people do when things are just too awful to understand. Like I said, it [the church she attended] was nondenominational, but that didn't matter, he preached the Bible, and that's when I started going to Biblestudy and studied the Word. I never studied like that before. When I came down here, it was a natural extension to keep [looking for] that, you know. I just felt so alone. The one thing about it, when you have the Lord in your life you're never alone. You're never alone. You understand that He cares for you and especially with men. He's [God] the only man that I've ever found, and I include all the men that I've dated . . . He's the only man that I've ever found and I include all the men that I know—my father, and Reverend and my brother, just all the men, my uncles—He's the only man that's never disappointed me.

The sources of their diminished personal regard were numerous. Relationships, intraracial discrimination, displeasure with their personal physical size or beauty, inadequacies in school, and a sense of failure as a mother were some of the precipitating circumstances. These women regarded the church as invaluable in helping them confront these situations and eradicate negative understandings of themselves.

Denise grew up with a sense of insecurity that often manifested in her withdrawing from others. She thought she was mentally retarded for many years because she found education an extreme challenge. At forty years of age, she discovered that she was hearing impaired. She now had an explanation for her difficulty with the educational system and for her tendency to misunderstand verbal comments. Her esteem rose when she found there was medical treatment for her hearing impairment. However, another biological condition, infertility, was not as easily addressed. She spoke of her past trauma and of her intense desire for a child. She believed for a long time that being a mother would make her feel "womanly all the way." She knew her husband loved her regardless of the infertility, but she was in a spiritual battle. Her frustrations about infertility became magnified when it became necessary for her to have a hysterectomy.

After the hysterectomy, the desire for a child did not diminish, and she considered adopting one. Now able to laugh about it, she said, "I used to tell the Lord . . . I don't want to be Sarah, Lord," referring to the biblical character in Genesis who bore a child at the age of ninety. At other times, she would pray, "Lord, you say if I believe and trust in you, you gonna bring it to pass." Now she's "at peace." God receives the credit for her current peace. A scripture that she once thought referred to barren women—"if a tree doesn't bear fruit cut it down"[6]—no longer bothers her, and she has reconciled herself to the idea that every woman is not meant to bear children. She has "learned to be thankful in all things" and counts among her "babies," her many nieces, nephews, and goddaughter.

A final word about the correlation between faith and the reconstituted self. Repeatedly, women spoke of God as "my everything," "my life," "my breath"—"God is the beginning and end of everything." Their words reveal a conception of the self transformed by God but also suggest a submergence of the self, a sense of incapacity without God. Several women have been suicidal, and others have suffered severe depressions. Reliance on God is the factor they credit for their having survived these crises. Women wondered out loud about the outcome of their lives without God. God is credited with healing their physical and emotional wounds. Reminiscent of a black preacher approaching the climatic moment of a sermon, one woman's voice quickened as she said with firm conviction, "He's my hope, he's my dream, and he's just everything to me. He's a friend when I'm friendless, he's a doctor when I get sick, He's a lawyer when I need a lawyer. He's everything to me."

God is the friend, the comforter, and the one who can be reached and talked to when one is lonely, when one doesn't want to tell anybody else. God is the being that gives purpose to life. God is a power mediated by the church but is not synonymous with the church. Several women acknowledged that one can "have church at home" if one is hindered from getting to the building. A member of Layton Temple spoke of how people are misled in making God and the church synonymous: "Even though I go to church, I know that he lives in me. A lot of people have those misconceptions that if they miss church . . . that God is in the church. I think it is good and healthy to go to church, but God, the church lives within you."

Most of the participants made a clear distinction between God and the church. The most important learning the church teaches them—an ultimate reliance on God—can be realized whether or not one attends church. Their consistent participation points to a realization that perhaps there is a qualitative difference in private worship compared to collective gatherings. The church adds a dimension to their religiosity, but it does not control the life-changing power of knowing God. Ernestine, a fifty-eight-year-old member of Layton Temple, affirms that God is present in her home, as well as in the church. She prefers her encounter with God when it is also an encounter with others.

Without it [church], it's like I lost my mother. I have a real deep love for my church, and I just wouldn't be me without it. It's just a part of me. Some people say they can worship God at home as well as at church. I know I can worship God at home, but I feel more free [when] we come together to worship Him. Look like, it means more to me to worship with somebody. I guess like you'd say, [that if] you eat by yourself all the time, you don't like to eat by yourself. I don't like to worship by myself. I feel we can give Him more praise together than we can by ourselves. The more praise that goes up, the more blessings come down, that's the way I feel. And He did say fellowship one with the other. If you stay home praising God all the time, you're not fellowshipping with [anybody] but God.

She spoke of how God's presence is a strong reality for her in church. "It feels like God is just right there and all I've got to do is just reach out and touch him." She acknowledges this is just a mental image she maintains and that she carries God in her heart wherever she is. Still, her concluding words were poignant "it look like when we go to church, that's when it [God's presence] really comes out!"

Discussion

It is often said that black women are in the "habit of surviving."[7] History supports that assertion. Certainly, one has to acknowledge the church's centrality to that survival and to black women's tenacity. One of the functions ascribed to black religion is that it is a "coping agent," providing a spiritual response to myriad challenges and forms of discrimination and oppression. Delores Williams writes of "a survival/quality-of-life" tradition among African Americans resident within African American religious culture. By "quality-of-life tradition" Williams means

persons, families and or communities attempting to arrive at well-being through the use of, search for and/or creation of supportive spiritual, economic, political, legal or educational resources. . . . In the context of much black American religious faith, survival struggle and quality of life struggle are inseparable and are associated with God's presence with the community.

This quality is found in the Black Church, but not exclusively. This tradition is evident in how African Americans have appropriated the Bible.[8] Williams asserts that for African Americans, "emphasis is put upon God's response to black people's situation rather than upon what would appear to be hopeless aspects of black peoples' existence in North America."[9] This indigenous hermeneutic strategy is a latent quality of slave religion itself and one that enabled slaves to resist oppression. The belief that God was on their side fostered slaves' survival by giving them an alternative and ultimate sense of worth. According to John Blassingame, their selfhood was not defined by the master's conception of their persons. Rather, it was shaped by a concept of God that could not be destroyed by the rigors of bondage. Blassingame states:

> One of the primary reasons the slaves were able to survive the cruelty they faced was that their behavior was not totally dependent on their masters. . . . In religion, a slave exercised his own independence of conscience. Convinced that God watches over him, the slave bore his earthly afflictions, in order to earn a heavenly reward. Often he disobeyed his earthly master's rules to keep his heavenly master's commandments. . . . Religious faith gave an ultimate purpose to his life, a sense of communal fellowship and personal worth. . . . In short, religion helped him preserve his mental health. Trust in God was conducive to psychic health insofar as it excluded all anxiety-producing preoccupations by the recognition of a loving providence.[10]

Here we see a distinct connection between reliance on God and desire for survival. Religion ameliorated the constant threat of nonexistence because, indeed, slaves had a belief that God was on their side. In addition to Blassingame, Gayraud Wilmore provides further evidence of this survival/quality-of-life tradition among African Americans:

> If whites thought they were dealing with children who could not discern the difference between white professions and white behavior, they were sadly mistaken. As John Lovell, Jr., has observed, "The slave relied upon religion, not primarily because he felt himself 'converted' [to white Christianity], but because he recognized the power inherent in all religious things." That power had to do, first of all, with the necessity of survival—with the creation of an alternative reality system that could keep a person alive and possessed of some modicum of sanity.

The protest and resistance elements we found in early forms of black folk religion in the Caribbean and in the southeastern United States express the determination of the slaves to "make it" against all odds.[11]

In other words, slaves embraced religion because it served to create a "sacred canopy," a worldview by which to interpret the daily horrors that sustained them against constant demoralization.

This survival thrust of African American religion is also a prominent theme in black cultural productions, especially literary canons. A recurring theme in African American literature is the depiction of religion as a source of stability for black mothers. However, all portrayals do not depict the relationship among religion, church, and black women as healthy ones. Williams demonstrates how this portrayal as cast by black male protest writers of the twentieth century varies from depictions by black female writers.[12] We cannot venture into the multiplicity of explanations for these different depictions. Nevertheless, this corpus of work lends credence to the cultural perspective that black women are peculiarly religious. They are persons who have a profound sense of connection with divine presence and power and a deep commitment to the church, and both are regarded as sources of psychological and spiritual empowerment. The consequences of that connection for the well-being of the community are the subject of ongoing deliberation.

These women's lives allow us a glimpse at the multifaceted intersections between religion and black women. This linkage is an empowering and transforming one. In most cases, the connection was forged in the Black Church, and it is within this institution that their faith continues to be sustained. Living in a different century and social context, contemporary black women have not had to find God in the brush arbor or been seated in a "Negro pew" like slave women of generations past. They have been nurtured in their faith within denominations founded and maintained by the labor and spiritual might of others like themselves. Yet there is enough resemblance in the function and "holding power" of religion in their lives to situate them within the same "survival/quality-of-life" tradition suggested by Williams. This tradition gave antebellum black women the strength to carry out the multifaceted tasks of laborer, mother, nurturer, cultural repository, and moral teacher on a slave plantation, a strength that has been interpreted pejoratively in the image of the "black matriarchy."[13]

The power of the church to facilitate survival and spiritual transformation cannot be underscored enough. The women I studied recounted the difference God has made in their lives and spoke of the inspiration they receive in church. They did not provide a critical evaluation of what is unique about the processes in the church that allow them to navigate crises as well as everyday tasks. Cheryl Gilkes's use of mental health processes as a construct for interpreting the functions of the Black Church is insightful. Given the relatively low rates of mental illness among blacks, she posed the question of what structures help maintain the sanity of African Americans. She contends that we must seriously regard the church and certain forms of religious practice as a conduit that allows African Americans to alleviate stress, renegotiate traumas, and ward off more severe forms of psychological dysfunction.[14]

The church accomplishes this in four ways: by articulating suffering; locating persecutors; providing asylum for "acting out"; and validating experiences.[15] These functions are mediated via fervent and lively worship services that allow for and sanction emotional release as "okay" and appropriate. The minister helps by naming the oppressor and reinforcing black persons' interpretations of the oppressive forces they are experiencing, rather than rendering the state of affairs from a majority perspective. These processes are also present in prayer meetings where members are able to share their sufferings and are reminded that members, as well as God, understand their troubles. Gilkes writes:

> Black women, particularly, are able to avail themselves of the forum of the prayer meeting to talk about their troubles with their husbands and sons. . . . not only are prayers offered up against the offender, plans of action may be formulated to attempt to change the offending behavior. Ministers and deacons may pay visits to the offending spouse.[16]

Some black churches are therefore capable of being an asylum, a place of refuge and protection, "a non-punitive setting within which blacks are able to act-out and work-through whatever happens to be troubling them on Sunday morning or prayer meeting night."[17]

Gilkes's analysis of the church as a place of shelter is applicable to this study. In the midst of all sorts of challenges—familial, racial, political, work-related, and psychological—the church has been a mainstay in the lives of these women. An important dynamic that enables transformation is the nonpunitive quality of the congregation. In these settings, persons give accounts of some of their most traumatic and saddest life experiences. Gilkes does not suggest that sanctions are never rendered but emphasizes that, often, the response does not stop at alarm but moves beyond sanction to some expression of support.

> When problems such as unwed motherhood and divorce arise, the prayer meeting is both a forum for announcing the impending trouble and for gathering the social supports necessary to endure and actively cope with the situation. Church members may render various forms of social support besides prayer. Church members may organize "showers" for the offending daughter, thus removing some of the punitive social pressure from the stricken parents.[18]

The impact of this nonpunitive atmosphere is borne out by the participants in this study. Within this group of thirty-eight women, fifteen had had out of wedlock pregnancies, occurring when the women were of different ages. Some were very active in the church at the time, others only marginally so. All were members at the time of their pregnancies. Overwhelmingly, they did not have to leave the church because of this violation of Christian moral behavior. One woman reestablished her connection with the church while in a common-law marriage in which she had two children. She never stopped going to church and didn't feel that she had to. Another woman told of relocating with her mother to a new church while she was a teenager and pregnant. The decision to change churches was precipitated not by her pregnancy but by other familial needs. In the new location, the visibility of her pregnancy and the absence of a husband were never questioned. The women were welcomed into the new community.

The qualities of refuge, caring, and nonpunitive treatment can be seen most vividly in Sister Parker's life. Sister Parker was seventy-seven years old when I met her. She lived in a large old home, which showed its age and was in need of repair. She was on a fixed social security income and a great grandmother. She spent most days seated in a recliner because of her weak knees. Sister Parker has had six children; five of them were born out of wedlock. She grew up in a rural area and worked the fields. Having united with a church early in her life, she was a church member and still living at home when she got pregnant at the age of seventeen for the first time. I asked her how the church reacted. "Well they would pull you out of the church if you had a baby [out of] wedlock. But I went back to church." I inquired what being pulled out meant.

> They withdraw the right hand of fellowship from you. They take your name off the church rolls and then you rejoin. You're not supposed to take communion then. You can go to church, but then you won't be recognized as a member. . . . I went on to church. As soon as I could get back to church, I went back to the church. No, I didn't ever stop going; what I mean is I just rejoined the church. Along in them days, they made you stay in the house for about six weeks, I'd say about two months roughly [after having a child]. They would treat you nice [when you came back]. They're not going to help you unless [you ask]. I imagine if I had went to them and asked them to help me [they would have]. But I always was independent, and I don't believe in asking people for help.

Although she was "pulled out" for three pregnancies, she did not speak harshly of the church's treatment of her. I inquired as to why she kept going back. She answered, "Well, I knowed no where else to go but to church. And I felt like it was my place to go back and ask forgiveness for what I did wrong. And I just believed in the church." She also added that men weren't "turned out" for their moral failure, even when it was known that they had fathered a child out of wedlock.

In response to the critics who assert the church is not doing well by black women, this research suggests that it is in fact doing some things well. The church provides access to persons who can meet needs for direct household assistance or mundane tasks. It embeds women in a religious and social institution that serves as a haven and that provides spiritual fortification and opportunities for a reconstitution of the self. It helps to stem the tide against not only the "devil" but more subtle combatants—stress, emotional traumas, social and community isolation.

Women attest to the enduring power of the church to define, foster, and affirm a sense of "somebodiness" among African Americans. Amid social conditions that often denigrate and oppress black women—racism, economic inequities, sexism, pathological interpretations of black motherhood, Eurocentric standards of beauty, physical violence, cultural stereotypes ranging from Jezebel to Mammy—churches provide alternative constructions of the self. Churches empower them to reject and reconstitute these stereotypes and dehumanizing forces. For black women the church is a mediating institution where one is relieved of racial disease and psychological, emotional, and relational stressors. It is a place where one can build or reconstruct a life unhampered by the debris of attacks to the self. In other words, external and internal threats to one's selfhood can find resolution in this religious space.

Their regard for the church as a site of personal reconstitution is maintained at a time when many black women are attracted to the theologies of spiritual and psychological healing that have become a mainstay of national women's conferences and numerous popular Christian texts challenge women to be Christ-centered and self-actualized at the same time. American Christianity has incorporated and adapted to a new form of religious phenomenon. Women have opportunities to attend interracial, cross-generational, religious conferences and revivals that tout a peculiar mix of spiritual empowerment, American individualism, consumerism, and self-help spiritual psychology. With the goal of liberating women from defeating ideas, guilt, shame, and internalized misconceptions of themselves and God, these events provide women a unique opportunity for cathartic release and personal dissociation from their pain.

Among African Americans, the most prominent of these events are the Woman Thou Art Loosed and God's Leading Ladies Conferences, sponsored by T. D. Jakes Ministries. The first one targets women who desire to be "loosed" from debilitating conceptions of the self or "their past"; the second one is for women who have already dealt with their emotional past and pain. These "leading ladies" know who they are and now want to be directed toward their divine destiny. The first Woman Thou Art Loosed Conference was held in 1993, and attendance has grown dramatically; more than fifty thousand women attended the 1998 conference, held in the Georgia Dome. God's Leading Ladies was instituted in 2002 in Dallas, Texas, at Bishop Jakes's church, The Potter's House. That first conference was limited to the capacity of the sanctuary; eight thousand women attended. Subsequent ones have garnered much larger audiences and have been held in sports arenas and civic centers.

These events provide a plethora of nationally recognized preachers and musical artists, religious products, dramatic presentations, sisterly fellowship, networking, and services of "spirit-filled" worship. Attendees can establish new relationships or be anonymous as they commune with God, however they desire to, in these transformed sacred spaces. The intention of these conferences is not to siphon persons from the Black Church (or other faith traditions) but to return them empowered and less encumbered with "baggage" to live for God. These religious events are meeting needs that the Black Church has addressed on only a limited scale. The Black Church has a history of addressing racial, economic, and socially oppressive forces that impact African Americans in general; these conferences, in contrast, address the particularities of women's experiences, especially the negative ones. However, what they provide for the individual who wishes to be "loosed" and to star in her own life is not matched with a charge to the church to oppose or stop the generation of new victims or to eradicate the economic, educational, and social barriers that limit women's progress. The solutions offered at these events overwhelmingly emphasize tapping the power of God within you through Jesus Christ.

Some of the women in this study were aware of T. D. Jakes, but he was not a household word for them, nor was he a source that they constantly referenced. His popularity appears to have increased in the years since my interviews were completed. None of them revealed having attended one of these conferences. For them, the local black congregation is facilitating what other women find at these mass revivalist gatherings. The affiliative dimension—being known by your fellow worshippers—outweighs the anonymity of a conference. Preaching that recognizes that solutions are not all internal eclipses the constant emphasis on individual reliance on faith as the way to be triumphant. This is not to say that the Black Church is providing a better systemic analysis of the oppression of women than these national ministries. Many African American pastors are critical of these conferences and the slate of clergy who seem to become household names and spiritual gurus by appearing at a conference. They are also frustrated by pronouncements by these preachers that flavor church members' faith in a manner contrary to some of their own pastoral tenets and teachings. I am suggesting that the Black Church has not been replaced as a refuge for women's spiritual and personal growth by these religious events; it does have a competitor in this arena.

As the Black Church engages rather than remains aloof from these religious venues and the theologies that emerge from them, there are many directions to pursue and tasks to consider. Can the Black Church make peace with these bastions of emotional healing and provide the ongoing care that is needed for women who participate in such events? Is the Black Church willing to examine its own offerings of pastoral care so that women will not consider being present in an anonymous crowd the requisite context for relinquishing their pain? Will church women ensure that the Black Church does not yield to the nondenominational churches and faith movements the task of naming sins against women and creating contexts for their resolution? Will the church expand its resources and opportunities for women's economic, social, psychological, and spiritual empowerment? Can it provide alternative contexts for transformation that are rooted in justice seeking and societal transformation, rather than solely individual integration and change?

The conferences offered by T. D. Jakes and others need not be a threat to the Black Church. While they encase persons in a spiritual cocoon for a short duration, these spiritual conferences will need social and institutional structures to have an enduring impact, as well as sustainable forms of assistance for their maintenance. This help is what the Black Church has a record of providing. The women in this study found within the church a host of resources and creative responses for their material and spiritual needs. They attest to the availability and expectation of assistance in all areas of their lives. In addition, spiritual guidance is a primary resource provided by the church. Most people have greater need for the intangible spiritual sustenance than they do for the material resources. Access to counseling and biblical instruction, as well as the numerous institutional venues (e.g., worship, Sunday school, choir rehearsal, prayer and Bible band, mission ventures) promote positive regard for the church, meaningful personal associations, and transformation. To echo Lena Horne, "black women are in the habit of surviving." It appears equally accurate to conclude that the Black Church has been the paramount institutional nexus for that survival.

4

We Went to the Church for Everything

The Mission of the Church

Well, I think, back during the years and coming on up to maybe not so long ago, the Black Church was the center of the [community], the place where we went for everything, for the Word, and political things, and community activities and all of that, so that's the difference that I see. . . . Black churches had to shoulder all of those responsibilities, and I think that it has made us [African Americans] stronger. . . . White churches and the white race, they have always had a place for everything, whereas we always came together in the church. But I don't have any regrets, or I don't think we should look back on that as a negative, 'cause I think it is the only thing, one of the only things that have made us stronger, you know? If it [the church] would continue to be so, maybe we could be much stronger persons; if we commit to the church and everything came from the church. But now, well, we get things from everywhere. [Our lives], they're just not centered around the church, and [yet] more people [attend]. Churches are crowded every Sunday, churches are having two to three different services, but we still ain't getting it. So I think we should go out and [do] mission work.

—Thelma

The mission of the Black Church has fundamentally been shaped by its dual commitments—to the worship of God and to the remedying of the oppressive social, political, and economic conditions of African Americans. As reflected in Thelma's words, in the past the Black Church filled roles for African Americans distinctive from the roles of white churches. Having fewer institutions to mobilize persons or amass and distribute resources, African Americans turned to their churches.

The Black Church teaches persons to see themselves as loved by God—as persons who have dignity because they are created in God's image—and to manifest ethical conduct that will bring honor to God's name. In some instances, this has meant an emphasis on holy living—refraining from immoral sexual and social practices and relationships. The focus upon personal holiness has not obscured the church's work of justice and ministry to the least among them. The success of the church and its centrality to the community has been largely a result of its outreach beyond its membership and its willingness to articulate a vision of a different society to persons who have lived and who continue to live on the margins of the American dream.

Thelma's words suggest that the Black Church is facing some contemporary competition for prominence. The church has been impacted by African Americans' access to economic, social, and political opportunities once denied them and by the creation of multiple voices and organizations that champion African American concerns. It is no longer the only articulator of solutions or disseminator of resources. Additionally, new theological commitments and forms of religiosity have influenced the historic foci of the Black Church. In the past two decades, individuals have been more public about personal professions of spirituality unmoored from any denomination or institutional grounding. The prosperity gospel, charismatic and "full gospel" forms of worship, the interpretation of spirituality via television talk show hosts, and the blending of religious teachings with inner psychological healing are available in American society. The Black Church and its members are not immune to these competitors.

While no one has fully assessed the impact of this religious marketplace upon the Black Church, its influence has resulted in varying adaptations within congregations and by members. Some churches have become innovative in their presentation of the gospel as they remain committed to their traditional foci. In congregations that perceive this eclectic religious milieu to be a threat, we find a retrenchment of traditional roles, polity, and worship styles. In addition, we see a more individualized approach to faith among the church members, which increases the difficulty of maintaining the historic identity of the Black Church. As we examine women's assessment of the work of the church and its priorities, we see indications of one or more of these trends.

In this chapter, I present both description and critique of the church's ministry, deciphering what it should be doing for the larger African American community and world. The religious landscape of America has changed since the civil rights era, a period when the Black Church's work had a very public face. Do women see the work of the church as similar to or distinctive from the work of past years? How expansive are women in their interpretation of the church's tasks? Should attention to the individual's spiritual needs preempt or compete with the church's historic commitments to fight for justice, provide material assistance, and encourage economic empowerment? Has the church become inwardly focused, responding to the maintenance of church members to the detriment of healing the larger black community?

In the church, the role of the pastor is to articulate the vision of the local congregation; often, it is assumed that this is done with minimal influence from parishioners. It follows, then, that everyone else has the responsibility to implement the vision or mission. Yet, if we see the tasks of vision molding and implementation as discrete components, we do not adequately represent the symbiotic relationship between pastors and congregants. Such a view also assumes that women have no significant role in helping to constitute the vision of the church, since men in the Black Church have usually occupied most top leadership positions (and presumably have greater access to the pastor). As we will see, such an assumption does not match the experience shared by these women.

What Is the Church?

It has become common to label the Black Church as the religious, social, and political nexus of the black community. But is this the label that church women employ for it? My survey provided a set of church descriptors that they were asked to check if they believed them to be applicable to their church. In descending order, the images selected were extended family, a spiritual center, a place of comfort, an educational center, a social center, an advocate for the poor, a hospital, and a political organ. Within the group, at least 80 percent agreed on the first three descriptors on this list.

Rosalind's description of the church included more than one of these choices. We find suggestions of hierarchical and vertical relationships in her comments. Mutual support is also present in her concept.

> I've always seen the church as a spiritual family. . . . It is like any normal family. Growing [up], you have your father, your leader, you are bring-

ing up the children, but you are doing it in a community type, it's like a community-type family. What are those things they used to have during the hippie stage? . . . Communes, that type of thing, where it's the patriarch, the matriarch, the children. I see that all in the church, us nurturing each other.

Throughout my interviews, women offered myriad church images, some in overtly theological language (the church is the body of Jesus Christ), others not. The idea of the church as a family and healing station reverberated throughout many of the interviews. Women spoke of the church as a rock, a solid place, a place where you feel at home, and a context where you get something to offer back to others. It is also a place that teaches parents how to build a spiritual foundation for kids, the place you go when other pressures are on your back. Susan described the church as a watering hole.

> The [church is a] watering hole. . . . You'll still be a [empty] pitcher if you don't go to church regularly. . . . It's better if there's something in there, something to offer. [In church] it gets filled with water and it makes you more pleasing, . . . like God is more pleased. If you see an empty pitcher and ain't nothing in it, well, you just see an empty pitcher. If you see a pitcher with something in it, that makes you want to get with the pitcher . . . it has something to offer me now, the pitcher has something to offer other than to [be] look[ed] at. [When] you go to church, you get filled. The pitcher is filled with water and now you have something to offer back, because you've been filled with knowledge, understanding, or what God reveals in his laws, his ways.

Some of the terms women offered implied that the church should have a congenial familial environment. A focus on the internal culture highlights their attention to the priestly aspects of the church's ministry. Belief in the priestly dimension was, however, held in tandem with expectations that the church would extend its welcome and services beyond its own membership. The church is there for its members, but it is also "a place where the needs of the community could be met, and a place where we meet for everything." Identifiers like "refuge," "safe place," "community center," and "hospital" lend themselves to multivalent interpretations. For instance, the church should be a place where persons can bring their spiritual woes and concerns, as well as a place where community members feel free to come and ask for material assistance. Beverly envisioned her church as being very community oriented.

> I think that the church plays a big role in the community to me. Let's go back to children. How about establishing some type of foundation within the community, to get the kids to come in and participate? For example, [have] after school programs for parents who don't get off till 9 o'clock at night. I mean [we're] right there in the community. Why can't we have some type of Bible study going on? . . . I say Bible study, but why can't they [have] some type of programs going on and teaching some type of trades, while the parents are at work? Or [kids can] come in and we can help them with their homework while the parents are at work. Not only that, but I figure, [given] where Calvary is located now, that there should be some type of outside community work going on.

Lynn argues for a more relevant ministry that responds to its immediate geographic community. It cannot continue to do the same thing repeatedly. Her church had moved from a quiet residential neighborhood of private residences and tree-lined suburban streets to a major thoroughfare with numerous apartment complexes, new housing subdivisions, and a busy commercial district nearby. This new location called for new forms of ministry, in her estimation. When I asked her to expound upon what constituted community work, she said, "Mission work," which could take the church in a new direction. "The mission work that we were doing [was] mostly going to feed the AIDS patients, going to the nursing homes, etc. . . . [Now] we're talking about bringing the kids in off the street, you know, setting up some kind of foundation like that, for teenagers and stuff like that."

The interpersonal, emotional, or spiritual needs of church and community members were primary in the women's minds, ahead of systemic or structural injustices. The church's priority should be to help individuals survive their immediate crises and challenges; the precipitating conditions that created these crises are not the first point of response for the church. The women believe that the church is there to take people's hurts seriously, not just to be a social place. Rene made this point strongly as she talked about what the church is and about the danger of forgetting whom it is supposed to serve.

The church is not an organization; it is an organism, it is something that lives, and it breathes. But people get too caught up in calling it an organization. When you forget that it's an organism, then a lot of things get bypassed. You forget that people go there who have abuse in the family, who have been neglected, [who come from homes] where mental, physical, and sexual abuse is going on. When you think of it just as an organization where people come, put in their dues, maybe say that was a good message or whatever, then something gets lost through the cracks.

To Rene, the church is more than a sociological entity. Her use of the term "organism" implies vitality and dynamism. Her words also included a criticism of the attention given to building the membership rolls of the church at the cost of attention to people's "real" needs. Bernice, a member of Layton Temple, echoed Rene's emphasis on ministering to the needs of people. The church is not just a place with material resources, she emphasized, but one with unique spiritual resources to offer. In response to my query "What is the church," she stated:

[It is] a gathering place for all kinds of people. I mean rich people, poor people, whatever kind of issues there are out there. I think the church should have a role in helping to deal with those problems, [be a place] where anybody can go if there's a problem and find somebody that can help them. Whether there are marital issues, whether there are substance abuse issues, whether there are incest issues, whatever it is there should be somebody there that can counsel with those people through the Word. Not necessarily having that much wisdom in how to deal with the psyche of folks, but having the wisdom through the Word to show folks, how Christ would handle that and to just of kind of help them through a crises. If we can't do that, I don't think we've accomplished very much. I know that it's a gathering place for the saints, cause a lot of the scriptures are really directed to the church itself. I know that we're a community or a family, but we have to be able to [be] the place that when the world fails you, you can turn to and not get rejected. I don't think that the church should hand out money freely. I've never been an advocate of that, but I think that we should have enough resources there that we can provide whatever the community needs.

The Work of the Church

One method I used to obtain women's definitions of the church's work was to elicit descriptive terms from them. Another was to gauge their answers on two survey items. The first question asked for the type of information they expected to receive in church. The most essential types of information this group expected the church to provide were the preaching of the gospel, information on strong families, and moral statements. Items that were seen as important but not essential were issues specific to the black community, information on global church concerns, and information on health initiatives. Several items were only somewhat important: birthdays, weddings, funeral, and job announcements, political announcements, notice of community and civic meetings, and voter registration information (in descending order). Possibly, the respondents did not consider these items as explicitly related to the black community and thus selected them less frequently. Furthermore, given the educational and economic achievements of the majority of these women, and the variety of African American media outlets in this area, it is likely that they have established other networks that keeps them abreast of these matters. This would decrease their need for the church to serve as an information conduit as it once did in black communities.

The second question asked the women to rank what should be the essential services the church provides. There were three answers that more than half of the women regarded as essential: (1) to provide aid and services to people in need, (2) to prepare people for eternity, to share their faith, and to resist worldly temptations and (3) to have an active evangelism program. All these priorities outranked involvement in the political arena as an essential service.

Given the on-and-off relationship the Black Church has had with emphasizing political action as a Christian value, these responses are not surprising. Answers to the survey item that asked women to select images of the church confirmed that "a political organ" is not among the dominant conceptions of the Black Church, but this item cannot be categorically dismissed as irrelevant. My interviews provided a bit more clarity about the relationship between church and politics. The political role of the church was neither strongly supported nor rejected by women in their conversations. Some women saw a role for the church in political tasks such as encouraging voter registration or allowing political candidates to be recognized in church services. Just as Bernice thought the church should be there to assist with the relational issues of its members, some women included politics within the scope of the church's work.

> There's always a place for the Word, even in the middle of the Olympics. . . . I don't think there is any place that the church is not needed, even in a political situation, if it's nothing but teaching us to at least cast [our] vote, to try and get somebody in there that's right. . . . I can't think of any area where the church would not be of use.

Others weren't so sure about the need for politics in the church. Lynn was still trying to decide what she thought of the intersection between the church and politics. She is a member of Calvary Baptist, which has a political action ministry.

> This is the first time that I've ever seen political action going on in the church. . . . Coming from the church I'm from in South Carolina, they didn't have that. So when they were talking about the political action, [it was] like, I have to figure out what really goes on with them. I'm still learning it—the political action—and what role it really plays with the church. [Although] I see a lot of senators and people like that come out to the church and what have you, I'm still trying to understand what role that really plays in the church. . . . I sort of see the connection with it [the church and politics], but I'm still learning a lot about it.

On a related survey item, the women deemed it "very important" (not essential) for the church to be involved in fostering a sense of patriotism and good citizenship. They also asserted that the pastor and congregation should be actively engaged in speaking or participating in the community regarding social issues. While they do not regard the church as a political organ, the women do desire the church to have an impact upon the society, as well as to respond to the needs of individuals. They considered it somewhat important that the church disseminate political information such as voter registration information.

In my interview with Michelle, I asked whether her vision of the Black Church included sharing announcements and information about black candidates or issues that seem to particularly impact the African American community. She responded,

Well, that is part of [our church's] vision. . . . To help educate the person, the whole person, and that's part of educating the whole person, and I buy into that. If it didn't happen, possibly in time it would click that something was missing [but] because it does happen, I don't make, it's like I'm glad that it does happen. I may or may not take the time to seek out some information that I need to know. . . . [When] he [the pastor] thinks that it's important enough that we need to know, he'll either intertwine it into a message or have somebody come and speak about something, and it helps you to be a better all around citizen.

The women also articulated the church's role in encouraging self-determination and fighting for civil rights. They felt that the church should give its assistance to organizations like the National Association for the Advancement of Colored People (NAACP) and should encourage entrepreneurial enterprises among members.

Holistic Help

The work of the church does not focus on just one or two tasks. It is multidimensional and has to function on many fronts. The ranking of priorities does not tell the whole picture of these women's concept of church work. Certainly the mission of the church is to evangelize and to share the gospel with all who will listen, but this task is the reverse side of meeting the practical needs of individuals in the community. There was no evidence that the women were concerned only with a person's profession of faith. The church's mission to "save souls" was not detached from its responsibility to help people survive their present living conditions and challenges. Repeatedly, they emphasized that the church must meet the whole needs of the person. For instance, Mother Cooper saw both evangelistic efforts and helping people as the church's task.

The church is supposed to be bringing people to Christ and caring for the widows and orphans. That's what the Bible says.. . . . I think we're doing a pretty good job of it. People are joining, and we do help people that's in need. We have missions for that. You don't have to be a member of Calvary. If you call and tell them that you're in need, they'll tell you that they going to do something to help you. We help a lot of people that don't even belong to our church.

This sense of holistic ministry was evident in statements like "reach the overall human being" and "there are no areas the church should not get involved in." Women had many ideas about where the church should focus its energies. It should be about helping "the least of these," sending the van to pick people up and assisting single parents to raise their children. It should reach out to the community, whether black or white, and deal with its issues whether or not people become members. It should keep people aware of political announcements and their Christian responsibility, sponsor political forums, and advocate for voting.

Anita, who imaged the church as a "filling station," described how the church should approach others. The church should "take the ministry outside the walls of the church and help when help is needed and just try to compel the lost to come to Christ and to help those who are less fortunate, those who are in need." Women defined "those in need" as including those beyond their own membership. It meant the community at large. Lori, who was in her twenties, made this link very explicit. She spoke of the necessary links between church and community. The church should feed people but should also tackle the tough issues like AIDS and homosexuality.

> I think that with any church that it needs to serve the community. Whether it's feeding the homeless or doing the ministry, going out to the prisons. The church should be the anchor for the community. I think the church is not serving its purpose if it's not involved with the community. It's like living in a glass house and inside my house everything is perfect, but when I step out everything is chaotic, and I'm not doing anything about it, so what's the purpose? We don't live in the church. We have to go back out into the environment, so it's important that the church participate. Do I think the churches are now participating? There are a couple of churches I hear may be doing something out in the community. But, as a whole, I don't think so.

The services that the women felt the churches should offer were endless, and the range of concerns to be addressed was quite broad. Many of the ministries their churches offered were part of the services they enumerated. The work of the church consists of implementing mentoring and tutoring programs; offering drug prevention and rehabilitation programs; teaching trades; organizing political forums; feeding and clothing the homeless; visiting shelters; and building strong families. Dealing with discrimination and "welcoming everyone regardless of station in life" are also considered important obligations for the church. There were no limits upon who could receive these services. The only apparent boundary pertained to means, not motive. It was suggested by some that the churches might want to refrain from distributing money directly to individuals. However, this sentiment was not widespread and contradicts the actual practices of both churches, which distribute cash assistance to persons in need.[1]

Women in these congregations were not restrictive in their definition of community. Community was neither geographically nor racially bound; it referred to their immediate geographic neighborhoods, as well as to African Americans collectively. There were women who were somewhat critical of how well their churches were actually reaching out to the local community. The voices of criticism were more apparent among members of Layton Temple COGIC, which was located in a low-socioeconomic-status urban neighborhood with more visible pockets of impoverishment and drug activity than were evident near the Baptist congregation. Nonetheless, the majority of the women agreed that neither race nor membership status was a reason to disregard the needs of those in the larger metropolitan area. Women were poised to render assistance to whomever inquired at the church or to whomever they might encounter.

At Layton Temple, members were ministering at halfway houses thirty-five miles away, as well as transporting the homeless from live-in shelters and under bridges all over the city to the church for meals. They were also in the process of establishing a new prison ministry during my time with them. I attended one of their planning sessions. As they planned to go into the local county jail, a woman already ministering there came to address the Tuesday night prayer and Bible band group. After an abbreviated prayer and study time by one of the church women, the guest instructed them on prison regulations for religious groups, proper decorum during a visit, and the challenges of providing ministry in this context. I could sense the members' enthusiasm for this ministry. The impetus for this ministry did not appear to be convenience or racial commonality. It was an initiative predicated on the desire to demonstrate God's care to the incarcerated. It was also a venture initiated and being spearheaded by a woman in the church.

In addition to not restricting its outreach to its immediate neighborhood or to meeting church members needs, the women said, the church should continue to function as a cultural womb for African Americans. It should provide services and be a clearinghouse for other resources in the community that it may not itself offer. They believed that if the church cannot meet a need directly, it should be able to help the person in need to find assistance. In describing her understanding of the church's mandate, Karen connected her present vision for the church with her understanding of the historic centrality of the Black Church. She stated:

> You know how the Black Church, the traditional Black Church, [according to] sociological studies and stuff, it was the avenue to which black people could have their say, 'cause at one time there were no other avenues really open to you. It was a social outlet, and church could help you find a job, you know you worked with a church, worked for the church, and, I mean, I see it as that kind of thing. I think it should be everything Jesus says it should be. . . . Jesus said he came to declare the acceptable year of the Lord, and so we're, that's what the church is. It's Jesus Christ, the body of Jesus Christ, and we need to do what he put us here to do and that's all these things, you know feed the hungry, clothe people, mend the brokenhearted. . . . I see the church being all those things. I really do, I mean that's why it's so vital, and we support it.

This group of women approached outreach to the community with more than just a missionary appeal or charitable intent. The idea of working along *with* the community, not simply on behalf of others, informs all that they do. Their choice of words—should provide, teach, help, give, instruct—could be misinterpreted as paternalistic. Rather than sending out a group of well-meaning do-gooders to assist the less fortunate, the church collaborates with community persons who just need some assistance. Members "ought not be elitist or thinking you're high and mighty" when assisting community members, offered one of the younger respondents.

Robin stressed that the church should make sure it is fighting what the community sees as its "most pressing battles." A former director of a church shelter, she learned in her years of experience about the symbiotic relationship between community and church. She knew firsthand the importance of the church's doing a community needs assessment rather than automatically replicating the work of its peers. Her work experience had led her to the conclusion that unmet material needs can be an impediment to receiving spiritual guidance.

If we as a church don't take the time in the community to really seek out, to see what the needs are for these particular black people in this community, then we will not be able to serve them. We can do the traditional things that churches do, get up and preach on Sunday morning and then go home, come out Wednesday night and do Bible study and then go home, which might be serving the spiritual, sometimes spiritual needs, sometimes not. Again, like I said, people cannot hear that Jesus can give them food if they don't have food and don't know where the food is coming from. So, the church could serve the needs of people in the community, but I don't know if they are, and it's a lot of work, it's a lot of work, and it's a thankless job.

Discussion

Earlier I argued that the centrality of the church in the life of black women results from its ability to meet their spiritual and instrumental needs and to mediate personal transformation for them. This chapter establishes another contributing element. Beyond their experience of personal transformation, black women have been and continue to be committed to the church. It is the institutional locus through which they can address issues that threaten the community. The church is involved in the implementation of programs and in the development of strategies to hold off the full impact of nihilism.[2] The religiosity of African American women is not one of self-absorption; their definition of the mission of the church and the necessity of giving that vision concreteness circumscribe it, as well. These women, and I risk saying Black Church women in general, articulate the need and embrace the challenge of maintaining the church's centrality in the black community. The intersection of religion and black women's lives yields both individual empowerment and community uplift in numerous ways.

As the spiritual nexus of the community, the church has a legacy of extending its assistance to persons beyond its doors. As we have seen, a sense of responsibility and duty underlie these efforts. The work must get done, and black Christian people must be about carrying it out. Black women have donated an enormous number of volunteer hours to these tasks—feeding, cleaning, planning, singing, gathering clothes, visiting the sick, teaching, organizing, and more. It seems almost rhetorical to inquire why they do it. Who else can be depended upon to carry forth this work?

Who would do it if they did not? Perhaps men would; perhaps not. Church women aren't waiting to see who will rise to the occasion.

It should be noted that women's labor for their church is not carved out under coercion or with an air of resignation. There is choice and gratification in laboring for the Lord and community. These are not women bearing burdens but godly women responsibly embracing tasks motivated by Christian faith and commitment to those in need, African Americans in particular. They help define the appropriate response and volunteer to implement the answer.

In *Acts of Compassion,* Robert Wuthnow has documented the consummate volunteerism of Americans. He makes the case that Americans are a volunteering people. It is one of the ways we demonstrate our care and compassion for others, as well as make our communities better places to live. In America, 31 million people volunteer in churches and synagogues, 20 million in schools, tutoring programs, and educational organizations, and 16 million in hospitals, nursing homes, clinics, or health agencies. Since Wuthnow's focus was on the formal organizations through which Americans volunteer, he didn't include the ways persons come to each other's or community members' aid informally and spontaneously.[3]

His analysis of the demographics, limits, and motivations for American volunteerism is useful in understanding the labor dimension of black female religiosity. Within the cohort that claimed that personal faith was *very important* to them, nine of ten persons also noted that helping people was *very important.* Wuthnow found that church members were more likely to have given service to social service type groups than were nonchurch members. He also reported the likelihood of involvement in a charitable activity was positively correlated with the frequency of church attendance and that the activities persons chose to become involved in were usually mediated by their church.[4] Church participation does not generate general convictions about helping others, which people can live out in many contexts; rather, Americans' altruism is "channeled by what they see and hear in church . . . into programs the church as an organization is trying to promote."[5]

As I look at the labor of this group of church women, Wuthnow's conclusions have a certain resonance. For the majority of them, service given through church-initiated ministries or efforts is the most efficient means to address social problems and still balance commitments to family, work, recreation, and personal enhancement. Volunteering at other nonprofit organizations or civic or service agencies can take more time, one must identify the organization, be trained, and learn to understand the particular role one can play. This required the luxury of time most women did not have. Lori, who volunteered as an AIDS educator, Anne who volunteered at her son's school, and Mother Williams, who collected clothes for redistribution, were the exceptions. Most of these thirty-eight women were not regularly involved in volunteer activities in lodges, sororities, or civic organizations separate from the initiatives of their church. Those who held memberships in the NAACP or National Council of Negro Women were only nominal members, rather than actively involved.

The church facilitates women's giving back to the community, diminishes the threat of an increasing privatization of their skills and relations, and disseminates pertinent information on vital political and civic matters to them. Most of these women are middle class, but not all. They are full-time workers, heads of households, and retirees. Two are full-time employees and have established home businesses, as well. Within this context of multiple commitments, they regard activity in the community as a requisite part of their Christian faith and an essential part of the focus of any church's mandate.

Congregations identify worthwhile causes to support and supply motivation for members' engagement and flexible parameters for carrying out the work. In the Black Church, an overt connection is made between Christian character and helping others. In both congregations, members were admonished to give back to the community and to realize that their well-being is impacted by the degree to which they embrace the theological axiom "You keep your blessings by sharing them." They were challenged to fight the inclination to work hard to provide the finer things just for their families while forgetting about others.

These teachings foster an expectation of service laced with ideas of duty. The church provides immediate opportunities for members to fulfill the mandate. It does not leave it up to them to establish a ministry; it encourages them to participate in one. The level of sophistication of services and the range of things one could get involved in varied between the Baptist and the Pentecostal congregations.

Earlier, I discussed one outreach endeavor in Layton Temple—ministry to inmates at a women's prison. This ministry included a set frequency, defined time parameters, communal support that allowed those with transportation constraints to participate, and clearly defined steps for ministry to those in need. Another example of the importance of having well-defined parameters for community engagement and uplift were the cell groups organized around members' birth months at Calvary Baptist. Every member is automatically a member of her month's cell group. The twelve months are subdivided into four clusters of three months each. Each cluster decides upon a focus for its outreach to the community, and once a month members from a particular month are asked to participate in that particular focus (i.e., visit a shelter, go to a prison, mentor children). The following month, they gather for a time of socializing and fellowship at a member's house.

The organization and procedures of these ministry groups allow women to be actively engaged in a personal way with others in the community but within a very limited time frame. People within a specific cluster of months share one missionary endeavor, giving everyone the opportunity to participate but avoiding placing an undue burden on just a few members. This allows members to balance activities geared toward the internal maintenance of the church with those of outreach. It also provides increased exposure to the needs of the disadvantaged for church members who otherwise might have been able to disregard their plight. This is particularly true since clusters periodically switch missions (e.g., the January-March cluster may stop visiting the boys' home, but the April-June cluster may pick it up).

While I believe that black church women are similar to other Americans in volunteering to better our society, their vision of the church and service to it reflect more than a magnanimous humanitarian spirit. Their definition of church and religious service continues the historical link between black women's commitment to social and racial uplift and the welfare of African Americans and Americans. Their practices of service have been constitutive of black church life. Although this group does not appear to have initiated ministries in their congregations (or I may not have unearthed this information), black women have worked in and outside the church and have invented creative strategies to address the oppressive conditions that affect African Americans. In our modern period, discretionary time is at a premium, so churches often makes volunteering more feasible by structuring opportunities in manageable tasks and time periods. Historically, of course, black women have labored on behalf of the community, whether or not it involved inconvenience, personal sacrifice, absence of recognition, or minimal appreciation.

One church woman who symbolizes these qualities is the recently deceased Mrs. Mamie Till Mobley. A member of the Church of God in Christ denomination, she was active with ministry to young people into her senior years. She came to national attention nearly fifty years ago when her son, Emmett Till, was savagely murdered in August 1955, four months before Rosa Parks refused to change seats on a Montgomery bus, igniting the modern civil rights movement. Mrs. Mobley (Till at the time), against the advice of authorities, decided to return her son's body to Chicago and to have an open-casket funeral. Nearly a quarter of a million people attended his funeral, and photos of his maimed and disfigured body appeared in *Jet* magazine, which circulated nationally. The resulting outrage and horror were a decisive factor in turning sentiment against segregationists and racial prejudice. It also heightened African Americans' consciousness of the conditions in which some blacks were still living.

Over the course of her life, Mrs. Mobley was dedicated to educating others about the destructive force of hatred. A school teacher, she founded the Emmett Till Players, in 1973, addressed various audiences, and coauthored a book about Emmett's death.[6] Mrs. Mobley's life is one example of women's willingness to make hard decisions for the good of many—to take unpopular stances; to share one's personal grief with the public—even when their own sacrifice is great. It also shows how the Black Church has been the institutional locus for actions with far-reaching political consequences.

The women I came to know through my research continue in the traditions birthed in the African Methodist Episcopal women's missionary initiatives of the nineteenth century, the work of the National Baptist Women's Convention in the twentieth century, and the labors of church women in the segregated YWCA, settlement houses, and missionary circles. They also extend the work of Christian women who did not limit God's work to the church walls or spiritual domains. Black church women have given expression to God's work by establishing schools, lobbying for women's and black people's rights, and being involved in the political arena. Nannie Helen Burroughs, Fannie Lou Hamer, the Women's Political Caucus, Charlotte Hawkins, Mary McLeod Bethune, Pauli Murray, Mother Coffey, Bishop Ida Robinson, and Olivia Pearl Stokes are but a few of the notable persons who make up this legacy.

There are countless unnamed women as well who have established the connection between faith, the church's social ministry, and the public good. At the dawn of the twenty-first century, the work of the church grows out of and builds on its heritage. Just as the vision remains consistent, a holistic response to the spiritual and material needs of the African American community, so do the women continue to render their "labor of love."

5

If It Weren't for the Women
Female Labor and
Leadership in the Church

Since the 1970s, there has been increased scholarly attention given to the role of female clergy in American religions. Whether women should be accepted in the ranks of the clergy, and the effect of such a step is still debated in Judaism and Christianity.[1] In Reformed Judaism, women can become rabbis. Globally, the Catholic and Orthodox churches continue to exclude women from ordination. In America, nearly half of the Protestant denominations ordain women. Change has occurred, but this greater access has not come without struggle as women encounter stained-glass ceilings.[2]

The research on female clergy has taken several directions. Foci have included the impact of women clergy upon the occupation and congregational adaptation to women pastors; women's distinctive ministry styles; their vocational satisfaction; and their path toward ordination. Women clergy are being celebrated for their homiletic abilities and for their social ministry. Historians are providing a much-needed historical assessment that allows us to measure perceived changes and gains resulting from the acceptance of women ministers. Sociologists have been analyzing the denominational forces, internal and external, that influenced the changes of the past quarter of the century.[3]

It is easy to presume from the increased recognition of female clerics that past barriers have been removed and that female preachers and pastors are faring well. It has also been assumed by some that denial of clergy status to women is synonymous with shutting women out of leadership roles and power in the church. Cheryl Townsend Gilkes cautions us against putting too much emphasis upon who fills the pastoral office within African American churches. To equate the official ordination of female clergy with female power obfuscates other manifestations of women's power and agency. It also negates the creative ways that women have garnered power in religious institutions and the very important labor of lay women and community mothers. Furthermore, she reminds us that much of the analysis concerning access and mobility among female clergy has focused upon clergy in mainline traditions, leaving unexamined the experiences of female preachers in African American contexts such as The Sanctified Church.

These insights are useful as a corrective to how we chronicle the history and labor of the Black Church. We have not told the story as often or as loud of the smaller Holiness and Pentecostal churches that sanctioned women preachers throughout the twentieth century.[4] It would be an error to simplistically equate the treatment of female clergy in the Black Church with the church's regard for women. Neither is the acceptance of or resistance to women clergy the definitive marker of the actual power women have in the business and liturgical aspects of congregational life. Women have exercised influence with or without the title "preacher."

In this chapter about women's contributions to the leadership and work of the church, I consider female leadership from two vantage points. First, I discuss their recollections of female leaders in their former congregations. I then examine of their labor and influence in their present congregations. I ask, What were the limits of female power in these congregations? To what extent is the adage "if it weren't for the women . . ." true in their congregations?

My second approach to female leadership engages the topic of female clergy and women's support (or lack of) of them. Repeatedly I have heard from clergy (male) that women are the strongest opponents to female clergy. Throughout my years as a participant in the African American church, as a professor, and as a cleric, I have found only isolated anecdotal support for this claim; yet it remains an accepted rationale by some pastors for limiting women's access to the pulpit and to official boards. This study provides more data that refute this assumption than support it. As we look at the issue of support, we also gain access to women's understanding of the structural and cultural forces that have shaped such a reverence for the black male pastor. What do lay women know about the process of becoming clergy? Are the reasons for or against ordaining women clergy based in theological, sociological, or pragmatic reasons, or a combination of these? The answers to these questions are more complex than one might think.

Female Leaders in the Black Church

All of the women but one in this group are lay women. They were introduced to the faith in congregations in which women were in the pews as well as in leadership roles. Many of these congregations also had gender-specific roles for men and women, which is not surprising since some of the women in the study came of age in the 1930s and 1940s. In these more traditional churches, men filled positions such as deacon, trustee, preacher, pastor, and elder. Few women ever saw other women in these offices or questioned women's exclusion from them. Those who were disturbed by the gender divide kept their dissatisfactions private. Women served in the choir, on the usher board, and in the Sunday school and worked with children of all ages. They also constituted the Mothers Board and the Missionary Circle and sometimes served as secretaries of committees.

Business meetings were open to youth. However, the women did not attend with regularity during their youth. There were no expectations that they would participate, and the women who did attend remembered them as boring. Among the women who attended these meetings (with a parent), there was no uniform interpretation of these gatherings. Many recalled that men were more vocal in the meetings and more responsible for conducting the business of the church. Women were not excluded formally from contributing to business meetings as a rule and did have a voice. A couple of women had been in denominations (e.g., the Church of the Brethren and the Worldwide Church of God) where women were prohibited from participating in business meetings.[5]

Examples of women exercising influence in these meetings were few. Jerri recalled hearing her mom speak out in a business meeting at which a young girl had been brought before the church for public sanction because she was pregnant out of wedlock. In the judgmental climate and fearing that the girl would be treated harshly, her mom stood up and gently but firmly shared some seasoned words about how the officials ought to handle this matter graciously, reminding them that they were not without fault in their own lives. This happened prior to the actual levying of sanction, and in Jerri's assessment her mother's intervention had the effect of averting a severe punishment and additional disdain being heaped on the teenager.

Can young children or teenagers distinguish the dynamics of power in a congregation or differentiate between formal and informal power? It is evident they can to some extent, even if they lack the clarity of adult eyes. This woman observed her mother inserting herself into a business situation and affecting the outcome of the proceedings. Whether she perceived her mother as out of line we don't know. Youth learn about the divisions of labor and about restrictions on the sexes through such communal events as worship services and business meetings. They decipher the expected roles for men and women and learn how children are to act in the sanctuary or when someone has violated a norm of the congregation. Each public service, meeting, or fellowship is an occasion for children to learn the expected behaviors and the intersections of gender and power. The involvement of women in business meetings neither reveals nor conceals the limits of women's power in the church. However, it does reveal that while in some black churches women are discouraged from participation in the corporate decision making, others defy these norms. Their children are not unaware of their resistance.

Labor and Leadership of the Women of Layton Temple COGIC and Calvary Baptist Church

This group of women makes significant contributions to the vitality and work of their congregations; they are not bench warmers. Only two or three could possibly be labeled "minimally involved." The lesser involvement of these few is the result of medical and physical limitations, intense involvement in educational programs, or transportation problems, rather than a lack of interest.

Women were involved in two categories of labor in their congregations: *church extending* and *church maintenance* activities. The first category consists of the community and social outreach programs of a church—its political activism, voter registration drives, ministries to the homeless and hungry, evangelism, and so on. The second type includes functions that create and enhance the worshipping environment and that build a sense of community among the membership. The first category focuses outward, the second one inward. Most congregations have both types of labor, even if one dominates the other.

Involvement in church maintenance activities occurred more frequently than in church extension ones. At Calvary Baptist, this took place primarily through cell clusters. Persons are assigned to a group according to their birthday. Each group has a responsibility for a community service project. Participants commit time in alternate months to work on their project. Some of the projects were visiting a homeless shelter, providing clothing for the homeless, and visiting a children's home. Layton Temple's outreach to the community took the shape of ministry to homeless men and visitations to the local women's prison to lead worship service and to offer spiritual counsel. The lesser emphasis on church extending is underscored by the women's frequent participation at functions that took place largely at the church.

As a group, nine out of ten attend worship services weekly. Nearly half attend Sunday school or a Bible study or engage in some type of church fellowship activity. Since these activities often mandate a personal devotional life, that two-thirds report daily prayer and meditation practices is not surprising. In contrast to their active involvement in activities that enhance their personal relationship with God, fewer than half participated in a community or social ministry a few times a year. Slightly more than a fifth sought new converts a few times a year, and less than a fifth participated in some type of civic, school, political, professional, or community group. I do not mean to imply that community outreach activities do not enhance one's relationship with God. However, these activities were treated more as secondary aspects than as vital to the churches' work and in the thinking of some of the women. In interpreting the participation levels in different activities, we should be mindful that some types of activities are offered less frequently. While there may be myriad church fellowship opportunities offered over the calendar year, community and social ministries tend to require a short-term commitment or a period of intense activity. Organizing voter registration drives or collecting food at Thanksgiving are examples of seasonal commitments.

Both congregations offer more opportunities for church maintenance activities than church extension ones. This was a source of frustration for some women. Several women in the Baptist church used the terms "church work" and "work of the church" to describe the two categories I have been discussing. Although they are committed to their churches, their volunteer labor lacks the satiation level of doing "the work of the church." This was less evident among the Layton Temple women. This may be attributable to the fewer demands on their time, the smaller number of ministries, and what I perceived as a greater congregational emphasis of the "hands-on" ministries to the community. Karen is active in several ministries at Calvary Baptist. She has headed one area for several years. As she talked about the distinction between these two areas, her desire for more "work of the church" was evident.

> Church work is those things you do to keep programs going, and ministries functioning. But the ministries are really supposed to do the work of the church. It's like, Jesus said, I come to set the captives free, I come to feed the hungry, I come to heal the broken hearted. That's the work of the church. We're supposed to go out and help people. I mean help people within the fellowships but also touch people who don't even know Jesus and that kind of thing. I've been looking at my job [her employment] in a whole different light. I think of a job as just something I do to earn a living so that I can do those things that God wants me to do; maybe He needs me to do something within that job. I mean there are people there who don't know Him. I mean maybe there's a reason that I'm there, and that's the work of the church. Putting together programs? I don't know. I'm just at a point where fashion shows [don't interest me]. I think I'm needing to go another direction, and as long as I'm calling meetings or reminding people of stuff they should be remembering themselves and that kind of stuff, I feel like somebody else will come to do those things. They need to be done, I'm not minimizing them, but there may be other things the Lord wants me to do. And they may be (not that I'm going anywhere) outside of Calvary's programs.

Karen's words point to the toll that constant service takes on some women, how tasks shift in their value, and how women look for the spiritual significance of their labor. Considering the list of ministries these women either led or participated in, she was right that church work eclipses the work of the church. Women were active in the following ministries of these churches: the praise team, the political action committee, the children's chapel, the coordinating council, the women's fellowship, the annual church celebration, the advisory council, YPWW, the Under the Bridge Ministry, the Prayer and Bible Band, the Mothers Board, early morning prayer, the new members committee, the singles ministry, and the married couples group.[6] They also worked as ushers, pastor's aides, and missionaries. They have organized and convened many of these initiatives, not just implemented them. The women do participate in the leadership roles of the church. Of the ministries and groups I have named, the majority are led by women.

I defined leadership roles as those that carry decision-making authority or that involve heading an auxiliary or ministry. Persons with responsibility for implementing tasks were considered to fill a supportive role. Positions on an official board or as director or codirector of a ministry or special emphasis, teacher, or financial officer were included in the first category. There was no uniformity to how women acquired their responsibilities. The pastor appointed most of them; others were elected by their particular auxiliary. Women recounted having been asked directly by their pastor to lead the Sunday school, to be on the Pastor's Aide, or to join the Mothers Board at Calvary Baptist.

Besides contributing their time and leadership to the church, women were also consistent financial contributors. In both congregations, tithing (giving 10 percent of one's income) was taught as the acceptable minimum contribution to the church. Neither church specified whether the basis for calculating the tithe should be an individual's net or gross income, or whether the tithe should be based on individual or family income. I did not make this distinction on my survey or in my interviewing. The interpretation was left up to the individual. The survey contained two items related to finances: "How much does your household contribute to the congregation each year?" and "What is your approximate total annual household income?" Overall, the inconsistency in the two figures reported did not support the women's claims to be tithers, yet thirty-two women reported in their interviews they tithed to the church.[7] Of the thirty-two, only one used the qualifier "sometimes." Two women reported they tithe as a couple, and one woman said her tithe was figured on her husband's salary because she was unemployed. Five did not give at the 10 percent level. The exact figure is less significant than the fact these women do indeed give significant amounts of financial support to the church and respect the idea of proportional giving. Teaching about tithing was not new to the majority of them. Only two had recently started tithing as a new practice when they joined their present church. Seven remembered it was a strong part of their teaching as children. Tithing was part of one's Christian responsibility, a behavior maintained by some even when other dimensions of their life did not conform to expected Christian behavior. None of them questioned the tithe as an unreasonable level of giving. In the vernacular of the older generation, several women considered it "just paying my dues."

Tithes support the general functioning of the church. In addition, various appeals were made throughout the year to fund special missions, to respond to unexpected crises, or to plan long range for capital improvements. Women also supported these special campaigns, over and above their tithe. Calvary Baptist was in the midst of a building fund drive and had asked members for a contribution of an additional $1,000 for that initiative. Sixteen of the twenty-five women supported the campaign. Four indicated their support was partial ($500 or less), one paid the $1,000 as a couple, and one woman said both she and her husband gave $1,000. Support for special initiatives was also present in Layton Temple. Members were asked for several special offerings, although none as large as contributions sought in the building fund drive at Calvary Baptist. The appeals at Layton Temple were to aid a minister who would be out of work indefinitely because of an accident and to send the "First Lady" to the national convocation.

Female Clergy

Access

The churches in which our respondents were reared during their youth exposed them to models of female leadership, but rarely were women in the leadership role of preacher or pastor. More Pentecostal women than Baptists had been exposed to women clergy. Among the COGIC, the offices of evangelist and missionary are highly recognized and provide women the opportunity to preach. This is not the case in Baptist churches. National policies governing access to the office of preacher vary by Baptist denomination, and the role of missionary and church mother do not have the same institutional power as within the Church of God in Christ. Historically, in Baptist churches, the women who were most likely to address the congregation were upstanding religious women, the pastor's wife, or an educator or a community activist chosen to bring the Women's Day message. With the increase in female clergy in recent decades, this is changing, and some Baptist churches are utilizing female preachers, licensing, ordaining, and hiring these women.[8] Women in the

Church of God in Christ and Sanctified Churches have had more opportunities to hear women preach.[9]

The exclusion of women from the leadership roles of preacher and pastor has been so pervasive that it was not a significant source of discomfort or frustration for the majority of the group. They accepted the exclusion of women preachers as normal when they were growing up, even if they didn't agree with the mandate for the exclusion. Rosalind, now in her fifties, thought back to her early years in Wisconsin. She remembers learning the lesson that women weren't supposed to preach. It was told and modeled. Women didn't even go in the pulpit in her former church. I asked her whether she had ever questioned women's exclusion from preaching. She replied:

> No, not then. Don't get me wrong, 'cause we had very strong women leadership in our church. They just were not to be in the pulpit. [They were in] mission work, even speaking; every aspect of the church except preaching. I really didn't think about it that much. 'Cause that's all I saw, were men preachers. I never believed that women shouldn't preach though. But I didn't believe that. Just like I didn't believe that priests, 'cause Milwaukee is very Catholic, that priests shouldn't marry.

While female clergy were scarce during their early years, all of the women in this study have heard a woman preach. Calvary Baptist had two female clergy on staff during my fieldwork, and a third one had left the church in late 1997. Layton Temple does not have female clergy on staff. However, the pastor does invite women to preach, and these visitors are accorded the same respect as male guest preachers. Female preachers at Layton Temple are missionaries, evangelists, or state mothers. I attended services when women preached in both of these locations. Outside worship services, some also watch religious broadcasts that feature female clergy and tune into radio shows with female clergy.

Women perceived their pastors as supportive of women preachers. In Layton Temple, the pastor has periodically admonished those who still seem disgruntled about women being preachers. The women applaud this public support. In Calvary Baptist, the pastor was also regarded as supportive of women preachers. They cited his stories about being brought up Church of God in Christ, and also his mother's influence, as factors that have predisposed him to support them. At Calvary, some did think

Reverend King favored men. They pointed to various things they've observed; women preach less than male guests, usually work in the area of women and children, and are addressed differently. Here's how one woman who is also a church leader put it:

> Sometimes I think [women preachers] are somewhat limited at my church. Pastor is very much in favor of women ministers. He has no problem with a woman being a minister and stuff, but I look at how duties are regulated, and it's more often than not that the women ministers are going to be over some aspect of children's ministries. I personally don't think it's coincidental. . . . Let me put it to you this way. We used to have a woman associate minister that was at our church, and before she was ordained, she was always Minister Green. When Reverend Miller, who's not ordained yet, came on board, he was automatically Reverend Miller. She didn't become "Reverend Green" until after she was ordained. He started calling her Reverend Green after she was ordained, but Reverend Miller is still Reverend Miller. He's always been Reverend Miller, and he hasn't had his ordination yet. I'm sure he will soon, but you know, it's a difference, and that's just an example. It's slight, and you know it's probably just a title. It's not all that important, but to some degree [it is]. I'm not saying he's persecuting the women ministers or anything like, but there's a difference, and I think its because they're women. I really do.

Several women have relatives or friends who are preachers. There was little doubt in their minds that women encounter roadblocks and glass ceilings as they strive to fulfill their call to ministry. A member of Calvary mentioned that the trial sermon is the first roadblock to preaching that many women encounter. This is not the same roadblock that faces women in the Pentecostal tradition. The COGIC has a clearly delineated process and requirements for women to be licensed as evangelists and missionaries. Pastoring is the glass ceiling against which women are likely to bump in this context.

However women come to be preachers, the struggle is not over once they are licensed. A consistent problem is access to paid positions. In addition, female clergy contend with basic rebuffs and slights. Eva recounted her hairdresser's experience. The hair stylist, Mary Brown, is a preacher, has gone to seminary, and serves as assistant pastor at her church. Eva recounted Mary's story.

She [Mary] went to another church and she was supposed to speak, but they didn't know that [the preacher] was a "she." They [had] just said "Reverend Brown." So she got to the church, and the pastor told her she couldn't preach. She said fine. It was some kind of big service. It wasn't Women's Day, obviously. It was another service. She got back at them. She said, "Okay, I won't preach." He said, "You're going to do the scripture." Well, she did the scripture, but she "preached the scripture" so that by the time she finished the scripture half the church had fallen out, the minister that was supposed to do the sermon had fallen out, matter of fact he didn't even preach. So I told her, "Good for you." I guarantee you she'll be asked back, now that a woman can preach. I told her, "It's sneaky and underhanded, but it worked."

Whether accurate or somewhat embellished, this story contains an instructive aspect: Eva made note of the unequal treatment of women clergy and was pleased with Mary's assertive behavior. By exploiting this small opportunity to demonstrate her spiritual abilities, Mary claimed for herself the right to share in the pulpit ministry of the church. When I asked Eva whether she thought this was a desirable strategy for women clergy, she responded yes. In spite of its obvious subterfuge, it was a necessary strategy to make a point in the face of this discriminatory treatment. She responded, "Sometimes you have to work around roadblocks. I think in order for women to succeed in this arena as in any other arena, they will have to work around roadblocks."

Support and Opposition

On the whole, these women were not opposed to female clergy. The majority of participants quickly acknowledged that women have the ability to preach and pastor. Women in both congregations acknowledged that women could preach as well as any man; they just aren't given legitimation or the same recognition. Some were sensitive to differences in delivery style. They attributed a teaching form to women and a preaching form (more proclamation, whooping, louder and more vibrant presentation) to men. While making reference to some of the differences in delivery or acknowledging their preference for one over the other, they did not indicate that any style of preaching disqualified one from the task at hand. Rosalind has been exposed to several women preachers now. She noted that some preach differently from men, but that is not a handicap. "Her [a Methodist minister's] preaching was different from Reverend King's, but I know other female preachers that are completely opposite [to her]. I know other evangelists who preach on his level."

The litmus test for women preachers was the same as that for male preachers: Are they anointed? Do I get ministered to? Karen spoke about a local pastor who has distinguished herself in the pulpit. She has been invited to Calvary on several occasions. She is powerful as well as personable.

> One pastor that I'm thinking about in particular, she's just, she's a very powerful spirit to me and being a woman and so obviously a woman lends to her ministry. There is a warmth there that generates I think just from her personal style. . . . I just have a great deal of admiration for her. . . . To me God can call anybody he wants. I know there have been struggles placed on women ministers and since I've learned that and that kind of thing and have more appreciation for it, I think they're even more powerful because of what they've had to go through.

As we continued to talk, she elaborated on her belief that this pastor's femininity was an asset.

> To me [her femininity], that's a compliment. A lot of women, and not just in the clergy, but women in general, when they take leadership positions you have to give up some of your things that might be considered more feminine because they'll be considered as liabilities or weakness. You have to give up, you know, in terms of a lot of areas, dress or speech or approach. But, to me, I mean she's warm, she's giving. It must be very hard to keep her up in that pulpit because before you know it she's just down there where the people are. And it's her personality, but I think it's also because she's a woman. She doesn't have any problems leading the church, . . . she doesn't have any problems leading, giving direction and that kind of thing, but she's still a woman.

She gave the example of how this pastor openly shared her own feelings at a singles event. Karen and others were sitting in the session with some reservations about talking.

She got very personal and said, "You all must think I'm going to tell your pastor on you or something. Look, I am a person. I am a woman. I just know that I'm not going to be single the rest of my life. I'm looking forward to who God has planned for me." I mean, she just started talking real open, and it just kind of broke the ice.

Women acknowledged that women have been preaching all along. One member of Layton Temple pointed out the fine distinction between what women were doing and how their activities were recognized or labeled within the denomination. Sharon's words expressed the sentiments of the majority, as she spoke of the women missionaries and evangelists she has heard: "They don't ever try to call a woman's [proclamation] preaching. They call it anything else." This struck her as odd because in her eyes the women are doing the same task as the men. Rhetorically, she asked, "Why does it have to be called something else just because it's a woman [doing it]?"

The case for women clergy is argued by appeals to equality, justice, and pragmatism more often than by appeals to biblical authority. The reasons given included the disproportionate representation of women in the church; the absence of a clear, convincing biblical basis for preventing it; the need for young children to see models of male and female leadership; and the belief that that women's abilities and talents bring different strengths to the clergy role.

Rene, a member of Layton Temple, has been dissatisfied with the limitations on women. Although she was taught at an early age that women could not pastor, she rejected this idea. She has seen that women are allowed to do basically anything else in the church. She talks with her husband about this biased treatment of women and has shared her sentiments in the church on numerous occasions.

I believe a woman can be a preacher [and] a pastor, and I have said that openly. That's my belief. I'm not going to hell because I believe that way. I believe that a woman can work outside the home. The church just has this [practice], men are put up here [elevating her hand in the air]. Because the Bible says the women are the weaker vessel, the men are put up on such a higher plane.

At Layton Temple, every fifth Sunday is Women's Day. This is not a large formal celebration as much as the day that women have responsibility to oversee the service. Usually, a woman preaches, as well. Ruth conveyed an incident that happened one fifth Sunday.

> I don't know who this man [was]. I don't even know his name, I don't even know if he was a member of Layton. I haven't seen him there in a while, but he had a problem with Women's Day, and every fifth Sunday is Women's Day. He happened to come to church on that Sunday. I understand that [before] there was a man who got up and left because he found out that the women were in charge of the whole service so about a few Sundays later (now I say that's kind of ridiculous) I guess it was the same man. I happened to be standing outside the church waiting for my daughter to come up, ('cause she wasn't coming to church, but, anyway, I'm standing there), and some people got out of a car and it came around. And this man was there, and I was standing outside. I don't know if I had on white, a white skirt or something, but, anyway, he looked at me and said, "Is today Women's Day?" No, he said, "Are the women in charge today?" So I looked at him, and I said, "No, but why, you got a problem with that, the women being in charge?" "I just don't like that kind of thing," [he responded.] I said, "Well, that's your opinion."
>
> So he went on in and there was a woman leading the praise service. So he accepted that, because he praised [along with them]. After service was over, he was talking to somebody and I passed by him, and he says, "Oh, what I said to you outside, I would like to explain why I said what I did." So I said, "If you choose to, I'll listen." But he never did. He left, and I was gonna ask him, "Why do you have a problem with women carrying on the service?" because he said that's something he don't like, he don't think women should be in charge of nothing.

Ruth's exasperation was evident as she recounted the story. The disdain for having women in charge is linked to opposition to women's having the right to exercise authority, whether preaching or performing other functions, in the church. She is frustrated with the way women are challenged for being bearers of the message. She longs for the day when the message is more important than the sex of the messenger.

> I think that I would like to see the day come when there is no competition in the church between the males and the females. Like, uh, I don't want to do this because the women are doing this, or I don't want to do

that because the men are involved. When we go to Bible study, we can disagree without [one] being dominate as "I'm the male and because I said it, it's right and because you're the female, [it's not]," you know? I would like to see a time come when we can just be Christians without gender becoming involved, or you can listen to a message from me and receive it as if God gave it to me, because I'm a female, the same as I can accept it from you as a male.

While support for female preachers was strong, there were dissenters. Women on the other side of the issue predicated their arguments upon interpretations of key Bible passages or essentialist gender ideology. Mother Williams was strongly opposed to women preachers. She arrived at this position after rigorous study of the scriptures. The topic of women preachers seemed to ignite a passion within her. At one point she told me how women were sometimes allowed to pray at church on prayer meeting nights and then shifted into an extensive narrative about women preaching. I quote her at length to demonstrate the intersection of her biblical interpretations and gender assumptions.

> I think, the belief then is much [as it is now], maybe that's why I believe now that men are the head of the church. As I grew older and it was controversial and women's rights gained momentum, I had to go back and search why I didn't prefer or didn't like the idea of women pastors. And I'll tell you what I learned. I always measure everything with Jesus and what happened during his ministry. I went back and I say, now Jesus picked twelve men. Twelve men, he taught and started his church [with], okay? It was no mistake that he didn't pick one or two women. God has control over all those things. Christ was predicted. It was predicted that he would come. Isaiah told of his coming. God is all-knowing, omnipresent and all that. And so I thought about that [shifts into another train of thought]. I have a cousin who after we grew up she went into the ministry. She sang beautifully, her and her sister sang in a quartet, and when she was ordained, I was happy for her, and I love her. She and I are very close, but I said to her . . . , "If people want to say that times have changed, of course they have changed, but the Word of God says Jesus Christ the same, yesterday and forever. So whatever Christ did, it was forever." So I said, "God bless you, hope He uses you mightily," but I had trouble with her in the pulpit. I do.

Here, we hear Mother Williams appealing to Jesus' selection of the disciples as a reason to oppose women clergy. Her words also demonstrate her opposition to allowing cultural shifts to influence the stances of the church. As she continued, she appealed further to women's nature.

> The nature of a woman is altogether different than a man. God did not make them the same. You see, he made the man from the dust, but he didn't go back to the dirt to make the woman. He made her from a rib of the man. During his ministry, [Jesus], during his lifetime, he loved women, and I believe that when he spoke to the woman at the well she went about telling everybody about it. But it didn't say that the Lord, that Jesus called her at the Last Supper and set up the church with her. I can't find and have not found yet a precedent for women pastoring the church. I love the ministries that support the church, and I believe the women are great in that, and that's where [they should be].

Mother Williams came at this issue from yet another angle. Her cousin who went in the ministry had settled into a prison ministry with her husband. She sounded pleased that her cousin had turned down pastoring a church. Although she doesn't think women should pastor, she admitted that she didn't think God would punish women who do choose to pastor churches. As she spoke about a woman who pastors a nearby church, the degree to which she believed women should not be in the pastoral roles became clearer.

> Just recently a friend of mine told me about a church over here on Main Street that's pastored by a woman, and she elevates the women in the church. Her brother is one of the pastors who was there with the former pastor, who was a man. She was telling me how belittling [she was] and the menial assignments that she would give to the men, and I said, "we women aren't cut out to [be there]. We were cut out to have babies, and we don't need to be up there in the pulpit with our [bellies]. We don't need to do that, you understand?"

This senior woman was not the only one opposed to women clergy. A minority of the group opposed having women as pastors, although they accepted preaching by women. They did not express the same opposition to women's serving as deacons, trustees, or finance board members. One participant adamantly asserted that a woman could not lead her as a pastor, appealing to the "nature" of women, rather than to biblical precedent. Another respondent spoke of her discomfort with a woman's fulfilling the role of bishop or elder. She struggled to articulate her discomfort, only partially conveying why she found women clergy bothersome. "I just don't receive it, I couldn't sit under a woman preacher, and that's not saying men don't keep up a whole lot of mess, but women have a tendency to chastise, to embellish, borderline to start telling stories." Drawing upon her experience with woman managers and supervisors in the workplace, she added that once a woman is in a position of power, she is "overly possessive . . . [becomes] a respecter of persons, chooses one over another."

Bernice, a member of Layton Temple, opposed female ministers on the basis that it is disruptive of God's ordained structure for the family and church.

> I guess I see the church more like a family, and in my family my dad was the head of the house, and my brothers are head of their homes and it just seems that things function better. Men are just more responsible. I think they're more fulfilled when they're in those positions of responsibility, and I see that in the church. I don't view the NAACP and all of those [organizations] as a family. That's an organization like a job, you're trying to get a job done and who ever is best to do that job, whether it's male or female will be the one who's doing that job. . . . I view the church as a family, the structure itself, as a family, our pastor being our spiritual father. These are the people he has watch over, and in that leadership role our men are helping him and then the women are falling into their positions. [In] my job I wouldn't have a problem managing men if I had to, 'cause it's a job, it's not dealing with your psyche. Maybe it is in a way, but I'm not trying to develop your family or your children, or having an effect on [them] and how they grow up. We're trying to get a job done for a corporation, that is an inanimate object. But for the church I don't see that it's inanimate. It is a spiritual thing, and I think it's better headed by men.

Janice incorporated into her understanding of church a family structure. The church is a place where everyone has his or her place, with the men leading. She differentiated between spiritual leadership and leadership in the business world. As a manager on her job, she can supervise men and women, but she does not regard authority over men as appropriate for women in the church. She believes that men have a greater capacity for leadership and that governance is a requisite role for men, rather than women. Janice spoke of gender roles as divinely purposed and of her own comfort with women in positions of authority.

> Maybe it has to do a lot with the way I was reared, but I just don't see the woman being over the man. It does something to the man's self-esteem when women take control from them, and I just advocate [for] them and love to see the men be up front, do what needs to be done, take control and the rest. There are places where we fit better, I think we work with the children better than the men, but that's kind of a God-given talent, I think. The Lord has put us as the mothers, anyway. I just believe that men should be in that position. It makes them stronger men, [having] that responsibility of being in control of things, for being responsible for the success of whatever organization you're in. I don't think that gives anybody the right to take advantage of anybody else; that's not Christian behavior, anyway. But as strong Christian men, if they're true Christians, they're not going to take advantage of anybody, anyway. But I just, I like them being in that position. I'm more comfortable with them in that position; I feel safe, if that's a good word, that our men are in control. They've got it going on. I think it's functioning the way the Lord would want it to function.

Lynn articulates a similar view of women pastors, also connecting her position to a divine design for the home and church.

> I feel like, I guess I've been convinced of the order that God intended us for—for the man to lead—and so I feel that it's important and even in a church environment I believe it's particularly important for young men, for children in general to see strong men in those kind of leadership roles—men subjecting themselves to the will of Christ, men leading, men being upright, doing what is right and a positive role, a positive impact. And I think it's important for women, too, to see men in a positive leadership, doing one's right role.

Her stress on male role models in the home led me to ask, "Are you assuming that people aren't seeing this [men] in their households and other places?" She replied, "No, not necessarily, but the church is supposed to be something, the example for so many things, so I think when you go, there are a lot of things you might not see in place, but they should be as the scriptures intended for things to be."

Although the opposition to female clergy appears on the surface to be about a theological mandate, upon closer inspection it is as much based on biblical grounds as on the perceived need for strong male role models and family models in the Black Church and community. In light of these concerns, a new trend must be given serious consideration. In the past two decades, a new form of pastoring—husband-and-wife teams—has become popular, and many clergy couples are receiving national attention. It is too early to know the impact of this new phenomenon on female clergy. It may become another challenge to female ministers (especially single ones) trying to enter into the vocation of pastoring in the twenty-first century. On the other hand, it provides an avenue to the pulpit for married women while suppressing members' reservations about male self-esteem. It also may have the effect of providing dual leadership models and affirming the model of church as a family with a two-parent ministerial team at the helm.

It would be misleading to leave the impression that opposition to female clergy is simple and straightforward. Women affirm the value of having strong male models of leadership in the church. Their support and their high regard for their pastors provide evidence of that commitment. Intellectually, some are uncomfortable with uniform acceptance of men but not women as "official" leaders. There is a tension between the needs of men and women that gets exposed as women strive to reach the position of preacher and pastor. On the one hand, men need to be exposed to strong male role models. On the other hand, female youth in the church need to be exposed to a more gender-balanced sharing of power in the church. These competing concerns become even more complicated as the traditional family model preached in many churches (i.e., a nuclear one) is losing dominance to various family configurations of the church membership. A woman who was in favor of women clergy commented on this dynamic. She affirmed that it is positive for boys to see men in leadership roles "because I don't think our young men have enough role models as it is. But, on the other hand, I think they should see both as leaders. Because there are so many homes where the woman is the leader. There is no man. If the woman can be the leader in the home, why can't she be a leader in the church?"

Advocacy

Women are not taking an active role in instituting structural changes concerning women in their denominations. The conceptual divisions of reality into sacred and secular realms are operative among church women. Reliance upon these dualities informs their evaluations of what change is necessary and their assessment of strategies for implementing change. The women I studied have not formulated a comprehensive analysis of sexism in the church and were not conversant with the works of womanist and feminist scholars who have offered critiques and alternative visions for the church. While racism is a legitimate phenomenon to oppose in the church, sexism does not appear to be evaluated as the same order of injustice. Among those who identified sexism as present in the church, few were convinced one should or could utilize the same mechanisms to fight sexism or gender discrimination in the church as one could outside it. Women were hesitant to support the appropriation of business or secular strategies (e.g., affirmative action) to redress the treatment of female clergy. The church is a distinctive sort of organization, a spiritual entity, which should not be run by the same procedures as other institutions.

Many women noted the changing prospects for women clergy in the local church. In both locations, participants have been exposed to female preachers. This personal exposure may have an unexpected effect upon lay women; personal exposure may serve to lessen their frustration or concern for the status of women clergy beyond their local congregations, because there is a female cleric in their midst. This appreciation may, in their minds, obviate the need for a more systematic or collective advocacy. Attempts at structural changes are also hampered by their limited knowledge of the processes and politics for hiring a pastor. Few have ever been a part of such a process. Some women had a personal acquaintance with or knew of a female cleric who had encountered hardships in gaining access to preaching and pastoring opportunities. Sympathetic to the frustration of their friends, they had not taken any direct action in these situations. There was no evidence that they had built formal alliances with these women. Some women did provide a listening ear, which could be regarded as a demonstration of solidarity.

The absence of a collective response is possibly better understood when one seeks to understand the concept of "a calling" from these women's perspectives. Preaching and pastoring are regarded as vocational choices predicated upon an irresistible "calling" from God. It is assumed these roles are neither merely nor primarily the result of a self-initiated choice. This establishes the preacher as one who should have the determination to assert herself in fulfilling her ministry, or the patience needed to gain opportunities if she encounters obstacles. The called person is a model of conviction and is expected to trust God to "raise her up" in due season. Thus, the assumption of the preacher's persistence proves the authenticity of the call while alleviating any incentive for involvement or advocacy on the part of the laity. The women I studied have confidence that God will create opportunities for women in this arena in due time. Linda did not oppose women preachers or pastors but was averse to the idea of intentionally selecting women for that role; it offended her understanding of calling, and she regarded an attempt to intentionally add women to the pulpit as inappropriate. Her words reveal both trust in inevitable change and opposition to human intervention in these matters. Linda said:

> It didn't shock me, and I didn't go into spasms when I walked into Layton and there were no women sitting up there. It was like, well, it will happen when it happens; it will happen when it's supposed to happen, when that leader comes forth. I mean intentionally trying to put someone up there, I think when you do that, sometimes that then you end up with the wrong leader, it seems. It's not by your choice, it should be by God's choice, it should be by the choice of the Spirit, and that person will come forth, and when that person comes forth let it happen. But when we start appointing it, it's wrong.

There is a general lack of preoccupation with the issue of female clergy among the group. They have been members of congregations with very few women ministers and did not expect that a church would or should have female clergy on staff. None intentionally sought a church with a gender-inclusive clerical leadership. In fact, as I posed questions about women clergy, members of both congregations looked rather surprised (others looked amused) at being asked to give serious consideration to the presence or absence of women clergy in their congregations. Some remarked that they don't even think about the division of labor in the church or the gender of the preacher. Others affirmed the positive attributes that women bring to the preaching and pulpit ministry. None went as far as to emphatically state that they were bothered by the unequal representation.

There was no organized support among these women for female ordination. Among the Baptists, several women said they had never heard any negativity about the female ministers or about the fact that Calvary has women in its clergy ranks. Does this indicate that debates over female clergy are restricted to those women who are actively pursuing ordination and are not pertinent to the overall well-being of the local congregation? Or is it a consequence of women's being included in the church hierarchy? Women have accepted and adapted to the polity of the church. Any vestiges of discontent are mitigated by the senior pastor's regard for female preachers (and other female leaders). Access to and familiarity with women clergy serves to correct what was previously considered normative. As youth, the women considered the absence of female clergy as normal; now the opposite is true. Female ministers' present involvement in the ministry of these churches can be treated as part of the congregation's identity, rather than an anomaly.

This is particularly true at Calvary. When I first started attending Calvary, there was one female minister present. Since then, she has been ordained and is no longer there. There are now three women ministers active. Two seem to have higher visibility than the third one. However, they are all part of the ministry; they do preach occasionally and are acknowledged for their contributions to their specific area of ministry.

Male leadership in the church did not disturb Betty, a member of Layton Temple. From her vantage point, there is too much to do in the church to "bicker" over who is in charge. She recognizes that she has friends who hold different positions, who are more vocal and push "much more than me about women's equality." She is content to do the work of the church regardless of the position or status it is accorded. While some of her church friends are more vocal about egalitarian treatment in the church, she also thinks the impetus for change is lessened by the power women have in the Women's Department; it "keeps them from pushing even more aggressively for equality in the denomination."

Discussion

Black women's religious lives have been impacted by the increasing presence of female clergy. Women have been exposed to these models and appreciate them for their abilities and spiritual gifts. On the other hand, the increasing number of women clerics has created neither a collective demonstration of support nor opposition. Personal commitment or responsibility for altering the institution's responses toward female clergy is lacking. On the whole, these church women are affirming of female preachers, exclusion from the office of pastor is a limitation that some women think should be maintained.

It is also evident from this study that women's lives are defined by often conflicting constructions of womanhood. They are participating in congregations that continue to disseminate a paradoxical message: women are powerful, but there should be limits to the exercising of their talents. In Layton Temple, preaching and teaching cast women as having a prescribed place in home and church, yet they are encouraged to use their spiritual gifts freely. Many of the women in this church had no problem reporting what their church has taught regarding women's place: women are not to exercise formal authority over men in the role of pastor. However, it does not elude them that some women in their denomination have been allowed to pastor churches, assuming the position upon the death of their spouse. In Calvary Baptist Church, there were less direct pronouncements concerning women's role and more emphasis on "saving" the black male, socially and spiritually. The social problems that impact men are cast as the primary problem of the black community. I did not hear any messages in either congregation that addressed the unique social, cultural, or economic realities of black women independent of the problems of black men.

Women's attitudes toward female clergy are influenced by other factors as well: the high regard for female labor in the church; the absence of black male role models in the community; the lack of a discourse on sexism in the church; reluctance to apply "affirmative action" strategies in a religious context; and perceived satisfaction with the "benefits" of church participation and the church's fulfillment of its mission. Together, these elements form a sacred context that makes acceptable the current state of affairs and impedes a comprehensive critique or discourse on gender relations in the church, of which the role of women clergy would be one facet.

Another characteristic that calls our attention to the gendered nature of the Black Church is its perception of women's contributions to church life and its acceptance of the exclusivity of the ministerial leadership of the church. For instance, while Calvary Baptist Church has had a couple of women as part of the ministerial staff, only two respondents reflected on the inclusivity of women in the leadership of the churches they were raised in, and none identified inclusivity in ministerial leadership or pastoral responsibilities as a desired or essential feature they looked for before joining Layton Temple. I believe their lack of preoccupation with the gender of the pastor brings to the fore women's self-understanding as essential to the constitution and maintenance of the church. There has been no agitation for women's ordination among black lay women of the magnitude found among mainline Protestants and Catholics.[10]

The discourse about the role of women in the church among the COGIC women cannot be understood without attention to the prominence and active role of evangelists, missionaries, and mothers in that denomination. All three are officially licensed positions and part of the episcopal structure. Women in these roles may exhort, preach, lead revivals, conduct prayer meetings, and found churches. In addition, they work at regional and national levels as the leaders of the Women's Department, developing publication materials and providing oversight for all of the Women's Departments in local congregations. The importance and visibility of the office of "Mother" in this denomination can not be underscored. The Women's Department manual describes this position as vested with authority:

> The role of the local church mother is indeed one of great importance and a "must" for a growing church. She is to a pastor in the local church what a wife is to her husband in the home. The day has far passed for a pastor to teach from the pulpit things that women should know. It was never proper, but accepted because of the time. Today, such teaching and instructing would only embarrass and drive our present-day generation from the church. . . . An effective church Mothers Board cannot operate without the authority released by the pastor and officers of the church. It is unfair to appoint a chairwoman of the board and tie her hands and the hands of the board. Women who cannot be trusted should not be appointed because the responsibility is too great. A failure in operation will only impede the progress of the church. . . . There should be a pastor-church mother relationship going on at all times and the pastor should be able to request anything within reason to the church Mothers Board and look for results.[11]

The position of National Mother corresponds to that of the Presiding Bishop of the Churches of God in Christ. Women reared in this denomination do not hear women officially "preach"; they "speak." Nevertheless, the prominence of missionaries, the historically strong women's department in this denomination, and the administrative and spiritual contributions of the Mothers Board serve to undermine a view of women as second-class citizens in this context. They are active agents, coleaders with the pastor, visionaries, program developers, ministers to the sick, teachers, and community activists outside the church.

In neither church were women oblivious to the general state of affairs within their denominations regarding women's lack of access to the role of preacher or pastor. Betty, a member of Layton Temple, told the story of a pastor's wife she had known in Florida who had started several churches, but every time she got them "up and running," the district would send in a man as the official head. She stated this not with any sort of consternation but more with a sense of resignation— that's how things are. Although Betty portrays the women's actions as subverted by the selection of a male pastor, the work of Cheryl Townsend Gilkes provides an alternative interpretation of this historic pattern. The founding of churches was a demonstration of women's agency, not capitulation. Within the context of urbanization in the South and then migration in the North, women sought "to recreate and reconstitute" the communities of which they had been part. The institutionalization of "church mother" in the Church of God in Christ and the similar position in the Baptist church (either honorific or formal) are evidence of women's autonomy and self-determination, while serving the larger national body. Often women gathered the initial congregation together, "sending home" for a pastor only once this community of women had been organized.[12] Considering the importance women played in the expansion of this denomination, to conclude that women were simply thwarted by the ecclesiastical powers would be erroneous and would minimize women's power in determining who would serve as pastor.

It would be misleading to suggest women do not contribute significantly to the selection of a pastor. Yet, even with their involvement in selection committees (in the Baptist church), on the whole they are unfamiliar with the processes, negotiations, and guidelines that accompany the process of ordination and selection of pastors. Linda's comments suggested her opposition to increasing the presence of women in pulpits. She appears resistant to any institutional or denominational changes that would mandate more equitable treatment.

The "calling" of a pastor is a hidden process in most congregations; it is a task overseen by a select few. Congregations discuss this process in terms of a "spiritual compatibility" and appropriate "gifts for ministry." These spiritual overtones obfuscate the reality that churches are relying upon resumes, reference checks, employment banks, credit histories, and other processes standard in employment searches. Linda's words could, with slight alteration, have been the voice of someone voicing opposition to affirmative action policies in another arena. It is also likely that her hesitation about intentionally expanding women's roles in the church is rooted in the fact that male leadership is not a liability to the church or its ability to fulfill its mission. While women do not preach, they are perceived as having influence in the church. The contribution of time and resources that black women give to the church reinforce the interdependence of laity and clergy, and ensures that women are not treated as an expendable constituency in the church. One must also bear in mind the lack of a comparative context from which to judge the impact of a woman pastor's leadership. Women's speculations about how the church might operate differently, whether the culture within the church would change significantly, or whether female leadership would be distinctive from what they've encountered are loosely based upon judgments made about women's impact in other, previously male-dominated vocations in and outside the church.

In the African American free church tradition, the individual who preaches for a given service is compensated, often by the raising of a "love offering." Women, like men, receive these offerings. However, absent from women's discourse was any reflection on other resources, opportunities, and compensation that accompany ordination and the denominational endorsement to which women are not privileged. I think this points directly to the presumption of the ministry as a task one is "called to," rather than a profession one chooses. With the emphasis on being chosen to fulfill a task, there is often the presumption that one's needs will be provided for by God.

The women in this sample had differing exposures to female preachers. Many recalled that, while women could preach powerfully, they usually had to do so from the floor, not the pulpit. The site of proclamation made only a marginal impression on the women, since the actual opportunity was not denied. My observation in both churches proved that this is not the case presently. I heard one woman preach in both congregations. At Layton Temple, it was a State Mother. At Calvary, it was the assistant minister. Both women delivered messages from the pulpit.

While the male leadership in their churches was regarded as a fixed reality—"that's just how it was"—some women noted how the prevalence of male leaders in the church has subtly influenced more than just the position of clergy. A single mother and member of Calvary Baptist has desired to be a deaconess for a long time. She was denied this opportunity in a former congregation. She could not fill that capacity because she didn't meet the criteria for this role in her church—a woman had to be married to a deacon.[13] She was frustrated and bothered by this but in her words "did not push it" and just accepted that her members were "old-fashioned." Another woman attested to having had a strong desire to be a deacon since joining Calvary. She never told the pastor, considering that the board is all-male. She recalled how the pastor sometimes asked women if they wanted to join the deacon's wives ministry, but not the deacons. She knows someone has to "test the waters" to make that board coed, but she's not willing to be the test case. She has put this desire on the back burner and rarely thinks about it.

The view of female leadership in the church among our women was varied. As already stated, they did not aggressively support greater access to the pulpit. There were a few signs of frustration with the limitations women encounter, and an occasional contesting of a woman's ability to pastor a church. The words of those who were opposed to women's preaching were not as harsh as the antipreaching sentiments that C. Eric Lincoln and Lawrence Mamiya discovered among their national sample of clergy. As already stated, the women in our study accepted the status quo.[14] Lincoln and Mamiya found almost equal proportions of approval and disapproval of women pastors among male clergy. Fifty-one percent approved, and 49 percent disapproved. The percentage of those who strongly approved (15 percent) was significantly lower than that of those who strongly disapproved (24.7 percent). This survey of 2,150 churches included sixty-six female clergy. Of the sixty-four interviewed, 82 percent approved of women pastors.[15] This study demonstrates that more progress must be made if women are to gain greater access to the pastorate; as a group, the Baptist and COGIC clergy were nearly three to one against women pastors.[16]

The reality that most women in the Black Church have been hindered from seeking the pastorate does not tell the whole story.[17] Some denominations have been formed precisely over the issue of female power in the church. In Pentecostal groups, the lines of discourse have not centered on whether to allow women to preach. Rather, the emphasis has been on equal access and opportunity for preachers. In practice, there remains resistance to female preachers, who are often treated as subordinate to male clergy. In the early twentieth century, two denominations that emerged as a result of these debates about women's roles were the Mount Sinai Holy Church of America and the House of God. They sought to correct injustices present in other Pentecostal groups, such as women's not being eligible for election as bishop and facing a more rigorous process to ordination. Thus, the history of black religion is not one of total exclusion from the pastorate. Where access to pastoring was not achieved, women created other enclaves where they could exercise power; often, the Women's Departments acted as these sites.

> [Black] denominations exhibit a range of shared powers and a diversity of opinions on the scripturally prescribed offices for women. Consequently, in those churches where women were barred from pastoring and preaching; there is a well-developed and powerful women's world which, while under the authority of male bishops has carved out its own space within the church while maintaining a militant consciousness concerning the areas of exclusion.[18]

My final conclusion about female labor and leadership is that it is a complex story. Women exhibit leadership in congregational life in numerous positions that make the Black Church the vital house of worship it is. The limitations upon lay women are minimal and yet remain in place regarding the roles of preacher and pastor. There is no evidence that women intentionally prevent other women from rising through the ranks of the clergy. While the folklore says otherwise, they are not a significant hindrance to the acceptance and treatment of female clergy in reality. There is support, and there is some opposition. Probably more than either of these positions, the lack of energy on this issue is most important. The absence of female clergy in the church is not regarded as a justice issue or a question of sexism, and it competes with concern for men's status in the church and society. In this instance, women's gender consciousness does not supersede their commitment to supporting black men, nor does it manifest itself in collective support for clergy women. In some ways, it is a recasting of the tension black women have lived with historically:

whether to align themselves along perceived gender lines (female clergy) or along racial lines (the state of black men). In this case, race trumps gender consciousness. I have more to say about these findings but leave it until the final chapter. First, in the next chapter, we examine another historic tension within the Black Church—the tension between race consciousness and Christian identity.

6

We're Part of the Same Culture
Racial Awareness and Religion

Enter the average church on any given Sunday and you are likely to notice the racial homogeneity of the people. Segregated congregations have defined the American religious landscape for nearly two centuries. These racially distinct congregations are rooted in two historical dynamics that converged in the nineteenth century—the quest for congregational independence by African Americans and the push of discriminatory practices from predominately white denominations and the nation at large.[1] What seemed like a momentary opportunity for the development of racially integrated churches in the post–Civil War era was thwarted with the end of Reconstruction and the rise of Jim Crow in the latter part of the nineteenth century. Law and custom enshrined white supremacy, undermining the possibility that white and black Christians could congregate in accordance with their professed Christian theology.

Racial segregation was the rule of the land until the last third of the twentieth century. It defined residential, social, economic, political, and ecclesiastical spheres. In the post–civil rights era, the legal barriers to integration were dismantled—schools, housing, politics, and the labor market slowly became integrated to varying degrees. Christian congregations, however, have remained largely racially distinct.

Given this state of affairs, in this chapter I examine the racial awareness and reasoning of black church women, how they articulate and live the intersection of being black and Christian at the dawn of the twenty-first century. A fundamental tenet of Christianity is that membership is determined by allegiance to a set of shared beliefs, not by membership in a certain racial, ethnic, or social group. Black and white Christians realize the failure of the church to realize this tenet in the composition of their congregations, yet they continue to impart this theological vision to new converts. In the following pages I explore women's perspectives and concerns about this racial divide in the Christian church.

Racial identification is defined as "a sense of common experience, group feeling, and shared interests with others of the same group."[2] It is the internal evaluation of the self, distinct from racial consciousness. Consciousness is outwardly directed; it is the evaluation of how one sees one's group in relation to the larger society. Previous forays into the study of racial identification have found that African Americans have a greater degree of collective orientation and racial identification than white Americans do. Moreover, among African Americans, church members exhibit stronger racial group identification than nonchurch members.[3] While religion has not been cited as the cause of this heightened racial identification, the positive correlation between racial identity and religious participation has been a persistent one.

My initial intent was to identify and assess racial consciousness independent of identity. Racial identity would be measured by women's support of black institutions, enterprises, and cultural institutions. The indicators for racial consciousness would be the respondents' patronage of black-owned businesses, involvement in black organizations and cultural events, support for black politicians, and views on interracial social relationships. Although I attempted to keep the internal and external dimensions discrete, women did not usually discuss these dimensions as separate aspects. Using a quantitative instrument such as a survey would have made it easier to measure attributes of each separately. It was more of a challenge using a semistructured interview. However, breaking down the women's comments into discrete dimensions would have blurred the content and elevated my own role as interpreter of their meanings. Therefore, I have chosen the broader rubric "racial awareness" to capture both concepts. I am defining racial awareness as one's perception of oneself as a member of a racial group and one's evaluation of how members of the larger society perceive that group.

In my conversations about race and faith, I examined how women construct meanings to support the incongruity between the ideological (what it teaches) and consequential (what adherents do) dimensions of their faith. Has their Christian identity superseded or transformed their racial self-concept? How did race factor into their choice of congregation? Do women reconcile their commitments to theological universalism with the practice of racial solidarity? Is selection of a black religious community indicative of a more generalized support of African American businesses and politicians? The responses to these questions are presented in two sections. The first one, on racial practices, demonstrates the women's individual and collective identification with the African American community. The second one, on race and theology, explores more closely the intersection of race, faith, and the choice to worship in the Black Church.

Racial Practices

Support for Black Businesses

The women in this study supported black-owned businesses and entrepreneurs with varying degrees of consistency and for different reasons. Some offered strong support; others felt no responsibility to support black-owned businesses. One woman attributes her support of black businesses to her established friendships. When I asked her about being intentional in her support, she said, "[I'm] not intentional . . . most of my friends who have businesses, I want to support them. Looking at the Chinese and the Koreans, they support one another. So why not put my money back into the black businesses? I do support the whites, too." Another woman anchored her support of black businesses in the desire to keep money in the black community but was critical of some of the dynamics she has observed in the delivery of services.

> We're the only group that does not pass wealth. You know, every generation has to kind of make it on their own. . . . I think that black people, we as a people could help ourselves a lot, I really do. . . . And as Christians we're able to help one another; we're supposed to help anyone that needs help. I try, I make an extra effort, and that's because I feel like I should shop at black businesses and stuff, and that's why it hurts so bad when black people [are mean] to one another, or disrespect one another.

For personal purchases such as clothing, hair care, particular ethnic products, and black art and literature, women turned to African American providers. As a group, they were less concerned about patronizing black doctors, lawyers, car dealerships, or other professional providers. They demonstrated the attitude of a modern informed consumer who goes where the best prices for the best services are offered. Thelma seemed to discount race more than the other women had when it came to frequenting black-owned businesses.

> Well, I don't go out of my way, you know, to give a certain person support, because I believe in God and I believe that we're all His children. As far as black businesses, if you're on my corner, and you're a grocer and you're black and I need something from the grocery store, sure, I wouldn't pass you by to go to another race, but I wouldn't pass them by to go to you, either.

I probed whether convenience was important. She responded, "Right, and I feel like regardless of what the statistics say about one supporting their own, the way I feel is that we're all God's children. I don't, believe in going out of my way just to get to a black." Lori was adamant that race does not determine where she shops. I asked her how important it was to her to support black businesses.

> It's very important to me. But I will not support a black business, just because it's black. I need to know that you are going to service me. That you are going to give me the best price for my dollar. I can no longer be of the mindset that just because you're black than I am going to come to your business. I'm going to come in, but you have to be just as competitive and do all the other things that any other business is going to do for me. Just because you're black is just not enough any more. . . . If you're providing a service for me and if all things were equal, and one was black and one was white, then I'd definitely go with the black one. However, if all things were not equal and you're going to give me some shabby service and say, "Well, she's black, I'm going to hook her up," [then] no, I can't shop there.

In our conversations about race and economics, I found many women had stories of being slighted or having to pay higher prices to black businesses than to white-owned ones. While they acknowledged that blacks often encounter higher costs in establishing and maintaining businesses, which are usually passed on to the consumer, some were not willing to pay the higher prices just to patronize black merchants. In addition, women expected equal or higher standards of customer service from black service providers. While they choose to support black businesses, the experience of being "burnt" feels harsher when the person is black. Joyce shared how supporting black business is important to her and her husband, yet it has its complexities.

> He [my husband] is really into supporting black business. I am, too, I am, too. I just get scared sometimes, because I feel like I've been burnt a lot by black people. And it's harder for me to deal with being burnt by black people than it is for me to feel being burnt by white people, and that just bugs me [laughter], you know? But we do support black businesses a lot. We were wallpapering the [room]. A white guy came in. I was not impressed. Carl heard a guy at church that was wallpapering. I said, "Let's give the guy a chance to do work on the house." My fear is [that] if the guy messes up the place, you can't sue the guy because he's a brother in two ways. He belongs to the church, and he's a black man. You can't sue the man. If he's a white guy, we'll stay in the court forever [laughs], that kind of thing.

One area in which the women indicated a degree of racial awareness and demonstrated their patronage of black businesses was in their home décor, specifically the presence of African or black artwork in their homes. I conducted the majority of the interviews in women's homes, usually in a living room, dining room, or kitchen. Present in some of the homes were images of African and African American persons and artifacts such as masks, fabric, and baskets. One woman took me downstairs to her family area, where she had various figurines and paintings depicting blacks. Another woman had a home-based business making flower arrangements, candles, and centerpieces with African fabrics and motifs. I saw one of her products carefully displayed on her mantle and another in the bathroom.

All of the paintings and other items I saw have been very popular for the past two decades and are available through black cultural markets, street fairs, and galleries and on the Internet. They are especially available in the region where this research was conducted. Given my limited access to their homes, I cannot be certain whether they collected these items as an expression of racial identity. The items may have been gifts, rather than purchases. Also, displaying portraits of African Americans or Africans may not signify the owner's disposition. For instance, one woman pointed out that her artwork by African Americans did not depict black persons or typical scenes of "black life." Artwork may also have been absent because of personal tastes or prohibitive costs. Notwith-standing, some women said they intentionally made such purchases for their home as part of an attempt to support a renaissance in African American culture.

In addition to the market for African American art, the city hosts several African American festivals and is home to several renowned black churches and ministries, cultural centers, research centers, colleges, and historic sites. This group of women had different levels of knowledge and familiarity with these local resources and sites. Most had supported or visited at least one of the historic sites or local cultural events, but they did not constantly patronize these centers. Their lack of support was more a consequence of time constraints than of lack of interest in the venues. Some visit the local attractions only when they have out-of-town visitors. As in any major city, it is likely that local residents take these events and sites for granted; the proximity may actually diminish their appeal, rather than enhance it. It is also possible that their support is influenced by local politics, persons, and debates about these institutions and churches.

Churches and community agencies in the city sponsor community wide celebrations of Kwanzaa.[4] Calvary Baptist Church has incorporated part of this celebration into its watchnight worship service. The origins and purpose of this holiday eluded some of the women. Some have celebrated it, but they said that in order to do so, they had to resolve what they perceived as a conflict between celebrating Kwanzaa and celebrating Christmas. Linda, a young married woman in her twenties believes that the concept of the holiday is valuable.

> I think it's a good thing. I guess it's just because it's just different to me because I went to church all my life and then somebody comes up with [a] Kwanzaa celebration in 1970 and all of a sudden I'm supposed to switch. So I guess it's just different; 'cause a lot of people just celebrate Kwanzaa and they don't celebrate Christmas. Granted, there are a lot who celebrate both. But I'd like to look at it just to see how you could positively do both. 'Cause I don't see not going to church.

When I was in Karen's home, I noticed some of the Kwanzaa symbols and asked her about them. She had observed the holiday with her son. She said:

This was our first year, and it took me a while . . . it took me a while for Kwanzaa because, you know, Christmas is, other than Easter, the biggest thing there is. And I thought that Kwanzaa kind of, you know, [was] not being really loyal [to] Christ. So it took me a long time for Kwanzaa. I had to; I had to really study [works by Karenga].

Support for Black Politicians

I raised the issue of supporting black political candidates with these church women. Would they support a black candidate over a white candidate because of his or her race? There was no unanimous answer. Only a couple of women were willing to support a candidate primarily because of his or her race. Many said they would not vote a race slate. They identified high-profile black politicians who had, once elected, disappointed them. They asserted that African American ethnicity is not a sufficient indicator of who has the well-being of the African American community in mind. Rather than vote for the black candidate solely on the basis of race, they would first assess the candidate's posture on issues important to the black community. Kelly goes out of her way to support black businesses. When it comes to black politicians, she isn't as committed.

[I go] part of my way, but another thing, too; they're gonna have to stand for what's right and wrong. No longer are you gonna take advantage of me. Because of your skin color, I'm supposed to vote for you? No, I'll still vote for you, but I'm gonna bend your ear, your arm, and everything else, cause you're gonna have to work for it. You're gonna be honest. You can't be like them [white politicians]. You've got to do what's right.

Michelle is a supporter of black candidates. She stated:

I like to support black candidates, not only because they're black, but also if they're saying the right things or at least have the right idea in mind, then I like to see that they get an opportunity. Now, if they're not doing the right thing after they get in, they need the same opportunity to go back home and think about that some more.

Choosing the person who could best address the collective local interests of African Americans was more important in determining their voting behavior than the national impact of having (or not having) another black elected official. Rene didn't put the interests of the African American community above the interests of others.

> I'd ask them [the black candidates] how they'd stand on issues that affect both the black and the white. All of my questions wouldn't be how you affect the black community, because he's going to be a representative for both black and white, why would I want him to just take care of me? I want to make sure he has the good of the people in mind, not just black or white. Yeah, I'd ask him about issues we see on the news that we see are affecting a specific group. They wanted to put an AIDS house in a particular neighbor. They call them colony homes. Most of the victims were white, and the community didn't want them in there. That was a white issue, in a white community. How do you feel about that? What do you feel about putting up colony homes in a regular neighborhood? We got twenty acres behind us. My husband and I are trying to get some of that land. We got twenty acres back there, and they gonna sell. What if they sold it and they put up an AIDS home back there? I mean, some issues are just colorless. They go beyond the color line.

However, all things being equal between the candidates (other than race), they would cast their vote for the minority candidate to redress past injustices endured by black politicians. As they had for black businesses, some women reported that failure by black politicians was more hurtful than failure by white politicians and that it would be weighed more harshly by them. Given the magnitude of hope and trust they invest in black candidates, women feel a personal let-down at a black politician's failure or lack of productivity and believe it harms black Americans collectively.

Support for Interracial Relationships

Another aspect I explored to determine racial consciousness was the women's views on interracial dating and marriage. Their public voices on these issues and their personal preferences did not agree. Like many Americans, they espoused the logic that persons should be able to marry whomever they desired. Personally, the majority preferred same-race couplings. Yvette said:

> I prefer a black man, but it doesn't bother me if anybody else doesn't or they cross over. I feel it's not set up that way. . . . God didn't intend for it to be that way. It's not necessarily blacks for blacks, whites for whites, Hispanics for Hispanics. He didn't set down any rules on that, to me. I don't believe He did. I can't believe He would, 'cause that would be saying then you're not good enough for somebody, and if none of us are perfect, then who's better than who? So that's what I believe, that's why I believe God didn't set it up that way. I feel there are things more important about a mate than their color, skin color, race, or nationality.

Some women had family members who have married across racial lines. The women with in-laws from other racial groups have accepted them as part of their families. Yet, they have tried to instill in their children a preference for someone of their own race as a marriage partner. The well-being of the children was cited as one concern in these unions.

Related to interracial relationships, two other sentiments surfaced. The first was that certain interracial mixes reflect negatively on black women. Tony has never dated a white man and concedes, "People should date whomever they want to date because it's them." Yet, her acceptance did not seem as convincing once she began to talk about unions of black men and white women.

> I have a serious problem with black men and women. I have a serious problem with that now. They need to date us. We are the ones that hang by these brothers, especially the entertainers and sports guys. They are rich and famous and have all this money and fame, and they are running to white women as quick as they can get them. These white women wouldn't be with them if they were not who they are. We struggle with them, we are with them when they have nothing and what do they do? They go to white women. With O. J. Simpson, Charles Barkley, I have a serious problem with them. Yes, I do. I used to love Charles Barkley until I found out he was married to a white woman. I cut him loose, just like that.

Because she cited only men with celebrity status, I asked her whether she'd feel the same way about the average black man. She responded, "Yes, I would. Come on. There are too many sisters out here. Yes, I feel that way, I certainly do." Another woman echoed her concerns about how African American women are treated in the mating game. She added to this perspective her concern about the loss of necessary resources in the black community.

> I'm for interracial marriages, but what I don't like to see is [pauses], I like to see people put money back into the community that they grew up in. I like to see them be concerned about that neighborhood strife. I think it gives us a sense of self-worth, but it also promotes growth for that neighborhood. So with the interracial [marriages], I think, black stars—I don't like to see them date black women when they're in high school, date black women when they're in college, and then marry a white woman. [They] move out of the black neighborhood, move into a white neighborhood, and get them a big old limousine. Why can't a black man be rich and live in a black rich neighborhood, or why can't he move into a mixed neighborhood? Most of the times they move into an exclusive neighborhood and they're the only black. . . . It's almost like their culture is good until they make a certain amount of money. That's what I don't like. I don't mind interracial marriages. If you love her, that's fine, but don't forget to put things back into the community where you came from. I think that when you rise to the top, why not take the girlfriend with you who helped put you through school and wrote out your test papers for you, you know did all that for you; maybe had your baby? So, in that respect, I think that should be a consideration. We don't see that maybe 1 percent of the black athletes have a black wife. . . . Very rarely do white successful men marry black women. If you look at the [white men] whom we see on TV a lot and look at their wives, they don't have interracial marriages.

A related sentiment expressed by a few women pertained to the idea that interracial marriages weaken the black community. They were not specific about how it weakens it. Lynn thinks blacks should marry blacks. When I asked her why, she responded:

> Part of it is support. You know it's getting more difficult for black women, so (I don't know if I'm being straight down on the line on this) but I feel like whenever possible, you should. I think there's something to be said for common cultures or common experiences being a better blend. I think that foundations are important, and I think you have a better chance of success if your foundations are similar. And I just happen to think that we need to support our people, you know. We need

to strengthen our race, if anything, and the way to do this is to stay within it.

Yvette, who counts all children of black-white marriage as African Americans, countered this idea that interracial unions weaken the race.

> What weakens [the black community] are our attitudes and the way we perceive [these unions]. . . . If we think, "Well, if I marry [or] if so-and-so marries a white man then that's going to weaken our race." No . . . as far as human society is concerned, if you got an ounce of black in you, you're black, anyway. So if they have any children, their children still going to be black, so why not?

The attitudes of these respondents reflect enduring racial and social dating norms. However, these positions, in some instances are intertwined with their theology and understanding of God. Some women admitted to having prejudiced views, or views that were contradictory to the Christian teaching that "God is no respecter of persons." Within this sample, only one woman has been in an interracial marriage; she was married to a Hispanic man born and raised in the North. She did not regard this union as having carried the same social stigma as white-black unions; in her community, marriages between blacks and Hispanics were common.

Race and Theology

"I Don't See Color"

My analysis of racial awareness uncovered a spectrum of racial dispositions showing how the women have reconciled their racial selves with their Christian selves. At one end were those close to an integrationist ideology; at the other end were those who leaned toward a nationalist posture. Of the thirty-eight women in this sample, I consider a third of them integrationists. These are the women who desire racially unified churches, believe in a common humanity among all peoples, strive to be color-blind, attest to feeling little discomfort around whites, and want racially specific concerns minimized in the life of the church. All but two of this group have visited white or interracial churches, and one of those two was exposed to white preachers at gospel conventions. This group affirms more stridently than the other women that God created everyone equal and that we must learn to get along.

Kenyatta's racial reasoning locates her at this end of the continuum. A preacher's daughter in her twenties, she doesn't go to church seeking news particular to blacks but listens if such news is brought up. The preacher has talked about blacks during February, Black History month. She watches various Christian broadcasts and thinks that the white ministers she watches preach as well as her father. She's always been a member of a black church but believes she could go to church with white people. She has dated a white man and has no problems with interracial marriages. As I spoke with her, she described herself as colorblind. A mother of two, she stated, "I'm not going to raise my kids to be prejudiced. . . . [I] think we'll all be in heaven."

Jerri, a woman in her fifties also strives for color blindness. She grew up "not seeing color" and believes that the Christian faith requires her to minimize attention to race. Her early Christian foundation was forged in an integrated Anglican Church in Jamaica.

> I didn't see color back home. I knew there was black and there was white, but it wasn't, they didn't talk about it like they do here [in America]. We had a motto there, we say, "Out of many, one people." There were white, black, Chinese, Indians, everybody. And I did not see color and racism until I came to the States. You know, because I had white friends and black friends. I still do now, but not so much as when I was home.

Her first choice of a church when she lived in New York was a "99 percent white" Episcopalian church. Some neighbors told her about a more integrated church. She moved her membership and attended there until she relocated to the South. She didn't give race as a factor in her decision to change churches or as a factor in her neighbors' having steered her away from the white congregation. Her experience in the South and her increasing awareness of American race relations appear not to have affected her comfort among and her ability to interact with persons of all races.

> I still don't see color really. It would not make a difference if I were in a predominantly black congregation or mixed congregation, as long as I go to church and get that Word. Even though I hear people talk about

racism, it's not a part of me. . . . I'm not prejudiced. I wasn't brought up that way, and I try not to indulge myself with racism, even though I know its there.

Likewise, Gail wouldn't have a problem going to church with whites. She acknowledges that there is still racism in the world and appreciates sermons that address this social ill, but she doesn't want a constant diet of it. She thinks blacks attribute too much of the unpleasantness of life to race and doesn't blame everything that happens to her on her skin color. Whites also give too much significance to race. In the past, she attended a "mixed church" but was turned off because members kept talking about how to get more blacks to join and to assume leadership roles. She considered the focus on a more balanced racial membership unnecessary. She also questioned the role of the Spirit in this approach.

> I walked in there, and it didn't dawn on me, and it didn't matter to me that all whites were standing up there in front of the stage. I think we need to separate the difference between race and spirit because they're not the same. They're not the same.

Gail believes there are sound reasons for blacks to have a separate worship space to address specific realities, but she's never thought she had to be in an all-black context in any area of her life.

Just as one's understanding of God is impacted by the theological context in which one is immersed, so is one's racial awareness. A member of the COGIC church since childhood, Ruth attributed her openness to racially inclusive congregations to the religious instruction she received. She was taught that it was wrong to hate people because of the color of their skin. The claims of salvation apply to everyone equally. She stated:

> I've gone to churches—in fact a cousin of mine goes to a mixed church, and she was brought up in the COGIC—so as far as race goes, we were always taught that it was wrong to hate people because of the color of their skin, because that didn't have anything to do with salvation. Blacks and whites had to be saved. And, also, when I was growing up, like, even though there were different denominations, we were always taught that you had to be holy no matter what church you belonged to. Holiness was not a denomination; it was a way of life for the Christian, for all Christians, whether you were black, white, Pentecostal, or whatever

you call yourself. If you said you were holy, you know, that's the way of life that you were supposed to be, but the denomination was the Church of God in Christ. I always understood that it had nothing to do with color, so I have no problem with [white worshippers].

Betty, also of Layton Temple, doesn't look for markers of racial awareness in church. The wearing of African garb, references to African Americans, and teachings on blacks in the Bible are tolerable within reason.

To me, it's [race in church] unnecessary. So many times now, they want to [do it]. I don't mind them saying that Zipporah, Moses' wife, was black, or Nehemiah was black, or whatever, something like that, but not a constant thing. I want the Word preached, and if it happened to be a black man during that day, it's good to know, but the culture and all that doesn't have to come into it. There's a time and place for all of that, and I believe it's to be taught at school, or during Negro History Week, you can bring a lot of stuff in. You can bring a lot of stuff in there [that month]. But I'm more interested in what the Word says. If it's a black person that did it, you know, did something, then it's fine, but to me it's not that important, 'cause it ain't gonna get me to heaven or hell. You know, I want the Word taught that's going to help my soul.

Karen, who admitted she had to get used to the idea of celebrating Kwanzaa, is not averse to attending a white church. If the Lord told her to join, she would.

As a black Christian, a black person who belongs to Christ, and a black American, we have an experience that we don't need to forget and that we need to support. Say the Lord told me, "Okay, Karen, go up to First Baptist in [city]. I want you to worship there. I want you to serve me there." I'd go because I was directed to go. But I would deeply miss the experience of what I've come out of. I can only believe the Lord put me there because there's something I'm supposed to lend from my walk and what he's brought me through. But I would miss the support and the fellowship of those who've been through that black experience with me, and I probably still would feel bound to help in some way. I would be there and serve. I'm sure the Lord would reveal to me what I'm supposed to be doing there and stuff like that, but I would probably still seek that kinship and still feel like I had to support the struggles of black people.

She went on to recall a recent conversation she had had with her son about black men being stopped by the police while driving. It was sparked by her son having seen a news clipping reporting that the actor Will Smith gets stopped regularly by the Los Angeles police while driving.

> He's a young black man in a nice vehicle. It's not because he's driving too fast or doing anything he's not supposed to do, [it's] because he's a young black man in a nice vehicle. That kind of experience and stuff, the [white] people in [city] probably don't know anything about that, and I can't just dismiss it because I now serve in [city] and work in a ministry there and that's where the Lord has directed me. I can't dismiss that that happens and that I need to support the kind of things that will make it not happen, because it's something that my son is going to go through at one time or another. As long as the world is like that for black people, then serving God and worshipping with people who don't have that experience, I would feel . . . I would do it [worship with whites], but I would miss it. I would miss my brothers and sisters, because, I mean, it's still going on. That's what shaped us, that's what we've grown up in, that's what our parents faced and it's still happening.

Among the integrationists, some attributed their posture to religious teachings, while others linked it to a specific "conversion" or transformative experience. Earnestine, a woman in her sixties, admitted that she used to detest whites. She never considered joining a predominantly white church when she was looking for a church. She attributed her feelings in part to what she knows about slavery and how "they did us so dirty." She recalled racist experiences in her hometown and remembered being attacked with racial epithets as a kid. "Since I've been saved, the Lord took all of that away from me. Honey, I'll hug a white person just as quick as I will a black person; [before], no way in the world you could've gotten me to hug one before." Her reformed attitude extends to white ministers, as well. They can preach to her just as a black minister can, because "God calls who he pleases." She doesn't think a white minister will necessarily talk about racism, but "if he was really up there carrying the Word of God, he would try to not have nobody talking about it, either black or white, really. 'Cause in God's sight, there ain't no color around; we all just human beings, and we are all his people."

A minister's wife who had grown up in a military family was one of the most critical voices of how exclusionary some African Americans can be. She spoke against blacks who confine the breadth of their interactions, knowledge, and community to a black constituency. The mother of a young child, she doesn't want her son to go to a totally black school. "I don't want nothing he has [or is exposed to] to be all of one [race]. I want him to see the world from both points of view." She attended interracial schools and was reared in racially mixed communities (many of them military bases), and she doesn't want to shelter her child from that type of experience.

She has not been pleased with how race influences her church life. She's heard some unpleasant things about whites in church and dislikes the Sunday school literature because its content and illustrations presume a black membership. She thinks the literature should be racially generic and that the church should be reaching out to all races. She rejects the idea that white people are keeping black people down; she believes racism exists on both sides. God is able to open any and all the necessary "doors" for her, so she doesn't perceive her life outcomes (e.g., getting a particular job or a car loan) as being a consequence of race.

> I believe that the world should get on to what the world is doing. The church has to set an example and has to say, yes, there are black and white issues, but we are yet one. We are yet striving for the same thing. The same thing a white person wants you want. They want to support their family, they want good jobs, they want stability, and a black person does, too.

"They Don't Know My Struggles"

Whether integrationists or nationalists, all the women I studied attend black churches. The women I label nationalists distinguish themselves not by their choice of church but by their reasons for attending black churches. They affirm their support for the creation of racially distinct churches as necessary for spiritual and socioeconomic empowerment. This group desires racial and experiential identification with the preacher, wants black issues to be addressed in the sermon, and seeks a church committed to strengthening black families and the black community. These women also regard the worship ethos and liturgical form of black churches as more appealing and culturally authentic. Some nationalists have visited white churches at one time or another; others have never considered even visiting one. This group has given serious thought as to whether a white minister has had adequate exposure to African Americans and the black experience to guide them spiritually. The challenges of being black in America and the ever-present racial divide between blacks and whites has made them consciously choose to join a black church. (One person contemplated selecting a white church over a black one.)

Joyce, raised in a predominantly white denomination, was initially ambivalent about selecting a church on the basis of racial affinity. She attends Calvary. Finding a church that could help her build a strong family and pass on spiritual values to her children was at the top of her priorities. She lives and works in a predominantly white environment. During our conversation, she initially excluded race from the aspects she considered when looking for a church home. I asked, "You didn't choose your church because it was a black church, would that be correct?" She responded,

> Well, that wasn't the main, let's put it this way . . . I didn't choose a church because it was a black church. But if I had to choose between a white church and a black church knowing that everything else was equal in terms of the quality of the ministry and all that kind of stuff, my preference definitely would've been a black church.

Sharon did intentionally look for a black church. She believed that a black minister could relate to her better than a white one. She wanted a pastor and spiritual role model who physically resembled her. She asserted that even while the pastor may be addressing common topics such as family and work situations, there is a particular kinship she feels with him and the way he elaborates on those experiences. She attributes that kinship to his race.

> I haven't specifically said [find a black church], well, maybe I have. I grew up in a black church; I look for a black church. There's certain things that are generic to our experience as it relates to life in general, plus the way the message would be given, that I would rather see a package that looks more like me.

Susan favors black churches over white ones because she can assume the existence of cultural similarities, one of which is language. She recognizes that with the increasing cross-fertilization of ethnic and racial groups, culturally distinctive patterns—behaviors, beliefs, idioms, worship forms—will diminish.

> Well, I favor the black churches because, not that I disfavor the white, I just more favor the black ones, . . . because of the cultural differences, even so much as body language and the way you say things, you're more accustomed to [it]. And sitting in the congregation, the response might be different, you know, real subtle things. Like if I'm talking to you, not that I don't know how to speak proper English, but there may be some things that I say, and this line is drawing thinner and thinner, but there are usually things that . . . blacks will use in their language [among themselves]. If a white person heard you say that or a Hispanic person heard you say that, [the person wouldn't understand]. Therefore, if you're my minister and you're white and I'm black and I'm trying to explain to you some of the things I feel, you may not be able to relate to them, and I say that, that line is getting smaller and smaller.

Similarly, Janice has visited a white church but wouldn't join one. She has concerns about what the pastor would preach and how she would be received. "I can't deal with people who say, 'Oh I love the Lord' and then can't sit beside me. I can't deal with that foolishness, that's foolishness to me." It is very important to her to stay in the black community, and that includes the church. She believes her energies should be used in activities that benefit the community, and she values her identification with others who know her struggles. She doubts she could find this in a white church.

> Hopefully, we should be doing something to encourage sisters and brothers to go on. The black community today is in chaos, and we as a people should be there in the community to try to make it better for everyone involved. So, yeah, I would say that it's important that I stay in a black community. If I'm going to focus my energies, I want it to be in a black community where I can identify with the people. Understand what I'm saying? Now, I can talk with white people, but they don't know my struggles, they don't know my fears, they don't know what I feel, but another sister will.

Particularly striking in these women's responses is their distrust of whites. They feel no desire to worship with persons who have not demonstrated a desire for significant interaction in other situations. In her earlier years, Rosalind was active in the civil rights movement and considers herself somewhat of a militant. She would not join a white or integrated church and can't imagine being comfortable there. While not wanting to take certain things about black people for granted, she regards the worship style of whites as outside her cultural experience. Perhaps more important than the cultural gap, she has experienced racial discrimination on her job and is convinced some whites still hold racist attitudes.

> [I'm] not violently militant, but militant to the point that I still feel that whites, not all whites, but a lot of whites, would love to see us back where we were. In fact, I think racism is greater now than it ever was, as far as keeping blacks back. And so I would feel almost as a traitor.

Anne remembers her mother's referring her to a predominantly white church when she first moved to the state. She visited once but didn't join. She had strong opinions about interacting with white Christians.

> I guess, [like] what I said before, in a church of black people I feel there were people who had a genuine interest in my well-being, or I feel like the pastor is not there for financial gain. I feel like he's there for a job; I feel like he's there, he's God-sent, and he's there cause he wanted to impart the Word and witness to people. . . . Even when my mom went to [a white church], and I think I went around there with her once, I just felt like this is somebody who, you know, like a Jim Jones–type thing. I felt like this is somebody who has found a bunch of black people and figured out ways to get money from them. And even though [he was] preaching from the King James version of the Bible and preaching some of the same stuff I've heard, I just could never get into it. I just always felt like they weren't genuinely interested in [us]. . . . It's kind of like, in no other facet of their lives are they wanting to be connected with us, so why all of a sudden does this white man want to move down here in the middle of this black neighborhood and start him a church?

Bernice has attended white congregations within the Church of God in Christ, white Presbyterian churches, and integrated nondenominational churches. The features that detracted from her experiences with these congregations were the worship styles and the size of the congregation. More important, in white churches her ease in relating to African Americans could not be realized. "I can relate better to black people than I can to whites; in the trust issues and sincerity and those kind of things, I probably relate better. I've never been in a white church for a long period of time."

I asserted earlier that nationalists intentionally seek Black Churches. There were exceptions to this, however. Bernice spoke of race as an unconscious parameter, rather than a conscious one, as she looked for a church. Race could either impede or foster the sense of religious and cultural affinity she desired.

> Oh, I probably didn't even think about that [race], but I'm sure underlying . . . 'cause if it had probably been a Caucasian church, I probably would have never even considered going unless the Lord really, really led me. I mean he led me to Layton Temple, so I guess if it had been His will for me to be someplace else, I probably would have gone to visit at least, but I probably wouldn't have joined. I wouldn't have felt that comfortable, and I wouldn't have felt that my kids would be comfortable, and so I probably wouldn't have joined. . . . There are cultural differences in blacks and whites. I think that black ministers can relate to those cultural differences much better, even in counseling situations, and I've been counseled by a white minister before, when my husband and I were having problems. But I felt very strongly that he had no sense of what was going on. He may have, because I think the human psyche is probably the same regardless of what race you are, it's just that, you know, the environment that you've been brought up in, and I just think there's just so many differences. . . . There's always that dividing [between races] that I know, and I always felt. I think that's just as much a racist issue on my part, a feeling I could never completely trust their sincerity and their loving us. I guess because of, it's probably been a self-esteem thing that they always put us down. So I would never feel that they would treat me as an equal or they would really consider me as an equal. Because if I trusted them in that area, then I would put my guard down and could then probably relate a lot better. But, because I don't put my guard down, I never truly trust their motives.

Kelly spoke of a certain level of comfort she has around black people. No stranger to whites and the bicultural world, she still affirms the commonality she feels when in the presence of other African Americans:

Just seeing my own people, I just feel more comfortable about being around black folk, period. There's a closeness there. I just think we have something in common. We can relate to some things. We have the same roots, that kind of thing. We're a part of the same culture. Usually, when things are alike, you are comfortable. I feel comfortable; I feel like these are my people, and you seem more at home.

Audrey's words poignantly portray the quest for a spiritual space that alleviates the tensions of a double existence—being black and working in a "white world." She balances belief in a universal God with her need for solace. Audrey has visited white churches but does not want to be in a white or integrated church context. She has encountered prejudice on her job and has no desire to experience it in church.

You know, I guess I'm a little militant. [I] might be a little prejudiced. When I get through with them white folk on my job being in charge of me, you know, I don't want that on Sunday or in my prayer life. You know we were taught too long of this white God in this white robe that we're praying to. What I have learned for myself is that God is no respecter of persons and that He is colorblind, and He is a spirit, with no color to me, you know what I'm saying? It was a revelation in my life that I didn't have to have them over me on Sunday, too, I guess.

Discussion

The women's varied responses demonstrate the complexity of racial reasoning and racial practices among African Americans, more so than a quick glance at the composition of Sunday morning worship services might suggest. Part of that complexity is evident in the fact that both the integrationists and nationalists are housed in the same church. A few women suggested that they could depart the Black Church without feeling a significant loss. I do not want to depict African Americans as a monolithic group. Yet, there is some uniformity in how they integrate their racial awareness and their Christian identity. They strive for integrity with each community they are a part of. Even as some speak as though the vestiges of racism have no hold on them and others are distrustful of whites, they all remain embedded in the Black Church.

What would make them leave? It appears the integrationists would leave if they found a predominantly white church where they could "feel the Spirit" or if divine direction led them to leave. The nationalists do not intend to sever ties with the Black Church. Race relations being what they are in America, they do not fixate on what ought to be but see the good in what is. They have decided not to be sidetracked into creating a racially inclusive church at the expense of building a stronger black community and maintaining a positive black consciousness.

Women's ideas about race are informed by multiple sources: the Bible, personal experience, social and economic analysis of the black condition, the historic role of the Black Church, and an assessment of white America and racism. They share no unified voice on racial practices but articulate norms for their behavior in light of the social and political realities that have circumscribed African American lives throughout the past century (and before). Marry whom you like, but recognize that interracial marriages might hurt the black community. Support black businesses, but get the best deal above all. Vote for the candidate who supports the best outcomes for the African American community (not the nation as a whole) regardless of race; vote for the black candidate if all things are equal. Support black institutions, but perhaps not if it takes all your discretionary time.

Their racial consciousness seems to reflect more folk wisdom than Christian theology; their concern that racial cohesion and the religious culture not be diminished is evident. We see among these women the negotiation of cultural values, American ideals, and theological principles. These are guided not only by an individualized ethic—do what feels good—but also by the value assigned to communal strength and vitality, that is, what is good for the African American community as a whole.

I found a few distinctions in the women's responses that could be attributed to their denomination. One was the composition of the integrationist group. I found more Pentecostals to be on this end of the continuum than Baptists. In addition, proportionately more Pentecostal women had been exposed (in various ways) to interracial congregations and recounted more explicit teachings about the racial unity that should be manifest in the body of Christ. This is not altogether surprising in light of the origins of these denominations. Of the seven primary denominations in the Black Church, the Church of God in Christ has been racially inclusive since its founding in 1897. Shortly thereafter, the denomination was strongly influenced by racial segregation, resulting in the birth of the

Assemblies of God. With a new "white" Pentecostal denomination on the horizon, many white Pentecostals withdrew and joined the ranks of the Assemblies of God, but the COGIC remained open to a white membership and maintained some integrated congregations. As a denomination, it offered official (state convocations) and unofficial (local church fellowships and tent meetings) opportunities for blacks and whites to worship together. Throughout the twentieth century, even when congregations were predominantly of one race, it still preached the emphasis on the Spirit as the force that creates transformation and replaces former identity markers with Christian love.

In *The Social Teaching of the Black Churches,* Peter Paris asserts that one of the fundamental principles of black Christianity is the principle of universal humanity—the parenthood of God and the fellowship of humanity.[5] These women attest to the centrality of this principle in the Black Church. They also demonstrate the tension that has always plagued Black Americans who try to adhere to this principle faithfully. The negotiation of allegiance to faith above allegiance to racial group, which Paris named "the ecclesiastical dilemma," has no easy resolution. It is a phenomenon that has to be renegotiated by each new generation of black Christians. It can be resolved by locating oneself in a black church, yet espousing minimal (if any) commitment or need for racially homogenous congregations. It may also be resolved by attending the Black Church because one regards the health of the black community and families as dependent on the ministry that emerges out of these congregations. These churches are the best institutional site for addressing the plight of black Americans. Neither those who put faith first nor those who foreground race deny that racism exists or have accepted the racial conditions in America, but the two sides differ in the degree to which they believe church and faith have to acknowledge and respond to blacks' historic oppressions and current problems.

Given the tone and perspectives of the nationalists, one might ask whether their responses represent more than examples of prejudice overlaid with theological content? I assert that they do. Certainly, some of their comments reflect racial views popularized in our nation and held by blacks and whites. However, that is an insufficient reason to dismiss them. Race is an anchoring identity for black women. These women did not acquire racial selves after becoming Christians but embraced Christianity through a community already defined by and proscribed by American cultural and racial norms and by legislation. As the women embraced Christian teachings, the teachings in turn became a formidable influence on the construction of their identities. These teachings had to be internalized along with already acquired cultural and community values. One value that African Americans have historically affirmed is the equality of all persons. Christianity has taught this value, as well. However, the contexts in which most African Americans initially embraced Christianity did not create the conditions for this universalistic principle to be realized. Nor has society at large made it possible to have more than occasional visible expressions of this ideal. Therefore, rather than interpret these women's insights as mere prejudice, I believe they are evidence of the strong relationship between racial and religious sensibilities among persons of faith. They remind us that one can not easily dissect categories of identity and discard them at will. Our identities are supported by psychological as well as social structures.

The internal life and practices of the Black Church have been largely outside the purview of white worshipers and scholars. The church's distance and invisibility from white Americans has had a positive effect upon its self-development and its institutional strength. Outside the purview of most scholarly research, black lay women have constituted these denominations into sites of healing, resistance, political empowerment, and social change. That has meant ensuring that the Black Church retains its roles and influence in the community, even when the women's biblical knowledge might suggest that they should be more inclusive. These church women are not willing to participate in white churches at this point in their lives. Neither do they want to redirect the energies of their congregations toward efforts to become more racially inclusive if it means that the Black Church would lose any of its effectiveness or stature. Their loyalty to the Black Church is informed by their degree of racial awareness.

This connection between racial awareness and participation warrants a deeper examination. Utilizing the concept of the Black Church as a "semi-involuntary" institution, the sociologists Christopher Ellison and Darren Sherkat analyzed the determinants of religious participation and church choice among blacks and whites. The semi-involuntary thesis, developed by Hart Nelsen, Raytha Yokley, and Anne Nelsen, states that religious attendance among blacks has been motivated by the visibility and respectability accorded the Black Church, particularly in the rural South. In the absence of other outlets, the Black Church provided contexts for leadership development, community involvement, and social activities.

The stature of the church, coupled with the fear of social sanctions for nonparticipation (such as loss of reputation and loss of access to other social outlets and activities), has helped sustain participation in African American churches. Ellison and Sherkat have tested this hypothesis by analyzing church participation rates among blacks and whites and among those in rural and in urban areas. They also examined whether belonging to a black congregation is a conscious choice and a consequence of racial consciousness. They found that, in addition to the historical status of the Black Church and the threat of social sanctions, religious participation is determined by additional social pressures and incentives that propel black people's rates of church participation higher than those for whites. Among these are social perceptions, familial relations, social status, proximity, theology, and worship. While they confirmed that black church attendance is higher than white, they could not establish that blacks intentionally choose black congregations.[6] Although their research was focused on frequency of attendance, the semi-involuntary thesis has implications for understanding the persistent participation of church women. They affirm the earlier conclusion of Nelsen and others that "whether—and how often—to participate in congregational life are not only reflections of personal spirituality, but may also be influenced by the (real or anticipated) judgments and reaction of others."[7] In other words, actions that may be deemed an autonomous choice are actually determined by context, the expectations of others, and perceived social sanctions.

In many ways, theories about the influence of cultural factors on church participation among African Americans are borne out by these women's narratives. Their stories not only confirm Ellison and Sherkat's findings but also expand the thesis, or at least call attention to other determinants not specifically mentioned in these studies. I have found that church participation among church women is informed not only by the real or imagined reactions of others in their own group but also by the perceptions they hold of other racial and ethnic groups. In addition, they choose to participate not only out of fear of engendering punitive social sanctions but also because they fear causing harm or disruption to the primary constituency and commitments of the community (in this case the Black Church). These women's loyalty to the Black Church is informed by a positive force, not merely the threat of a negative one. Rather than give primacy to the role of social pressures in African Americans' church participation, I suggest that racial awareness and consideration of the social milieu in which African Americans live entice participation. Ellison and Sherkat did not find that African Americans intentionally chose to be in black congregations. However, this does not invalidate my argument that racial awareness informs the choices women are making about where they wish to be affiliated. African Americans do consider numerous factors when considering whether and where to participate in church. As we examine African American women's life, we must enlarge the list of variables that we consider relevant for understanding contemporary rates of church participation. Interpretations and perceptions of race relations in America, the merits of collaboration with white congregations, evaluation of appropriate religiocultural leadership, and desire for a context where whiteness is not institutionalized as normative are also considerations in where they choose to affiliate, if not whether to do so.

Women's racial awareness is not primarily constructed around victimization, they are not reacting to individual acts of racism or discrimination. They are not defensive, reactionary, self-protective, or unwilling to engage white Americans. As a group, they struggle against racially oppressive forces implicitly, rather than explicitly. They encounter racism or cultural denigration periodically. However, these events are not the primary shaping experiences of their adult lives. While they acknowledge that racism and prejudice are still a part of American society, the reminders aren't experienced as critical life-shaping realities that merit an overt personal response. Concerns about family and relational issues are more primary than concern about racism, employment inequities, or cultural repression.

This group of women is not composed of poor, disadvantaged black females on the extreme margins of the American dream, with all the harshness, economic fragility, and cultural stigmas that accompany such a location. The women are employed students, hourly wage earners, teachers, managers, and medical professionals. They live in urban centers, as well as suburban tracts. In the eyes of many, they have "made it," yet they are drawn to the one place that affords them a feeling of home, refuge, safety, understanding. They support the institution that has, unlike any other, attempted to carve out a dignified existence for African Americans and to provide for the spiritual and material needs of its people. It is to this place that they turn to anchor their racial selves and their Christian selves.

We see in the lives of these women, in a very concrete way, the incongruity between religious ideas and lived practice. What do Christians do when they believe that God has mandated one thing but find its realization hampered by social realities and forces? Several possibilities exist. They can disregard the mandate, devalue it, construct a response that addresses the spirit but not the letter of the principle, deny the authority of the mandate, or interrogate the mandate's authority and content in light of other, competing sources of authority or values. It appears that this group of women has chosen the last alternative. They are not dissimilar to Catholic women who interpret the church's teaching against abortion within the context of their families' ability to responsibly care for one more child. In this instance, the disparity is not itself a cause of significant discomfort. Whether because of the personal impact on them, the implication of lack of support for the Black Church's work, concern about encountering different cultural practices, or failure to find the appropriate interracial church context, all these women make their spiritual home a black church. This does not create a conflict for either the nationalists or the integrationists. One might have expected to find greater expressions of dissatisfaction among the theological integrationists, but this did not happen. Perhaps their acknowledgment of their openness to worshipping in more inclusive settings is sufficient to assuage any guilt they feel about not intentionally helping to build a more diverse institutional church.

7

The Conclusion of the Matter

I began this study with two major questions: Why are women so faithful to the Black Church? How is the Black Church faring in the eyes of women? Although familiar with the scholarly and commonplace explanations, I wondered how women would answer these questions if given the opportunity to speak for themselves. What reasons would they give? Which central concerns of the church would they discuss? How would they speak of the impact of God and church in their own lives? The prior chapters present their responses to these questions. In each chapter, I have engaged a different dimension of their religious lives, describing what I assessed to be the central positions of the group, as well as variations. I have provided description and interpretation of their thoughts and actions regarding each aspect. While this study provides a nuanced look at the multiple determinants of church participation and loyalty, it also leaves questions unanswered and points to new areas of investigation.

In these concluding pages, I invite the reader to consider the implications of this study, less from a sociological perspective than from a theological and pastoral one. These pages may be of particular interest to those in congregational ministry. I shift my approach from analysis of particular themes to a discussion of the implications of my findings for the vitality of the Black Church in this new millennium. I do not revisit all of my prior conclusions. Instead, I offer informed ministerial reflections about several dimensions of the Black Church that emerge out of this work and that warrant subsequent attention from the clergy, membership, and scholars.

Unity and Diversity

With a group of thirty-eight women as one's referent group, it is a challenge to generalize about black women's faith or about the breadth of diversity or unity among church women. While the degree of variation would be greater in a larger group, there are still some conclusions one can draw. This group of women showed similarities on several essential items. For instance, there was a consensus on the important worship dimensions of church—preaching, prayer, effervescent worship, fellowship, and pastoral leadership. These women are all committed to their present congregations and do not intend to move to integrated churches. Overall, they regard spiritual fortification and personal transformation as more important benefits of church participation than practical assistance. They are givers much more than receivers of the resources of their church. There was also consensus around organizational dynamics: the polity of the churches work fine, the male-dominated leadership does not require their immediate attention, and the absence of men is a consequence more of larger social forces or personal choice than of the church's initiatives, access, culture, or outreach. Furthermore, I found that the church is still a location for supporting families, teaching traditional family concepts, and helping the downtrodden. Congregations should be sites of equanimity and fairness, not exclusiveness and power hoarding. Women continue to revere the prominence of the church in the black community and affirm that their labor has been indispensable in establishing that position. Given these many commonalties, it appears that these women are monolithic in their religious valuations and concerns.

Still, we should note some distinctions. The women do not agree about the success of the church in actually encompassing neighborhood residents and in responding to the basic needs of their communities. Some happily report the official record of community activities completed by their church, while others are dissatisfied because of what's left undone and believe that the *work of the church* is being eclipsed by *church work*. Women do not agree about their role in increasing opportunities for female ministers. Whether greater acceptance of women preachers is seen as a spiritual transformation that God will bring about, a change they should be advocating for, or the responsibility of those women who are called to the ministry depends on who one asks. There is also disagreement about whether pastoring should be more accessible to women. Women's access to the preaching role was generally affirmed.

Pastoral Care

A significant area where opinions varied was the women's evaluation and use of pastoral care. The women are not equally satisfied with the pastoral care (including care by the pastor and by the members) extended to them, and they have relied on persons outside their churches to meet many of their spiritual and emotional needs. They question the trust and confidentiality levels in the church. The church's ability to resolve the personal crises of members and to serve as a refuge is also diminishing, in the eyes of some women. Some of the thirty-eight women did not share significant life crisis events with other church members; the church may be "home" for some women, but clearly not all. Not only did they not talk of the personal experiences with members; they also kept them from official leaders in the church. I learned of difficulties they had never recounted to another church member, from divorces, infertility, spousal/relationship abuse, substance use/abuse, unintended pregnancies, physical disabilities, poverty, and rape to a failed adoption process.

I am not suggesting that these women were suffering in silence. Networks of family and friends sustained them, but these were largely outside their immediate church family. The reasons for their maintaining their privacy varied. Some spoke of distrust, embarrassment, and shame about their circumstances. Others regarded the crises as a private matter or assumed they could handle them themselves. Some feared the content of the minister's counsel or worried that their confidentiality would be breached. These reservations were rooted in previous experiences when counsel had been sought or advice given in a similar situation. Two women who had been abused in their marriages remembered being told by former pastors that they were responsible for the marital discord. Each woman rejected this assessment, defied the counsel of her pastor, and resolved the situation on her own. In both of these instances, the abuse continued after the women sought counsel. Both women eventually left their spouses.

My experience in the church and particularly at gatherings at women's conferences and workshops confirms that it is not uncommon to encounter women who have been counseled to stay with abusive husbands. Such advice demonstrates the limited effectiveness of pastoral advice pertaining to domestic violence and the degree to which pastors sometimes strive to sustain marriages and intact families at the expense of a woman's safety. The two women's decisions to resolve it their way demonstrates their ability to resist further victimization and to reject the role of the dutiful Christian wife. It also demonstrates their willingness to evaluate theological and pastoral counsel in light of their own experiences and wisdom. By turning to resources outside their local congregation, they resisted further victimization.

Choosing privacy over congregational support appears incongruous for women who regard their churches as responding to the particular challenges of modern society holistically. While envisioning the church as a haven for the downtrodden and the undirected, they elect not to use it in this way themselves. The church may be a refuge for many, yet for some women it has not been a haven where they can share all types of life situations with confidence that they will receive the best-informed assistance and care.

My concerns about women's maintaining their privacy when in need of pastoral care are twofold. First, the church needs to enhance its pastoral care options in the local church. The size of the congregation impacts the access members have to the pastor's counsel, and the training of the pastor impacts how members assess the pastor's effectiveness. One of the pastors had been seminary trained; the other had not. I cannot speak to the level of expertise they had in dealing with emotional and psychological conflicts. However, given that many of these issues are perceived as "women's issues," churches have to prepare clergy to respond with a sensitivity that effects empowerment and healing rather than guilt and self-recrimination. Trained professionals as well as care teams of lay members are underutilized resources that the congregation could make available for women and men who are facing domestic or other crises.

Pastoral care does not need to take place in a one-on-one caregiver-care receiver relationship. Women have high regard for their male pastors, yet because of social mores and personal embarrassment sexually related traumas are topics they are not likely to share with them. This state of affairs is in part a result of the fact that most clergy are men, but not totally. One of the women is this study experienced posttraumatic stress syndrome many years after being sexually violated. She withdrew from church for a time and did not share her current symptoms or the past abuse with her pastor. She was able to find support from a male minister she considered a "brother in the Lord." The depth of her relationship with this confidant was more significant than his gender. She spoke glowingly of his support; however, at the time of our interview, she still had never shared her trauma with her biological sister. More than the sex of the pastor, the quality of the relationship matters in the administering of pastoral care.

Pastoral care can occur in small groups within the congregation, whether they are affinity groups, women's fellowships, Bible study cells, or literary groups. In *Godly Women,* Brenda Brasher discusses how the women's enclave in a fundamentalist congregation provided care for a woman dealing with infidelity in her marriage. Her husband was one of the pastors in the congregation and had an affair with a woman he initially began counseling. In the women's group this minister's wife found support and love. The group also became the site where women conceived and initiated change in the church's practices for counseling to prevent other ministerial-congregant relationships from escalating into sexual misconduct. *Dear Sisters: A Womanist Practice of Hospitality,* by Lynne Westfield, also points to the dissemination of care and "hospitality" that can occur in nontraditional settings. Westfield describes a Friday night women's book club that provides the ministering context. One of these groups (Brasher's) was an official ministry of the church; the other (Westfield's) was not. Both attest to women's abilities to create alternative sites for their own empowerment when the dominant institutions fail. The church must ensure that the presence of these sites does not foster a greater split between the public and the private spheres. Nor should the existence of these enclaves alleviate the church's responsibility to educate the membership about the societal preponderance and systemic nature of sexually related offenses or other abuses that have traditionally been made invisible or discussed only in same-sex gatherings.[1]

This leads me to a second reflection. Women who maintain their privacy highlight the limits of a discourse on gender and sexuality in the Black Church. The theologian Kelly Brown Douglas, in *Sexuality and the Black Church,* has brought to the fore what many scholars of black religion have long attested—that the Black Church does not have a well-constructed sexual ethic. Moreover, the discussion of sex has been hampered by the discourse about race, the construction of the black body, and the abuse of black women's bodies. Many of the issues about which women were silent concerned some aspect of sexuality. While the Black Church has moved beyond the days of imposing public sanction on women who violated its sexual norms, it has not replaced that harshness with a strident condemnation of other types of abuse or other forms of oppression of women.[2]

Many churches have yet to name these abuses as social ills to be excised from the community. Taking the risks of talking about issues that have been silenced by their very exclusion can be a formidable task. In *Between Sundays: Black Women and Everyday Struggles of Faith*, Marla Frederick writes of women who strive to protect their own bodies and also those of younger women in the community. Some of them have experienced childhood pregnancies and molestation. The older women have experienced the power of efforts to silence discussion of such topics and now strive to create a safer context and different discourse for their children and grandchildren. Part of what the women impart is a sense of sexual ethics in an effort to prevent teenage pregnancy and sexually transmitted disease; however, the conversation is broader than the teachings they learned about sexuality.

> Within this discourse is a larger discussion about the need for biblical ideals of sexuality in order to facilitate the regeneration of society as a whole, decreasing the numbers of abused and neglected children. In addressing these issues, close relationships between mothers and daughters or grandmothers and granddaughters become powerful points of departure for agency. Within these relationships, silencing is not permitted. While the women spoke of varying degrees of comfort in talking with their children or grandchildren about sex, they all felt that the discussion itself was important. Gone are the days when parents told their children to "be quiet" because they were asking about "nasty" stuff. These very attitudes, the women confirm have been detrimental.[3]

While these women strive to make discussion of sexuality accessible to young women, their efforts appear to be more of an individual crusade and commitment than a reflection of the church's commitment to the large community. The Black Church continues to send incongruous messages pertaining to sexuality. Because the churches do not name and confront these concerns, women (and men) continue to silence themselves or seek resources beyond the faith community for resolution. However, naming by itself is not sufficient. The engagement of the ministerial leadership in a public discourse on these topics or in worship services and the creation of ministries explicitly charged with assisting persons facing difficulties in areas of life considered taboo—infertility, rape, unplanned pregnancies, domestic violence, sexual orientation—would move the church toward being a more welcoming center where its members could get assistance. As one woman said, the church is a hospital where one comes to be healed. For issues still seen as "private, personal, or sexual" the care is not readily available.

Closeted Womanists?

In the past two decades, a new term, "womanism," has emerged in black theological scholarship. As mentioned, womanism was first coined by the author Alice Walker to describe the qualities of bodaciousness, assertiveness, maturity, self-love, community involvement, and faith manifest in the lives of black women. Walker constructed a four-part definition predicated on the folk expression "womanish." One of those definitions was "a black feminist." This fueled a debate about the distinctions and merits of feminism versus womanism.[4] Womanist theologians and scholars have expanded the term to describe both methodological approaches and particular ways of black women's being in the world. In the past two decades, constructions of womanist spirituality, Christology, ethics, and hospitality have grown significantly. The field of womanist scholarship is still expanding and is by no means confined to Christian women who have found usefulness in its appropriation.

A reoccurring use of womanism is as a marker that identifies significant women or their behaviors as expressing womanist consciousness or commitments. In this way, scholars recover and revise established historical narratives, situating black women as central rather than on the periphery of scholarly research. This also requires that we regard gender as a defining organizing principle of society and of women's social experiences, rather than an incidental circumstance or influence upon women's behavior. The label "womanist" has been applied to Anna Julia Cooper, Sojourner Truth, and Mary McCloud Bethune, among others. On the other hand, the Women's Auxiliary of the National Baptist Convention has been described as possessing a feminist theology but is not assigned womanist sensibilities.[5]

How are we to regard the women in this study? What definition of womanism is adequate as the measuring stick? Is it a label they would apply to themselves? The last question is easier than the first two. No, these women would not use the label for themselves. I did not consistently ask them about feminism or womanism, in part to see whether they raised these topics themselves. In a few instances, the term "feminism" was mentioned briefly or with an indication of distaste, so I thought that pursing an extended conversation would yield little. When I did ask direct questions about their knowledge of feminism and womanism, most wanted me to define feminism (a request I refrained from) and had never heard of womanism. The one minister in the group who was seminary trained was familiar with feminism.

The fact that they would not use the term "womanist" to describe themselves does not mean they do not fit a definition of "womanist." Historians, sociologists, and psychologists regularly apply new conceptual terms to past phenomena and personalities. The definition of womanist depends upon whom you ask. It also is a label one can choose to adopt.

> One does not get to be a womanist by virtue of her blackness and femininity. Nor does one become a womanist simply because one reads, understands and makes the appropriate adjustments in her life. The lived-world struggle to appropriate self-love as the operative principle is formidable. Black women entering the womanist enterprise commit to exploring further the contradictions that shape their collective and personal lives in the spirit of critical inquiry and in the spirit of hope.[6]

My reading of Christian womanist scholars leads me to the following list of characteristics. Womanists are not wed to biblical authority that is predicated on the Bible's being inerrant or infallible. They assert the need for inclusive language, although it is hard to determine how much this is embraced in practice. Most have not rejected the Bible or Christianity in total, as some radical feminist theologians have. They value and advocate for the physical and spiritual salvation of the family, redistribution of wealth, goods, and services in American society, and the end of race, sex, and class supremacy. In addition, they are devoted to articulating a theological liberative position for women even when it might be at odds with a black male perspective on what would enhance African American existence. They address society's dehumanization and oppression of black women. Finally, they resist grand narratives of history, which obfuscate particular realties and tend to universalize experience from the dominant group's perspective.[7]

Even as I penned this list, I was cognizant of how these traits seemed more applicable to a small cadre of socially prominent and influential black women and to the scholarly women who have defined the field of womanism than to the lay women in this study. Given womanism's focus on being a woman-centered individual and possessing a critical consciousness of and a commitment to the eradication of women's oppression, I find it difficult to apply "womanism" to this group of devout Christian women. If I truncate the meaning to indicate certain commitments to self, community, and church, then they fit the rubric.

In *God Don't Like Ugly*, Teresa Brown argues that women have been the resource for transmitting spiritual values and mother wit within the African American community. They not only transmit it, they have created it and we can locate many of these "truths" in the canon of black women's literary products. She argues that black women have their particular brand of spiritual values. They are able to stand up for black women and to speak about black women's lives. She identifies black women (churched and unchurched) as the wise bearers and vessels of African American values. Following the methodology of the womanist ethicists Katie Cannon and Emilie Townes, Frye agues that literature demonstrates the ethical paradigm and tenets that African American women have codified and lived by, as well as the culture of resistance that is central to any definition of womanism.[8] A womanist sees Jesus as cosufferer, not just redeemer and liberator. The solidarity to fight oppression comes from a God who suffers alongside one. While this may be the theological framework for womanists and black Christian feminists, I hesitate to ascribe this view of Jesus to the masses of laywomen who populate black congregations. Jesus is triumphant Lord, comforter, and enabler rather than cosufferer.

If one has to embrace all aspects of the definition to be a womanist, then one particular part of the definition is problematic. The inclusion of positive regard for women who may love women sexually or nonsexually as a defining trait of a womanist also disqualifies these women as womanists. Admittedly, whether to label these women "womanists" may be a misplaced preoccupation on my part. The resolution of this matter on my part rests finally on the breadth that the theologian Jacquelyn Grant gives to the concept of womanist.

> A womanist then is a strong Black woman who has sometimes been mislabeled as a domineering castrating matriarch. A womanist is one who has developed survival strategies in spite of the oppression of her race and sex in order to save her family and her people. Walker's womanist

notion suggests not "the feminist" but the active struggle of Black women that makes them who they are. For some Black women that may involve being feminine as traditionally defined, and for others it involves being masculine as stereotypically defined. In either case, womanist just means being and acting out who you are.[9]

Another significant element of womanist thought that bears on these women's lives is the criticism of the Black Church leveled by some womanist scholars. Do the women voice the same critiques of the Black Church that are leveled in the theological and ethical works of womanist thinkers? Grant considers the injustice that has befallen women because they have been considered the backbone of the church far too long.

> On the surface this may appear to be a compliment, especially when one considers the function of the backbone in human anatomy . . . the telling portion of the word backbone is "back." It has become apparent to me that most of the ministers who use this term have reference to location rather than function. What they really mean is that women are in the "background" and should be kept there. They are merely support workers. This is borne out by my observation that in many churches women are consistently given responsibilities in the kitchen, while men are elected or appointed to the important boards and leadership positions. While decisions and policies may be discussed in the kitchen, they are certainly not made there.[10]

This practice of locating women in subservient positions is maintained by certain theological ideas. Grant has argued that the constant image of suffering servant as the metaphor for the Christian life is an oppressive vise that crushes the lives of black women. Women need to be taught to embrace a more liberating concept of discipleship. In a similar vein, Frances Wood argues that black women's experience in the church has been romanticized and that their experience in the larger society has been the equivalent of silent suffering. Women are silenced, degraded, and ignored when they speak of their realities. On the other hand, they are complicit with their own oppression, not exercising their own agency and muting their voices "in the name of racial solidarity." Women who try to claim their voices are sometimes labeled man haters and have to compete with the larger number of women who suffer from "internalized misogyny."

Wood suggests this may account for some black women's reluctance to be identified with womanist thought.[11] I would add that questioning a woman's sexual orientation is another strategy for silencing her voice.

While I'm reluctant to label this group womanists, I do believe they are church women who demonstrate the paradoxes of faith. They are outspoken on some issues and silent on others. They fight some battles by stepping across gender conventions and others by staying within the appropriate lines of protocol. They alternate between stressing personal salvation for the hurting individual and faith that is focused on transforming communities, not merely individuals.

Another pillar of womanist thought is its reliance on a multiplicity of sources for theological and ethical reflection. Womanists are uncomfortable with extreme devotion to the Bible and to Western theological traditions at the expense of African traditions, African American social, economic, and political history, literary and cultural repositories of moral wisdom, the history of social resistance, and especially black women's social experiences. The constructive ethics and theological developments of womanist scholars emerge from a multidisciplinary analysis of these sources. Womanists are committed to identifying how black women have utilized their historical and social experiences as the context for developing creative responses to cultural oppression and sexism. The women I came to know depart from this womanist hermeneutical stance. They do not regularly employ experience as a category for interpreting Scripture or contemplating their actions in the manner womanism suggests. They are not immune to reflecting on their own lives, but they are much more evangelical than womanists in their commitments to biblical authority. They cannot discard the scriptures and do not see them as an instrument of a patriarchal religious system; they are trying to bring their lives in line with them. Where there is a tension, they have accepted the evangelical posture of trusting God to assist them in aligning their lives with Scripture. While a few women may question certain texts that have been used to oppress women, as Howard Thurman's grandmother did, it would be misleading to assert that women dismiss or reinterpret the biblical texts that do not reconcile easily with their lived experiences or that have been used to substantiate hierarchical relationships and oppression.

If there is an area where women are willing to interject their own experience in the hermeneutical process, it is the role of wifely submission. As is popularly advocated in many modern Christian women's books, they have learned how to replace the traditional teachings about submission with an interpretation of shared authority for the home. Still, they assign the role of headship to men.

Womanism is still largely a theology based in the academy. While it provides an analysis of the Black Church's strengths and weaknesses as part of the theological task, the church could benefit from having more models at the congregational level that translate and embody womanist principles, empower women, and encourage clergy to develop a critical ethical and biblical consciousness. I am not suggesting that there are currently no creative responses and avenues through which these theological systems impact local communities; programs that fulfill these goals to varying degrees are The Rites of Passage Program at Bridge Street African Wesleyan Methodist Episcopal Church, in Brooklyn, New York, and the Full Circle Intergenerational Project, the Back to the Kitchen Table Project (which evolved into the Northeast Denver Learning Resource Center), and the Sisters Working Encouraging Empowering Together (S.W.E.E.T.) network, all established in Denver. Each gives concreteness to one or more primary womanist commitments: strengthening the family, moving beyond a survivalist mode of reality, creating creative solutions to annihilating forces in the community, and empowering black women. S.W.E.E.T., which was founded as a church-based women's ministry, is a reproducible model for bridging the chasm between formal womanist theology and black church women. In its groups, distinctions of marital status, education, class, family structure, and physical appearance are subverted as each woman becomes a "sister" who is accorded respect regardless of her familial, social, or economic status. The goals of the groups were:

> to bring together a group of women that would eventually be empowered to look beyond social structures and see common ground. . . . Meetings varied in their degree of formality with annual seminars, weekly meetings, Bible Studies, monthly workshops, relationship-building exercises, small group discussion, potluck dinners, informal and formal luncheons, community action projects, intergenerational mentoring groups, individual and group counseling sessions, guest speakers, speakers from within the group, panel discussions, role playing, ethnographies, health support groups, and African American women's literature study and discussion groups. Each meeting began with prayer, praise reports of successes or blessings from the week, concerns, and group-building exercises. Women were not pressured to be a member of a

church but there was an understanding that the group was spiritually based. Each sister determined and articulated her own sense of spirituality, a spirituality that included the conscious awareness of God, self, and others in a total response to black life and culture.[12]

These groups, which began with a core of forty women, spanned five years. In that time, between five hundred and six hundred participated in them. Teresa Brown, who founded S.W.E.E.T., reported some of the outcomes.

> Sisters passed on their ideas of how to survive and thrive, and listened carefully to the "othermothers" in exercises such as "Who was the woman in your life who had the greatest impact on who you are today?" . . . As each woman shared, she also received affirmation of her situation or overcoming through similar stories repeated by another sister as well as a sort of embryonic sustenance from one another. If the situation had not been resolved, means for change were offered as possibilities, not exact solutions.[13]

Adding to these expressions of womanism are many sites on the Internet that disseminate womanist thought. A few sites promote critical reflection on women's experiences. One site, somethingwithin.com, established by the biblical scholar and A.M.E. minister Renita Weems, is in this category. An online journal for thinking women of faith, it posts articles about women in the Bible, reviews books about women, and invites articles about triumph. The site doesn't explicitly claim a womanist orientation, but Weems has established herself in the academy and through her popular writings as womanist-centered. Internet resources like this make the principles behind womanist action more accessible to contemporary black women, rather than remaining a subtle and diffuse presence within the African American religious tradition. Clergy-scholars such as Weems are also uniquely poised to provide models for biblical interpretation with a womanist standpoint. I have used excerpts from one of her sermons in several classes I taught during my tenure at Duke Divinity School to expose students to womanist hermeneutics. In a sermon titled "A Woman Who Fears the Lord," she exegetes the passage of Proverbs 31. Weems masterfully invites the hearer to understand how a text has been misused and made the servant of a particular type of theological picture that is oppressive to black women. Rather than preach a traditional rendering of this text, which reinscribes that a Christian woman should strive to multitask and be a virtuous woman by becoming a godly superwoman, she skillfully challenges the audience to consider what happens when cultural expectations are imposed on Scripture. Furthermore, her use of this text during a church revival may be an attempt to move women to the center of the biblical canon, forcing the church to consider the redemptive word for the entire membership in this passage. It is not just a text for the church women or for men who want a prescription for a godly mate.[14]

These signs are encouraging indicators that womanist work and consciousness are making inroads in local congregations. Yet, the tasks of improving the church, according to womanist scholars, will take much more rigorous analysis and sustained commitment to change. The womanist ethicist Katie Cannon has a clear sense of what will be required of the Black Church if it is to construct and embrace a more inclusive and liberating ethic. "We need to analyze the social organization of the Black Church—curricula, music, leadership, expectation, pastor-member interactions—as well as outright sex discrimination. Far too often, the organization of the church mirrors male dominance in the society and normalizes it in the eyes of both female and male parishioners."[15] Her words indicate that something is defective in the church that needs to be corrected. I concur. However, it seems that womanists should embark upon a sustained analysis of the church's "successes," not just its limitations. For womanism to have a decisive impact on the Black Church, it must engage more thoroughly what the church does well for men, women, families, and communities. In the midst of some African Americans' meager existence, others are constructing life options and a quality of living to which the church contributes. I also believe that womanists must make their theological contributions more accessible to lay women. This may mean engaging via pulpits, media, and popular magazines the topics that undermine the health of the black community and women. For the Black Church and womanist scholars and preachers, it may also mean responding empathetically to clergy and laity's concerns about the fragmentation that occurs along with the dismantling of familiar language, rituals, and organizational structures and providing theological rationales for the newly constructed forms that are deemed necessary.

Female Clergy

The acceptance of female clergy by the church is neither a divisive issue nor a justice issue for the women I studied. Women are considered able proclaimers of the gospel and leaders of congregations. However, not everyone is persuaded that God has ordained the acceptance of women, and so they resist sanctioning women as pastors. The women are not committed to being advocates for women ministers. This is due to several factors: their own theology concerning the process and meaning of a religious call; their limited knowledge of institutional and denominational processes; and the inward focus of most of their volunteer labor and power.

They feel a level of contentment with the progress women have made in the church and are confident it will continue. However, it is likely women's stature in ministry and the opportunities open to them would have progressed further if women organized collectively, were politically well informed about the process of ordination, and exhibited a womanist consciousness about these matters. While things move slowly for female ministers, women do fill important responsibilities in the church pertinent to the functioning of the church. Cheryl Gilkes has cogently described the importance and power of the church mother in Baptist and COGIC churches. This was solidified for me as one of the COGIC women spoke of the church mother's role in her church. In Layton Temple, the mothers literally pray for the pastor during the service. No one is to come between the women's section, adjacent to the pulpit, and the pastor. They are securing a spiritual hedge around the servant of God. This ritual function is more than just a symbolic posture. The church membership has assigned power to that role and function and believes in the efficacy of the prayer support. These women also have power beyond the time limits of the worship service. Church mothers are not ignored even when expressing their dissatisfaction with the direction of the church or pastor. They help select pastors and evangelists and soften sanctions against those who have violated the moral norms. Yet, as Anthony Pinn notes, this "does not fundamentally disrupt the male-centeredness of the denomination because church mothers give primary attention to the education and training of women."[16]

Teresa Brown acknowledges the male guard that presides over the pulpits in most black congregations and admits that even some women affirm this organizational position.

The black males and some black females cite biblical mandates against women preachers. They are accustomed to the male entitlement reinforced by the "man of God" image that parallels their male image of God. They also believe women will dilute the only power they have—leadership of the Black Church. The travesty of this is that the Black Church was created as a center of liberation. Yet due to assimilation of white patriarchal structures, many churches have become battlegrounds for sexual equality in the black community.[17]

This state of affairs calls for a creative response on the part of the Black Church, rather than acquiescence. The struggle should not be the province only of those women who aspire to be ministers but must be waged by and among women in the pews, as well. Within the S.W.E.E.T network, women embarked upon a reassessment of women's roles in their churches and in the ministry. In sessions facilitated by women clerics, they discussed questions such as "Who decides what you do at church and how?" and "What scriptural information is available about women's roles and responsibilities in religious settings?" These sessions helped women link their experience as laity to the oppression of women clerics and empowered them to make a difference.

> There were no right or wrong answers, just an opportunity to air opinions, strategize about ways to make the church more inclusive of women, and help other women identify instances of discrimination and role-stereotyped ministries in churches. One of the interesting finds from the meetings was that the majority of women had never questioned what women are required to wear or do, or that the positions in the church are traditionally closed to women. Nor did they question the language, songs, and sermons that excluded women or referred to them only as tools of destruction of men. . . . Some of the women had difficulty understanding how or why a woman would seek ordination and wanted to share pain experienced in their lay ministries and strengthen their resolve to support ordained women. Bible studies or sacred texts studies led by womanist scholars or an ordained woman were crucial to nourishing the seeds of change that these discussions had planted in terms of women's roles and responsibilities in the church.[18]

In developing this model of women's networks, Teresa Brown realized the necessity for consciousness raising among women in the Black Church.

She observed firsthand how this process can take place across generations in a context of mutuality, self-examination, and critical analysis. Central to this process is the task of connecting the reality of discrimination against women clergy to more subtle forms of male privilege and gender bias which affect lay women in congregations.

In this new millennium, I foresee greater inclusion of women clergy in established congregations and historic black denominations. Congregations will continue to slowly change as long as denominations continue the practice of "loose coupling"—the practice of having a formal policy that states the denominations' stance, yet allowing that position to be circumvented in practice at the congregational level. Loose coupling is in operation when women do the functional work of clergy without having the official sanction of the denomination to do so or when the church ascribes a different label to a task or activity depending upon whether a woman or a man performs it (e.g., men are regarded as "preachers" and women are called "speakers" or "teachers" when they publicly share the Christian message).[19]

Loose coupling is a denominational practice that protects the group's self-perception and maintains its relations with other churches in its denomination. It reveals the extent to which institutional rules are established to respond to external forces and environmental factors, rather than to regulate the internal operations of the organization. In other words, the denomination adopts a public posture of opposition to a particular change but in actuality tolerates it. The Black Church is not the only faith tradition that makes use of these practices; the pattern was first detected among mainline denominations.

In order for significant progress to be made, there must be consistency between rhetoric and practice, rather than a hypocritical relationship. As long as women are willing to perform the task of preacher or pastor without formal recognition, congregations will be able to receive the benefits of women's gifts without having to address their own structural inequities. This practice will also give legitimacy to the conception of "vocation" that I previously discussed. It will continue to validate a woman's persistence as authenticating her call and will undermine the fostering of solidarity and collective action on the part of men and women who desire greater acceptance of female clergy.

Any attempt to change the church's stance toward female clergy must address not just the work of women clergy but also that of lay women. This discourse must clearly situate women's work within a larger analysis of power and oppression. Although women diligently give their service to the church out of love and duty, the question of whether this is a maladaptive concession to the female-dominated membership in the church needs to be raised. Cloaked in Christian conceptions of service and fearful that the church's work will be thwarted if women don't step to the fore, the church encourages female labor while according the highest positions of recognition to men. Stressing the virtues of humility and of rendering one's works to God without fanfare, the church holds at bay any personal dissatisfactions or stirrings of collective challenge. To rectify this situation, women must forge alliances with female clergy (and male empathizers) to consider alternative models of power sharing. While absence of unity (or fear of such absence) in the church often frustrates acts of resistance, women must learn to rely on one another for support when being at odds with fellow members or challenging the church's sexism is more difficult than remaining the dutiful "willing worker."

Loyalty Forever?

As the twentieth century began, there was a group of faithful but agitated women in the Baptist church who loved God and hated distorted manifestations of God's presence in the world. They worked for change and justice in society and in their denomination. These women were not content with the state of affairs. They brought together personal, intellectual, spiritual, and financial resources to impact the social conditions of African Americans. They founded the National Baptist Women's Convention so that there would be a permanent institution where women could articulate their concerns, debate public policy, develop creative solutions to the oppression of women and blacks, and be confident that God's guidance and power was directing their actions. They were church women with a purpose and a fierce determination.

The women I have presented in this study are also women with a purpose. They want to live their lives to show love of God and to impact the world. They too care about the social and economic realities of African Americans. Yet, there is a distinction. These contemporary church women are not part of a unified women's network that looks systemically or sociologically at their conditions. They tackle the problems of the oppressed not on a global scale but on a local one. I believe they're more comfortable with the traditional universal claims of the Christian faith than with womanism's unmasking of the particularity of all theologies. Most of them will probably never write a letter of rebuttal or dismay regarding the actions of their denominations. Their reach is narrower and closer to home than that of the women Evelyn Brooks Higginbotham chronicled.

They are women of action, but a different sort of action. We cannot indict them for not being replicas of their early-twentieth-century sisters. Time and context have a way of defining the questions one raises, as well as the solutions. Church women at the turn of the twentieth century were unequivocally convinced that the Black Church was the only viable institution that could confront the strident racism and disenfranchisement blacks faced. It was the institution that could create and maintain a liberating sacred world to keep African Americans afloat. Women at the turn of the twenty-first century have to evaluate the church and their role against a different cultural, racial, and social reality.

The Black Church has been joined by a plethora of other social, civic, and fraternal organizations in the struggle. African Americans have experienced the gains of economic access, social inclusion, and political engagement. There are black intellectuals with nationally recognized prominence who serve at the top white and black academic institutions, and African American clergy who balance ministry with public service. Black women have made strides in government, lead the oldest continuous black ministers' conference, and have broken the glass ceiling of the bishopric in the A.M.E. Church.

African Americans still remain extremely loyal to the Protestant church. However, there are some signs of greater toleration of and collaboration with African Americans who practice other faiths (Islam, African traditional religions) or who are committed to the well-being of the black community but claim no faith tradition (humanists). The black (male) minister's voice, once the only one authorized to interpret and speak prophetically about the plight of African Americans, no longer has that exclusive privilege. Voices come from within the Black Church and outside it. Ministers, politicians, activists, professors, theologians, grassroots organizers, denominational policymakers, cultural critics, and hip-hop artists each have legitimation in different sectors of the black community to interpret the state of black America and to posit solutions. The Black Church is no longer the only public sphere for the debate of policy issues or current social ills.

I suspect that debates about the conditions of African Americans occur in the Black Church at the local level more than at the denominational level. As people increasingly change denominations at will, the influence of parent bodies or women's auxiliaries on local congregations is lessened. The local minister often holds more sway over his or her congregation than any denominational bureaucracy or adopted position. In the midst of this state of affairs, we find black women managing the church now as they did a century ago. Their loyalty is one of the defining qualities they have in common with their foremothers. I believe the story of the Black Church will continue to be one of female fidelity and faith. Women's loyalty can be anticipated for several reasons. One, their commitment to serve the church anchors them to the organization. Repeatedly, whether it was commitment to children's ministry or a couples ministry, teaching Sunday school, or working with the youth, women ask themselves, "Who will do the work if I just leave?" Even when they question the suitability of the church for them, I found that women do not want to undermine the Black Church as a meaningful spiritual house for others. They do not just "leave the job." It takes more frustration than most of them experience to just walk away from a task they perform as a sacred trust.

We can expect loyalty also because women's theological views militate against a quick departure. When conflicts emerge in the church, women look for the lesson to be learned. Having lived through a period of turmoil in her church, one woman said she learned "that this situation wasn't about me. It was bigger than the persons involved. God is doing something in the larger picture." One member who had considered moving her membership said, "I believe one has to have a church membership. [I'm] not sure I should judge what is going on, like maybe I can't see the whole picture." A third woman, whose confidence was publicly betrayed by her pastor many years ago, recounted how she felt compelled to stay in the church. Although she felt personally betrayed, she could not leave until she had worked through forgiving him. Leaving before this reconciliation would have been inappropriate. She eventually changed churches and joined Layton Temple, but she never considered denouncing the Black Church altogether.

The mechanisms women use to resolve conflicts are often spiritual strategies, rather than skills a business manager would use or alternative conflict resolution strategies. The effect is often an abdication of women's power to make changes in the church. Women rely on praying, telling someone else in a leadership role, or believing God will work it out. Even when these methods don't appear to have any immediate effect, or their private meetings with leaders yield no change, women still trust God's eventual intervention. Finally, the loyalty to the church continues because women distance themselves from intense involvement in the affairs of the church. Women begin to separate going to church and being spiritually fed from knowing how the church operates. They maintain a nucleus of established relationships but distance themselves from newer initiatives. Even when they suspect money is not being used appropriately, many still give financial support. Most of the women in this group said they would give to the church and not question how the money was used; "that is up to the Lord," and the leaders will have to give an account for its usage.

These mechanisms suggest that loyalty is not simply a function of internal motivation, spiritual renewal, spiritual sustenance, and positive regard for church members. It is also the consequence of valuing cohesion over disruption, the church's skillfulness at making women's work indispensable, and the triumph of select theological ideas set within a dichotomous frame (e.g., if you do X, you're not a good Y). I do not engage the topic of loyalty because I want women to be less committed to the Black Church. Nor do I want to leave the impression that these mechanisms are operative for all church women. A perusal of the frequency and pain of congregational splits is evidence that women do get to the point where "enough is enough" and they vote with their feet.

Women have been the dominant constituency in American congregations since the late seventeenth century. Since that time, their social roles, work and educational opportunities, childhood experiences, and commitment to a more equitable society have bound women to the church. Church women don't often recognize the influence of these social forces. They would say they choose to reside in the Black Church. As I've argued, the power of cultural norms and practices and the prestigious stature of the Black Church make the decision to participate semi-involuntary more than voluntary. We can conclude that social dynamics, cultural norms, and valuation of the church and its intersection with the life-giving God they find therein anchor this constituency to the institution. A radical change in any one of these components may shift their loyalty before the present millennium ends. For now, we must surmise that the Black Church would become a much less enduring institution if it weren't for woman's loyalty and love for it.

Righteous Contentment

Black church women take seriously the theological claim that the church is a unique institution. It is not merely an organization of people gathered together for a common purpose. It is the church of God. It has all the trappings of a sociological entity, but it is much more than that. The theological uniqueness of the church calls for an organizational distinctiveness, as well. Although the church is supposed to be "in the world but not of it," when the church fails, women do not exhibit outrage or reimagine their image of the church. Because the church is "not just another organization," women can acknowledge the church's similarity to secular businesses and agencies, yet still maintain a perspective that keeps the sociological and organizational mechanisms of the church as invisible as possible.

This sort of rationalization suppresses the discourse I have said is warranted, one that examines the intersections of gender, power, and church labor. The Black Church must engage in a comprehensive analysis of how labor at the congregational level of the church supports the hierarchies and male power. Any discussion of power must begin with an acknowledgment of its presence and a description of who has it. This can be frustrated by dichotomous thinking that separates spiritual from secular mechanisms and commitments and by assumptions of good will on the part of the pastor or church. It may also be limited because any discussion of power has the potential to confront women with the reality of political processes that govern the church. For instance, as I spoke with one respondent, she reported that different terms are used for female and male preachers in her congregation. She provided an astute observation about this practice but quickly diminished the significance of the observation by saying, "It's only a small thing, it's not that important." In other instances, women supplemented or softened their own evaluations of the church's treatment of and teachings about women by calling attention to the pastor's passion to save black men. Since women regard their pastors and the church as having honorable values and commitments, a discourse that unmasks unequal consequences for women seems unduly critical. It also suggests that the church has become captive to relying on secular notions of equality to evaluate the church.

This struggle to maintain the church as a unique entity, unencumbered by what is considered secular ideologies and strategies, can be best captured in the words of one Baptist member. I conversed with her about the type of accountability structures that should be present in congregations to respond to leaders who have moral lapses or who violate the church's trust. I asked, "Do you think that churches should have processes of holding someone in a leadership role accountable?"

> I don't know that I can really answer that because [long pause], I guess my first answer would be yes. There should be, but then [pause] our shepherd is Jesus Christ, and very often we can't exactly take the systems of the world and impose them as is on the church, 'cause we're under a different model. Forgiveness and servanthood and the things that Jesus taught, very often they're diametrically opposed to world systems, to the way we do things in the world. Our corporate directors, vice presidents, and [managers] at Bell South do not consider themselves servants. . . . I'm not sure that those kind of values [of the corporate world], we can wholesale transfer them to God.

We talked further about the procedures of her company: the clear delineation within a corporate system for troubleshooting and the clear chain of command so that one knows "where the buck stops." She illustrated this point with a story of how she resolved a customer's complaint by going to top management in the company. She later was informed that she had ignored certain aspects of corporate protocol by going directly to the top. I probed further: "How do we go about holding people accountable, if you think that's desirable?"

> I think we really have to do it based on the scripture . . . [that's] the only thing I can think of. What we use at Calvary is Matthew 18. If you have an ought against your brother, you go to your brother. I think it has to operate at that kind of level. Because that's the only model that I could justify. I still, I guess I still feel that at whatever level it takes place, it's really going to your brother and trying to have your brother restored. That's the emphasis of it [Scripture]. Your first thing is to regain your brother and have him restored, and not only within the fellowship but have him restored in his relationship with the Lord. And that's why I say, I don't know whether we can just [didn't complete thought]. I know that's there's church government. I don't quite understand all of it, and that's probably why they've never put me in that area, but I don't think we can just treat each other any kind of way, because we're called to a different model. We're called to be Jesus Christ's physical presence until

He comes back again, so we have to treat each other differently than we might otherwise. . . . I think that pastors or church officials have a responsibility to God first and then to their congregations. They are accountable. They're always accountable. We're all accountable to the Lord. I'm just not exactly sure, except we go to regain our brother, how we do it. You know, friends of mine in my church used to say, "You know, you're really naïve." They say that to me a lot. Not so much now, but when I was over [a specific ministry area. They'd say], "You just don't know what's going on" and it used to hurt my feelings, but then I thought about it and I was glad. I mean, I'm very happy to work and to do what I can and not have to be embroiled in all that stuff, especially when I was working in that ministry. I'm glad to not have a lot of knowledge of the inner things that go on and that kind of thing, because it frees me to do what the Lord has for me to do.

This woman went on to name some of the dynamics to which she had been oblivious. Some related to personality conflicts, others to power struggles. Her words reveal the extent to which she believes that the church is a distinct domain, with theological commitments that must be rigorously embraced, even when they hurt or don't appear to go far enough. That is the price of being distinctly Christian. The cost of not adhering to a Christian ethic for restoration is spiritually frustrating and is proof of a diminished regard for the body of Christ.

Like, well with the split. It depressed me to know that people, it's a reality, but it depressed me to no end, that church folk treat each other just like and often worse than any old person out on the street. I think we have a higher calling, but we're in process, and people bring with them their experiences and stuff like that. Many people operate under the same value system that they operated with when they were in the street. And that's why the challenge to know more about Christ and draw closer to him in the Body is so great, because we need to be that peculiar people. We need to demonstrate Christ. I'm just happy not to know all that stuff . . . and I pray for strength. The more responsibility I've assumed in the working of the church, I've been privy to things I'd rather not have been privy to and that kind of thing, but it makes me pray harder, and that's why I know that's what the Lord wants me to do. That's my input. I'm not necessarily going to be able to go in there and offer the solutions that are needed to restore this and renew that and all that kind of stuff, but it brings me to my knees, and that's my work. That the Lord guides us, that the Lord's hand is upon it, and that what He wants is done. I am naïve, but I don't mind, I don't mind being naïve. It's a lot easier.

Not everyone in this sample would have echoed her comments exactly. But many respondents expressed some aspect of these theological ideas. They affirmed their reliance on God to work things out, their frustration that the world's issues seem to be unduly impacting the church (the sex of preachers, status seeking, unequal treatment of people, excessive emphasis on race) and their belief that it's easier to be loyal to a small task of the church than to learn too much about the church's overall operations.

My years of observing the Black Church as a scholar, minister, and Christian lead me to the conclusion that this is not an isolated view. These sentiments are more characteristic of "typical" black church women than of womanist voices, which stress where the church is falling short. Contemporary black church women do not want to take the risk of fragmenting the church. They are not as confident that they are called to be the change agents as they are that God can do all things.

It would be easy to see them as blind, to suggest they have a false consciousness or have learned too thoroughly the very theological positions that hinder the realization of a healthier or more just church. I hesitate to affirm any of these judgments because it privileges the façade of scholarly objectivity at the expense of honoring these women's constructions of reality. Rather than conclude that the womanist critique of religion is the only resolution or position that will ultimately empower the Black Church, we must consider womanist voices along with the more conservative sentiments of this Baptist church woman.

This suggests to me another direction that the Black Church will have to move in this new millennium. The church will have to create venues for the airing of different interpretations of race, class, and sex oppression and allow a discourse involving divergent theological perspectives. I think this is a particular challenge as independent and nondenominational churches multiply across the American landscape, as more Americans have multiple points of access to electronic preachers, and as the distinct markers of the Black Church become less distinguishable. In this postmodern world, individuals who identify with womanist or liberationist theologies cannot presume a privileged stance any more than the church women who reflect more conservative and traditional views. The competing voices requires that those in the Black Church revisit the basis for their theological convictions. Although a few women used sociocultural analysis or experiential learning to evaluate the church's preaching and teaching, I am comfortable saying that reason, tradition, and experience were all less significant than Scripture as the basis for their views of Christian authority. Along with relying on Scripture, many of the women are content to assume that there is a "correct" way to understand the Bible and are willing to rely upon interpreters to supply what the "correct" theology is. The creation of a venue where one can deconstruct hegemonic theologies and encourage women to regard themselves as interpreters and interrogators of the Christian faith, rather than mere consumers, would be a positive first step. In the final analysis, this type of religious context may allow lay women to define and expand what they regard as *righteous content* rather than accept the status quo and be *righteously content*.

Appendix I

Methodology and Research Design

The research design of this study incorporated methods used in the social sciences and in oral history collection. I collected the data using three methods that overlapped: fieldwork in the churches, administering a survey to church members, and conducting semistructured interviews. The field research and interviews were collected over a period of six months in 1995. This intense period of data collection was followed by intermittent visits. In the summer of 1998, I conducted follow-up interviews with most of the women to investigate further their perspectives on female clergy.

During my months of observation, I regularly attended Sunday morning worship services, prayer meetings, Bible studies, new-member classes, prayer and Bible band, and Sunday school. I also observed activities that met less frequently, such as special afternoon programs, fashion shows, church business meetings, and dedication services. I talked with church leaders, including members of the Mothers Boards, heads of auxiliaries and ministries, deacons, trustees, pastors, and one pastor's wife. I had access to documents and publications of the church, including bulletins, teaching materials, histories, denominational manuals, church anniversary booklets, membership records, and some financial records.

Adults age eighteen or older were asked to fill out a multipage survey consisting of close-ended items. A slightly modified version of the survey used in *Congregational Change in Changing Communities*[1] was administered to collect demographic information and to contrast the two congregations on significant indicators. I amended this instrument to include several items specific to cultural norms of the Black Church. The survey gathered information on basic demographic indicators, levels of participation, perceptions of local congregations, and views on what churches should do. The survey also served as a mechanism to identify any unique social indicators or theological positions among my respondents and was used as a vehicle for soliciting female interviewees.

Survey participation was encouraged through public announcements during worship made by myself and the pastor, printed announcements in the bulletin, and distribution of letters to leaders of small groups and through the Sunday school and Bible study classes. Since I was interested in the activities and attitudes of church members, surveys completed by regular visitors or nonmembers were excluded. Fifty surveys were completed from the Church of God in Christ congregation and 125 from the Baptist congregation. Between 40 and 60 percent of the adults in attendance on a given Sunday completed surveys during my visitation period.

To complement the quantitative instrument, I focused most of my attention on field research and the semistructured interviews. In participant-observation, the investigator's goal is to interpret a culture or social unit from the perspective of those on the inside. It requires that she immerse herself in that context and allows the members to guide her into their world. A researcher's credibility and the impact of her presence within the congregation may affect her access to information and the thoroughness of her understanding of that social world. The litmus test is whether church women and other interpreters of the Black Church recognize the portrait and interpretation of African American women's religiosity I have presented in these pages.

The third method used in this project was the interviewing of the women. Of the participants, thirteen were Pentecostals, members of the Church of God in Christ denomination. Twenty-five were from the Baptist church. Availability and access to the women were factors in the final shape of the sample. I identified some of the women through referrals or direct solicitation. The selection process leaned toward middle-aged participants and mothers, since these populations tend to participate more in church activities than younger women. However, the group has diverse characteristics. There are parents and nonparents, women without formal leadership or participatory roles in worship services, and women of varying ages and employment status. Some are from urban areas, others from rural ones. They represent two of the historic black denominations that have had strong female organizational structures almost from their inception. These auxiliaries helped develop and sustain a distinct female culture and feminine discourse within the larger national bodies and often were the forces within the denomination that challenged the domination of race relations as the most important struggle of black life. As inheritors of that legacy and as products of those gatherings, these women provide a particular entree into the life of the church and to an understanding of the impact of its rhetoric about family, religion, and gender. Furthermore, they demonstrate how women sometimes conformed, sometimes resisted, these gender constructions.

I conducted all the interviews and transcribed most of them myself. Interviews lasted between one-and-one-half and three-and-one-half hours. In most cases, the older the respondent and the greater the number congregations of which she had been a part, the longer the interview. The interview guide consisted of open-ended questions about the respondents' religious socialization, critical life transitions, familial roles and responsibilities, conceptions of gender roles in the church, racial consciousness, and views on the work of the church.

This research design was informed by the logic of feminist ethnography. Feminist ethnographers do not necessarily use new research methods. They employ the standard mechanisms of the scholar's particular field of specialization. The distinctiveness is more in the choice of problems to study, in the approach to content, in the inclination toward interdisciplinary approaches, and in the collection and interpretation of the data than in the tools of data gathering. They are also concerned to honor women's voices rather than speak for them. Feminist scholars are committed to documenting the lives and activities of women and to conceptualizing women's behavior in relation to the social contexts in which they participate.[2]

In the social sciences, one of feminism's most basic tasks has been to challenge scholars to consider how gender is a primary organizing principle in society and its institutions. Feminist scholarship has expanded our understanding of the differences between women's and men's social experiences. Women's lives have often been marked by social, economic, and cultural oppression. Feminism has demonstrated how these experiences influence both women's participation in society and the meanings that they assign to the roles they fill.

Feminist theory is a corrective to assumptions of universal human experience. It requires that we tend more closely to the particularity of groups and subcultures within a culture. It affirms rather than trivializes female activities, agency, labor, and perspectives. This study fits within this framework by focusing on an understudied constituency within American Christianity—black women. Feminist principles also inform this study by providing a caution against imposing a voice on the respondents and a reminder to tend to issues of reciprocity in the interviewing process. As much as I would like, one cannot let others have their say without imposing some categories and interpretation. I have taken seriously the task of hearing women's voices as accurately as possible so that my narrative does not occlude their perspectives.

Appendix II
The Interview Guide

I.

1. State your name, age, and marital status.
2. Do you have children? How many, and what are their ages?
3. Do you work? Where? When did you retire?
4. How long have you been in this field?

II.

1. Are you a native of this state?
2. How many people were in the household you grew up in?
3. Do you have siblings?
4. What are their ages?
5. Was there a division of labor/responsibility functioning in your household that was gender-specific?
6. Were there specific roles for the boys and girls?
7. Who was the disciplinarian?
8. What did your parents do for a living?
9. What could women get away with/be lax about in regard to family expectations?
10. Were there things that men could get away with?
11. Were you taught lessons of what girls do? Of what boys do?

III.

1. Was attending church or religious school a part of your upbringing?
2. What did a typical church service consist of?
3. Did you go to Sunday School?
4. Did your parents attend church?

5. Were your parents differently active?
6. Did other family members attend?
7. Did people in your immediate community or neighborhood go to the same church?
8. Did you see your classmates at church?
9. Did women go more often than the men?
10. Did you notice this or ever wonder about it?
11. What were the roles of men and women in your family church?
12. What was the social standing of the church?
13. Did the prominent members of the community attend your church?
14. If not, to what church did these persons go?
15. What did your church do in the community?
16. Did they give food, clothing to others? Were social functions held there besides religious functions?
17. Were community meetings, civil rights organizing, voting registration conducted there?
18. Did you ever question those roles/division of labor?
19. Did you have choice whether to attend or not?
20. What sort of devotional/religious practices did you observe or participate in at home? at church?
21. Are there persons whom you can recall that strongly impressed you as religious or very devoted to the church? Whom?
22. What behaviors indicated their commitment to you?
23. Can you remember any very significant religious experiences you had or you observed as a child or a teenager?
24. Can you describe the circumstances for me?
25. Did you ever formally join the church? What prompted that?
26. What was the process of becoming a member?
27. Did you ever attend a business meeting?
28. Did men and women participate equally?
29. Do you remember any disciplinary issues coming before the church? What kind of issue?
30. How were they resolved?

IV.

1. When did you start exercising choice whether to attend church or not?
2. What were the circumstances under which this happened?

3. Were you still living at home? Working? At college? Had crises recently occurred?
4. From the point when you started determining whether to go to church or not, how consistent has your attendance been?
5. How often do you go now?
6. Have you had any periods of nonattendance? How long?
7. Do you consider this a time of backsliding?
8. Were the changes in your attendance work-related?
9. Were there any major personal changes in your life during that period (relationships, sickness, moving, education, divorce, having children, death, etc.)?
10. Have you been a member of any other religious denominations or faith traditions (i.e. Islam, Jehovah's Witness)?

V.

1. How did you come to be at this church?
2. How did you first hear about this church?
3. How long did you visit prior to joining?
4. How long have you been there?
5. What were you looking for in a church?
6. How important was the geographic location in selecting a church?
7. How important was the activities for youth?
8. What activities are you involved in at this church?
9. Has your current level of activity always been what it is now?
10. How about in other churches?
11. Are there roles in the life of the church that women cannot fulfill?
12. Have you ever questioned any teaching of your church in regard to women?
13. What does your church, in general, teach is the role of women?
14. How do you feel about that? Agree? Disagree?
15. Do you financially support the church? Are you a tither?
16. Is there an aspect of the worship service that is most meaningful to you? What? Why?
17. Were these dimensions important to you in choosing to join this church?
18. Describe to me the content of the preacher's sermons?
19. What do you get from them (emphasis on content)?

20. Is there a part of the Christian year that is especially meaningful to you? Why?
21. Are you comfortable with your level of participation?
22. How would you describe your feelings for your church?
23. Are there people, activities that encourage (those) feelings for your church?
24. What do you like best about church?
25. What do you like least? Is there something you'd like to see improved?
26. Of your closest five friends, how many go to church with you?
27. What kind of outside socializing do you do with the church members?
28. Have you had members casually over to your house? Not for a meeting?
29. How has the church and its members been helpful to you?
30. Did you ask for the assistance or others took the initiative?
31. What sort of things should the church be about?
32. Are there things the church should not get involved in?
33. Do you think your church is sufficiently active in the community?
34. What other organizations, civic organizations are you a part of in the city?
35. Have you participated differently in the past?
36. Are you in any lodges, sororities?
37. Do you do volunteer work on a regular basis outside of the church?

VI.

1. Have you ever attended/been a member of a predominantly white congregation? Where? When? How long? Why not?
2. Are there differences between white and black churches that make one more preferable than the other?
3. Did race factor into your decision to join this church?
4. Do you think there are issues specific to the lives of African Americans which only a black minister can effectively speak to/about? What are they?
5. Do you intentionally make an effort to support black businesses?
6. Are you a member of any African American organizations or professional associations? National Association for the Advancement of Colored People?

7. Do you subscribe to black magazines, publications?
8. Have you supported/observed any of the black cultural festivals—Kwanzaa, Juneteenth, Martin Luther King Day, Black Family Reunion?
9. How do you do this?
10. Do you think blacks should support black candidates?
11. Do you think people should date interracially?
12. Is there any harm to the race when this occurs?

VII.

1. Do you have routine devotional practices that you follow? Prayer? Study?
2. Do you watch Christian television, listen to Christian radio?
3. As a family do you have routine devotions, or times of prayer?
4. What does God mean to you?
5. What does having God in your life mean to you?
6. Who is God to you?
7. How has God/faith been helpful to you?
8. Can you think of a metaphor to describe the church? Why did you pick that one?
9. Can you think of a metaphor to describe God? Can you finish the statement God is like _____?
10. How has the church been meaningful to you?
11. Has God helped you see yourself differently?
12. Can you elaborate please?
13. Have you always felt good about yourself?
14. Is there anything else you'd like to tell me about your relationship with God? With the Church?

Notes

NOTES TO THE INTRODUCTION

1. "Black Church" is used in this text to connote the seven historically independent and predominantly black denominations that have shared a significant
unity in their missions, cultures, and sources of origins. The founding of the Free
African Society in 1787 is considered the precursor of the first black denomination, the African Methodist Episcopal Church. I have appropriated this definition from C. Eric Lincoln and Lawrence Mamiya, *The Black Church in the
African American Experience,* as my own. The churches included are the African
Methodist Episcopal Church, African Methodist Episcopal Zion Church, Christian Methodist Episcopal Church, National Baptist Convention, USA, Inc., National Baptist Convention of America Unincorporated, Progressive National
Baptist Convention, and Church of God in Christ. No definition, whether coined
by a historian, sociologist, or theologian, is going to be inclusive enough to en-
compass all black congregations. This one excludes black congregations that are
part of predominantly white denominations. Smaller Pentecostal and Holiness
sects that have previously been marginalized in studies of American religion are
ignored by this definition, along with some very influential churches in urban
areas that are nondenominational. Universal Temple and Trinity United Church
of Christ are two examples of large, progressive congregations in Chicago that
do not fit Lincoln and Mamiya's definition. However, given the impact of these
seven groups on the collective life of America and African Americans, as well as
the estimated 80 percent of black Christians who belong to them, I am persuaded of the merits of these parameters. C. Eric Lincoln and Lawrence Mamiya,
The Black Church in the African American Experience (Durham: Duke University Press, 1991), 1.

2. Gerald F. Moran, "Sisters in Christ," in *Women in American Religion,* ed.
Janet Wilson James (Philadelphia: University of Pennsylvania Press, 1976), 47–
66.

3. Ann Douglas bases her analysis on the decline of New England mainline
Protestantism. It cannot be inferred that all denominations had suffered compa-
rable numerical declines in their number of male attendees and clergy. Sectarian

groups such as the Methodists and Baptists profited from the decline in mainline membership and from the cultural shift. All Christian denominations, however, have echoed the lament that congregations are populated primarily by women and have lost their influence in the political, civic, and economic arenas, arenas historically considered the domains of men. Ann Douglas, *The Feminization of American Culture* (New York: Knopf, 1977), 17–79, 97–117.

4. Joseph H. Fitcher, *Southern Parish* (Chicago: University of Chicago Press, 1951); Fitcher, *Social Relations in the Urban Parish* (Chicago: University of Chicago Press, 1954).

5. A thorough analysis of the development and expansion of the study of religiosity is documented in Daphne C. Wiggins, "African Americans, Gender and Religiosity," in *Culture and Difference: Critical Perspectives on the Bicultural Experience in the United States,* ed. Antonio Darder (Westport, Conn.: Bergin and Garvey, 1995), 169–184.

6. For a summation of each theory see David de Vaus and Ian McAllister, "Gender Differences in Religion: A Test of the Structural Location Theory," *American Sociological Review* 52 (August 1987): 472–484.

7. See Gary Marx, *Protest and Prejudice: A Study of Black Belief in the Black Community* (San Francisco: Harper, 1967); Hart M. Nelsen, "Unchurched Black Americans: Patterns of Religiosity and Affiliation," *Review of Religious Research* 29 (June 1988): 319–412; Darren Sherkat and Christopher G. Ellison, "Identification and Separatism: Religious Involvement and Racial Orientations among Black Americans," *Sociological Quarterly* 32 (1991): 477–494; Hart M. Nelsen and Anne K. Nelsen, *The Black Church in the Sixties* (Lexington: University of Kentucky Press, 1975); Robert J. Taylor, "Correlates of Religious Non-Involvement among Black Americans," *Review of Religious Research* 29 (December 1988): 126–139; Robert J. Taylor, "Structural Determinants of Religious Participation among Black Americans," *Review of Religious Research,* 30 (December 1988): 114–125. For studies pertaining to female religiosity and attendance see De Vaus and McAllister, "Gender Differences in Religion: A Test of Structural Location Theory"; Edward H. Thompson Jr., "Beneath the Status Characteristic: Gender Variations in Religiousness," *Journal for the Scientific Study of Religion* 30 (1991): 381–394; Marie Cornwall, "The Social Bases of Religion: A Study of Factors Influencing Religious Belief and Commitment," *Review of Religious Research* 29, no. 1 (September 1987): 44–56; Ellen M. Gee, "Gender Differences in Church Attendance in Canada," *Review of Religious Research,* 32 (March 1991): 267–272; K. Felety and M. Poloma, "From Sex Differences to Gender Role Beliefs: Exploring Effects on Six Dimensions of Religiosity," *Sex Roles* 25 (1991): 181–193.

8. See Lincoln and Mamiya, *The Black Church*; John Brown Childs, *The Political Black Minister: A Study in Afro-American Politics and Religion* (Boston: G. K. Hall, 1980); Aldon Morris, *The Origins of the Civil Rights Movement:*

Black Communities Organizing for Change (New York: Free Press, 1984); W. E. B. Du Bois and Monroe N. Work, "The Negro Ministry in the Middle West," in *The Negro Church*, ed. W. E. B. Du Bois (Atlanta: Atlanta University Press, 1903); and Ronald L. Johnstone, "Negro Preachers Take Sides," *Review of Religious Research* 11 (Fall 1969): 81–89.

9. Bishop T. D. Jakes is the founder of T. D. Jakes Ministries and the pastor of The Potter's House, a nondenominational church with a membership of more than 27,000 in Dallas, Texas. The author of more than two dozen books and CDs, he travels internationally, preaching the Christian message as well as leading massive spiritual rallies and leadership events. He has amassed a large female following through the popular text *Woman Thou Art Loosed* and the national conferences he sponsors with the same title. In September 2001, he was featured in *Time* magazine; the caption "Is This Man the Next Billy Graham?" ran across his cover photo. David Van Biema, "Spirit Raiser," *Time* 158, no. 11 (September 17, 2001): 53–55.

10. Lincoln and Mamiya argue that the effect of secularization on black religion has not resulted in a complete institutional differentiation or privatization of faith among African Americans. Lincoln and Mamiya, *Black Church*, 8–10.

11. Black women's religiosity is also chronicled in Clarence Taylor, *The Black Churches of Brooklyn* (New York: Columbia University Press, 1994); Judith Weisenfeld, *African American Women and Christian Activism: New York's Black YWCA, 1905–1945* (Cambridge, Mass.: Harvard University Press, 1997); Judith Weisenfeld, *This Far by Faith: Readings in African-American Women's Religious Biography* (New York: Routledge, 1996).

12. Evelyn Brooks Higginbotham, *Righteous Discontent: The Women's Movement in the Black Baptist Church, 1880–1920* (Cambridge, Mass.: Harvard University Press, 1993), 188–229.

13. Elizabeth Cady Stanton, *The Woman's Bible* (Seattle: Coalition Task Force on Women and Religion, 1895; repr., ed., New York: Arno Press, 1974).

14. Lincoln and Mamiya included 2,150 churches in their national church sample. More than 80 percent of the churches sampled had fewer than 600 members; the median size was between 200 and 250 members. Lincoln and Mamiya, *Black Church*, 142–143.

15. See note 8, this chapter. Other studies worthy of mention are Benjamin E. Mays and Joseph W. Nicholson, "The Genius of the Negro Church," in *Afro-American Religious History: A Documentary Witness*, ed. Milton Sernett (Durham: Duke University Press, 1985), 337–348; Edward L. Wheeler, *Uplifting the Race: The Black Minister in the New South, 1865–1902* (Lanham, Md.: University Press of America, 1986), 1–36; and William E. Montgomery, *Under Their Own Vine and Fig Tree: The African-American Church in the South, 1865–1900* (Baton Rouge: Louisiana State University Press, 1993).

NOTES TO CHAPTER I

1. Hart M. Nelsen, "Unchurched Black Americans: Patterns of Religiosity and Affiliation," *Review of Religious Research* 29(4) (June 1988): 398–412, 406.

2. Joseph R. Gusfield, *Community: A Critical Response* (New York: Harper and Row, 1975), xv–xvi.

3. Marcia Riggs, *Awake, Arise, and Act: A Womanist Call for Black Liberation* (Cleveland: Pilgrim Press, 1994), 10.

4. C. Eric Lincoln and Lawrence Mamiya, *The Black Church in the African American Experience* (Durham: Duke University Press, 1991), 309–345.

5. Ibid., 327.

6. Evelyn Brooks Higginbotham argues "pubic sphere" is a fitting label for the Black Church, because of its social and civic functions. The Black Church has been noted for its representativeness of the African American community; its accessibility to religious and secular groups; its provision of an arena for critical discourse and debate on community values; and its capacity to disseminate information to the larger constituency. This breadth of engagement in secular matters qualifies it as more than a religious institution. Evelyn Higginbotham, *Righteous Discontent: The Women's Movement in the Black Baptist Church, 1880–1920* (Cambridge, Mass.: Harvard University Press, 1993), 10–12.

7. Lincoln and Mamiya, *Black Church,* 307–308, 322.

8. The Promise Keepers is a recent religious movement in America that focuses on reclaiming Christian manhood and thereby strengthening family, church, and the nation. The movement originated in 1990 under the leadership of Bill McCartney, a former professional football coach and former Catholic who is now a member of the charismatic Protestant Vineyard Fellowship. Best known for its large Christian rallies that attract millions of men, the ministry in 1997 had more than four hundred paid staff and a budget of $115 million. All men who join the movement pledge to keep seven promises, which include honoring God first, working toward racial reconciliation, and treating women properly. Al Janssen and Larry K. Weeden, eds., *Seven Promises of a Promise Keeper* (Colorado Springs, Colo.: Focus on the Family, 1994).

9. This is the name for the Christian manhood conferences sponsored by Bishop T. D. Jakes Ministries. All are rooted in Christian teachings, and the Manpower services have attracted men by the tens of thousands, filling large churches and sports arenas for these two-day events. While T. D. Jakes Ministries and Promise Keepers events attract racially diverse audiences, the first is more African American and the other more Euro-American.

10. Gilkes makes a similar argument about the participation of young girls in the Sanctified Church. Church women perceived the society as a real threat, and men a posed a real danger to young black women in the early twentieth century.

Having their children in their purview as much as possible was one way black women sought to shield girls from undesired attention and danger. Cheryl Townsend Gilkes, "Together and in Harness: Women's Traditions in the Sanctified Church," *Signs* 10 (Summer 1985): 678–699.

11. This church was seven years old in 1997.

12. This is normative in light of Lincoln and Mamiya's finding that the average black church has at least 2.5 to 3.0 female members for every male member. Lincoln and Mamiya, *Black Church,* 304.

13. The Mothers Board is an official board of the Church of God in Christ denominations. Women are appointed to this position by the pastor, and all members of the church officially recognize it. Beyond the local congregation, there is a state mother and a national mother, as well. These women leaders all have governing power over the other women within the denomination, are looked to as spiritual leaders, and have a substantial degree of autonomy at the national level. See Cheryl Townsend Gilkes, "The Roles of Church and Community Mothers: Ambivalent American Sexism or Fragmented African Family-hood," *Journal of Feminist Studies in Religion* 2 (Spring 1986): 41–59.

14. The racial identity of these persons was confirmed by one of my respondents; one of the white attendees was her daughter-in-law. Her son and his wife were not officially members of the church at this time.

NOTES TO CHAPTER 2

1. W. E. B. Du Bois, *The Souls of Black Folk* (1903; repr., ed., New York: Fawcett, 1961), 141.

2. "Running" is a term sometimes used interchangeably with "shouting." It connotes the physical movement of a person who is experiencing the presence of God such that they move bodily under its power. Visually this may look like the person is spontaneously leaping from his or her seat and beginning to encircle the circumference of the sanctuary, unaware of what else may be taking place at that moment. Individuals may also run in a more circumscribed area, such as back and forth in front of the pulpit area. Robert M. Franklin asserts that these periods of cathartic shouting are often regarded as the most controversial feature of black congregational culture. "During designated moments of formal worship, shouters may stand, walk, dance, leap for joy, speak in tongues, or fall to the floor in response to an overwhelming encounter with the mysterium tremendum. . . . Persons who shout report that they feel better and that something therapeutically significant has occurred." Robert M. Franklin, "The Safest Place on Earth: The Culture of Black Congregations," in *American Congregations: New Perspectives in the Study of Congregations,* ed. James P. Wind and James W. Lewis, vol. 2 (Chicago: University of Chicago Press, 1994), 262.

3. The call-and-response feature in black churches has deep roots in the

African American religious traditions. A participatory and dialogical response to the preacher's pronouncements, it signifies affirmation of and identification with the proclaimed word and represents the communal nature of telling the story. Franklin, "The Safest Place," 264–266.

4. "Prosperity gospel" refers to a theology that asserts that Christians are entitled to material as well as spiritual abundance in this life. It is a consequence of one's faith. This theology has proponents across denominations and races. While some traditions within Christianity have always linked wealth and faith, this particular manifestation has gained renewed vigor in the past decade via the televangelists Creflo Dollar and Frederick K. Price and countless other protégés in local congregations. The prosperity gospel is just one strand of the larger Faith Movement teachings. This modern theology has roots in theological ideas promulgated by Norman Vincent Peale's *The Power of Positive Thinking* (New York: Prentice-Hall, 1952) and Napoleon Hill's *Think and Grow Rich* (Greenwich, Conn.: Fawcett, 1961). Fred K. C. Price, pastor of Crenshaw Christian Center in Los Angeles published one of the defining books on this theology in 1992; Price, *Name It and Claim It: The Power of Positive Confession* (Tulsa: Harrison House, 1992). Also see Marla F. Frederick, *Between Sundays: Black Women and everyday Struggles of Faith,* (Berkeley: University of California Press, 2003), 147–153, for a discussion of how black church women have responded to this theology within a North Carolina locale.

5. I am not affirming the merit of these allegations by referring to them in the text. The women who spoke of them were adamant that they had no proof of the allegations. I have referred to these recollections to elaborate on influences on pastoral regard. I am intentionally leaving out the specifics of the alleged misconduct.

6. The Mothers Board at Calvary Baptist has less institutionalized power than the same group at Layton Temple COGIC. The pastor appoints women to the Board. They have responsibilities for providing prayer support, serving as wise elders to young women, and giving some assistance during the communion service.

7. Franklin, "The Safest Place," 265.

8. Renita J. Weems, "Reading Her Way through the Struggle: African American Women and the Bible," in *Stony the Road We Trod: African American Biblical Interpretation,* ed. Cain Hope Felder (Minneapolis: Fortress Press, 1991), 57–77.

9. Ibid., 62.

10. Ibid., 57.

11. Ibid., 58.

12. Ibid., 63.

13. The Reverend Henry Lyons was convicted in 1999 on charges of grand theft. He accepted a plea bargain for more than fifty federal charges against him;

they did not add additional time. His misappropriation of funds through deceptive business practices became public after a lengthy investigation, sparked by his wife's allegedly setting fire to a second residence he had purchased with a female business associate. Lyons resigned from his post as president of the convention in 1998. His sentence was a term of five and a half years and a multimillion-dollar restitution payment. He was released on November 30, 2003, having received a reduced sentence for good behavior. Bethel Metropolitan Baptist Church fired Lyons in December 2000. The church was without a pastor upon his release, and Lyons is hoping to pastor in St. Petersburg again. St. Petersburg (Fla.) *Times,* December 1, 2003, p. 1A. See St. Petersburg *Times* online at www.sptimes.com for a comprehensive chronicle of the Lyons indictment and trials from July 1997.

14. The research on black male disaffiliation is minimal. Some sociological studies provide demographic information on nonattendees. However, these statistics may pertain more to unchurched populations than those who have defected. Some scholars and clergy have taken forays into this arena through group interviews and other market research techniques. See Robert M. Franklin, "Reclaiming the Souls of Black Men: The Mission of African American Religious Institutions," paper presented at the One-Third of a Nation Conference, Howard University, Washington, D.C., April 1988. Jawanza Kunjufu found several reasons for the lack of male participation in churches in his interviews of seventy-five black men. Twenty-one items were identified, most of which are critiques of the institution and its culture. The top items were hypocrisy, ministers' large egos or dictatorial tendencies, teachings of submission and passivity, tithing, irrelevance, eurocentrism, the length of services, and the emotional levels of the church. Jawanza Kunjufu, *Adam! Where Are You? Why Most Black Men Don't Go to Church* (Chicago: African American Images, 1994), 56–71.

NOTES TO CHAPTER 3

1. See David de Vaus, "Workforce Participation and Sex Differences in Church Attendance," *Review of Religious Research* 25 (1984): 247–258; Edward H. Thompson Jr., "Beneath the Status Characteristic: Gender Variations in Religiousness," *Journal for the Scientific Study of Religion* 30 (1991): 381–394; Bradley R. Hertel, "Work, Family, and Faith: Recent Trends," in *Work, Family, and Religion in Contemporary Society,* ed. Nancy Tatom Ammerman and Wade Clark Roof (New York: Routledge, 1995), 81–122. In addition to the quantitative studies, Brenda Brasher presents an insightful examination of women's participation among Fundamentalists. In this tradition, which tends to have a strict gender divide, she argues that women create a separate sacred enclave to address their life experiences and to have an alternative sphere of power in the church. Brenda E. Brasher, *Godly Women: Fundamentalism and Female Power* (New Brunswick, N.J.: Rutgers University Press, 1998), 8–29, 165–182.

2. The acclaimed author of *The Color Purple* Alice Walker coined the term "womanist" to capture the strident, audacious, and inquisitive behavior of a black female who is perceived as mature beyond her years. "1. From womanish (Opp. of "girlish," i.e., frivolous, irresponsible, not serious.) A black feminist or feminist of color. From the black folk expression of mothers to female children. "You acting womanish," i.e., like a woman. Usually referring to outrageous, audacious, courageous or willful behavior. Wanting to know more and in greater depth than is considered "good" for one. Interested in grown-up doings. Acting grown up. Being grown up. Interchangeable with another black folk expression: "You are trying to be grown." Responsible. In Charge. Serious. 2. Also: A woman who loves other women, sexually and/or nonsexually. Appreciates and prefers women's culture, women's emotional flexibility (values tars as natural counter-balance of laughter) and women's strength. Sometimes loves individual men, sexually and/or nonsexually. Committed to survival and wholeness of entire people, male and female. Not a separatist, except periodically, for health. Traditionally universalist, as in: "Mamma, why are we brown, pink, and yellow, and our cousins are white, beige and black?" Ans.: "Well, you know the colored race is just like a flower garden, with every color flower represented." Traditionally capable, as in: "Mamma, I'm walking to Canada and I'm taking you and a bunch of other slaves with me." Reply: "It wouldn't be the first time." 3. Loves music. Loves dance. Loves the moon. Loves the Spirit. Loves love and food and roundness. Loves struggle. Loves the Folk. Loves herself. Regardless. 4. Womanist is to feminist as purple to lavender." See Alice Walker, *In Search of Our Mother's Gardens: Womanist Prose* (San Diego: Harcourt Brace Jovanovich, 1983), xi. The term has been appropriated by African American women scholars, clergy, and laywomen across various disciplines and professions as a ideological standpoint for their commitment to a holistic response to any manifestation of oppression that impacts black women in particular and humanity in general. These methodologies range from the traditional ones of their particular disciplines and vocations to the construction of new ones for critiquing and ameliorating the intersecting oppressions of race, class, sex, and heterosexism.

3. This list includes some of the texts and essays which have helped define a womanist approach to religion and theology. Jacquelyn Grant, "Black Theology and The Black Woman," in *Black Theology: A Documentary History, 1966– 1979,* ed. Gayraud Wilmore and James Cone (Maryknoll, N.Y.: Orbis Books, 1979), 418–433; Theressa Hoover, "Black Women and the Churches: Triple Jeopardy," in *Black Theology: A Documentary History, 1966–1979,* ed. Gayraud Wilmore and James Cone (Maryknoll, N.Y.: Orbis Books, 1979); Katie G. Cannon, *Black Womanist Ethics* (Atlanta: Scholars Press, 1988); Toinette M. Eugene, "Moral Values and Black Womanists," *Journal of Religious Thought* 44 (Winter–Fall 1988): 23–34; Jacquelyn Grant, *White Women's Christ, Black Women's Jesus: Feminist Christology and Womanist Response* (Atlanta: Scholars

Press, 1989); Emilie M. Townes, ed., *A Troubling in My Soul: Womanist Perspectives on Evil and Suffering* (Maryknoll, N.Y.: Orbis Books, 1993); Delores Williams, *Sisters in the Wilderness: The Challenge of Womanist God-Talk* (Maryknoll, N.Y.: Orbis Books, 1993); Kelly Brown Douglas, *The Black Christ* (Maryknoll, NY: Orbis Books, 1994); Cheryl Kirk-Duggan, *Exorcising Evil: A Womanist Perspective on the Spirituals* (Maryknoll, N.Y.: Orbis Books, 1997); Joanne Marie Terrell, *Power in the Blood: The Cross in the African American Experience* (Maryknoll, N.Y.: Orbis Books, 1998); Katie Geneva Cannon, *Katie's Canon: Womanism and the Soul of the Black Community* (New York: Continuum, 1995).

4. Delores Williams's use of "black church" is distinct from my use. She uses two terms to describe what I see captured by the one term. African American Denominational Churches is a reference to the visible, varied black congregations that do not have a unified foundation. The Black Church is the invisible Godforce of Black people that cannot be contained. It manifests as "the heart of hope in the black community's experience of oppression, survival struggle and its historic efforts toward complete liberate." Williams, *Sisters in the Wilderness*, 206–209.

5. Robert J. Taylor and Linda M. Chatters, "Church-based Informal Support among Elderly Blacks," *Gerontologist* 26, no. 6 (1986): 637–642.

6. The scriptural reference for this verse as quoted to me could not be found. It is possible the woman was paraphrasing it. It may be an allusion to Jesus' cursing the fig tree for not having borne fruit in Matthew 21:18–20.

7. This phrase is a partial quotation from Lena Horne: "Having been a Black woman, you learn not to depend on anything. You get into a habit of surviving." In Kesho Yvonne Scott, *Habit of Surviving: Black Women's Strategies for Life* (New York: Ballantine Books, 1991,) 2.

8. Williams, *Sisters in the Wilderness*, 1–7.

9. Ibid., 35.

10. Ibid., 206.

11. Ibid., 223.

12. Delores Williams provides an analysis of the intersections of religion and church and black mothers in African American literature (and music). She examines these portrayals in the writings of male and female authors. In contrast to male authors, who often denigrate black women's faith commitments, she argues, women writers have highlighted the personal perseverance of black women because of their faith commitment; religion as a source for community survival strategies; and how black women's religiosity exceeded the limits of Christian norms and institutional forms. Williams, *Sisters in the Wilderness*, 34–49.

13. Williams dismisses the idea of the black matriarch as an appropriate interpretation of the slave woman's position. While black women then and now have been perceived as strong, "it must be emphasized that strength is not necessarily synonymous with power. . . . The antebellum black mother had no real

power. The power above her and her family was the white antebellum slave master and his family. But it is perhaps not too farfetched to suggest that in their struggle to survive and nurture their own, many antebellum black mothers often had as their helpmate not the black man but black religion. The black man was the lowest in authority in the slave system. Hence, black mothers and nurturers depended upon their religion for psychological and emotional support. And black Christian religion became, after the Civil War, greatly dependent upon these black women for its form and sustenance." Williams, *Sisters in the Wilderness*, 39–40.

14. Cheryl Townsend Gilkes, "The Black Church as a Therapeutic Community: Suggested Areas for Research into the Black Religious Experience," *Journal of the Interdenominational Theological Center* 8, no. 1 (Fall 1980): 29–44.

15. Ibid., 32.
16. Ibid., 35.
17. Ibid., 38.
18. Ibid., 36.

NOTES TO CHAPTER 4

1. The dissemination of money to individuals has often been a function of deacons and the purpose of the benevolence offering in black congregations. The processes for determining the level of need and the amount to be distributed vary widely. At Calvary Baptist, one had to make a formal request or present a bill or evidence of financial need through a deacon. At Layton Temple, there was a similar process, but also a stronger likelihood that the financial need would be met immediately through the collection of an additional offering, if the request was made during a worship service. I observed this impromptu assistance on several occasions. On one occasion, the congregation responded financially to the need of a woman who had suddenly lost her mother and had to travel out of state for the funeral. The second time, it assisted a minister's family because the husband had been in a severe accident and would be out of work for several months.

2. Cornel West defines "nihilism" as a sense of despair and lack of opportunity and a sense of hopelessness about whether conditions will improve. He regards it as a pervasive and threatening force among African Americans that is having dire consequences within the community. *Race Matters* (Boston: Beacon Press, 1993), 14–15.

3. Robert Wuthnow, *Acts of Compassion* (Princeton: Princeton University Press, 1991), 7.

4. Ibid., 127.
5. Ibid., 127.

6. I first encountered this story in Cheryl Townsend Gilkes's "*If It Wasn't for the Women*": *Black Women's Experience and Womanist Culture in Church and*

Community (Maryknoll, N.Y.: Orbis Books, 2001), 87–88. Mrs. Mobley died in January 2003, in Chicago. She was eighty-one years old and still an advocate for justice. Two days before her death, she was scheduled to be in Atlanta to give a speech about her son's death as part of the closing ceremonies for the exhibit "Without Sanctuary: Lynching Photography in America," at the Martin Luther King Jr. National Historic Site. Her book, *Death of Innocence,* coauthored with Christopher Benson, is to be released by Random House in 2004. See Ana Mendieta, "Mamie Till Mobley, Mother of Lynched Teen," *Chicago Sun Times,* January 9, 2003; www.suntimes.com/output/obituaries/cst-nws-xmob09.html; Adam Bernstein, "Mamie Till-Mobley; Civil Rights Figure," *Washington Post,* January 8, 2003, B06.

NOTES TO CHAPTER 5

1. Several studies that examine the status and inclusion of women clergy at the end of the twentieth century are Barbara Brown Zikmund, Adair T. Lummis, and Patricia M. Y. Chang, *Clergy Women: An Uphill Calling* (Louisville: Westminster John Knox Press, 1998); Frederick W. Schmidt, *A Still Small Voice: Women, Ordination and the Church* (New York: Syracuse University Press, 1996); Rita J. Simon and Pamela S. Nadell, *Women Who Would Be Rabbis: A History of Women's Ordination, 1889–1985* (Boston: Beacon Press, 1998); Janet R. Marder, "Are Women Changing the Rabbinate? A Reformed Perspective," *Religious Institutions and Women's Leadership: New Roles inside the Mainstream,* ed. Catherine Wessinger (Columbia: University of South Carolina Press, 1996), 271–290; Delores Carpenter, *A Time for Honor: A Portrait of African American Clergywomen* (St. Louis: Chalice Press, 2001).

2. For recent figures on ordination in mainline and some black denominations see Mark Chaves, *Ordaining Women* (Cambridge, Mass.: Harvard University Press, 1997) 16–18. This text also is a study of the factors within each denomination that served as an impetus for change.

3. A partial list of current research on the status of women clergy and the distinctive attributes of their ministry includes Edward C. Lehman, *Women Clergy: Breaking through Gender Barriers* (New Brunswick, N.J.: Transaction Books, 1985); Elaine J. Lawless, *Holy Women, Wholly Women: Sharing Ministries of Wholeness through Life Stories and Reciprocal Ethnography* (Philadelphia: University of Pennsylvania Press, 1993); Paula Nesbitt, *Feminization of the Clergy in America: Occupational and Organizational Perspectives* (New York: Oxford University Press, 1977); Jualynne E. Dodson, "Women's Ministries and the African Methodist Episcopal Tradition," *Religious Institutions and Women's Leadership: New Roles inside the Mainstream,* ed. Catherine Wessinger (Columbia: University of South Carolina Press, 1996), 124–138; Jackson Carroll, Barbara Hargrove, and Adair T. Lummis, *Women of the Cloth: A New Opportunity*

for Churches (San Francisco: Harper and Row, 1982); Sally B. Purvis, *The Stained Glass Ceiling: Churches and Their Women Pastors* (Louisville: Westminster John Knox Press, 1995).

4. Ordination of women is sanctioned in six of the seven largest denominations of the Black Church. Of the seven largest bodies that make up the Black Church (as defined in this research), the Church of God in Christ formally denies ordination to women.

5. Members of these two denominations reported the exclusion of women from the business meetings. Several women presently in the COGIC church also remember this dynamic from their younger years.

6. A coordinating council is a group that functions primarily as a board of directors for the Baptist church. The pastor officiates at the meetings. The council is composed of all deacons, trustees, heads of other ministries, and at-large church members who are selected by the pastor.

7. It is always hard to determine who is or is not a tither, even with superior church records. In most churches, gross and net salaries are not known. As noted in chapter 1, the level of giving can indicate a tithe; for example, those persons who earn a household income of $20,000 would normatively tithe $2,000 to the church. Otherwise, their contributions to their church would not reflect the traditional 10 percent donation that is preached in both congregations. Eleven reported donations of $2,400 or more, seven reported giving levels of $100–$599 and $1,800–$2,399. Five gave in the $600–$1,199 range.

8. The title of Associate Minister has various meanings. It can be a compensated position or an honorific title. It may refer to an individual who has a specific area of ministerial responsibility in the congregation. Probably its most common use is to refer to a preacher who is affiliated with this congregation and who is submitting herself or himself to the tutelage of the pastor. Such an arrangement affords the associate opportunities to preach, lead worship, assist in the ordinances of the church, and have the ecclesiastical endorsement of a local congregation to preach in the wider religious community. This person may or may not be ordained.

9. Cheryl Sanders, Saints *in Exile: The Holiness-Pentecostal Experience in African American Religion and Culture* (New York: Oxford University Press, 1996).

10. Black women were in the vanguard of the development of state and national Baptist bodies. However, their radicalism was tempered by a resident conservatism that was manifest in their disdain for the public displays of immorality on the part of blacks. It was also evident in their reluctance to agitate for inclusion of women in the clergy. "While the female leaders of the black Baptist church sought to broaden women's job opportunities and religious responsibilities, they revealed their conservatism in their unquestioning acceptance of man's sole right to the clergy." Evelyn Brooks Higginbotham, *Righteous Discontent:*

The Women's Movement in the Black Baptist Church, 1880–1920 (Cambridge, Mass.: Harvard University Press, 1993), 15. At the 2002 National Baptist Convention USA, Inc., in Philadelphia, there was a silent protest on the part of clergy women to bring attention to the denominations ban against women ministers. See Jim Remsen, "Women Take a Stand at Baptist Gathering," *Philadelphia Inquirer,* September 5, 2002, www.philly.com/mld/inquirer.

11. Mattie McGolothen, ed., *Women's Handbook, Newly Revised Edition of Organization and Procedure* (Memphis: Church of God in Christ Publishing House, 1980), 20–22.

12. Cheryl Townsend Gilkes, "The Storm and the Light: Church, Family, Work, and Social Crisis in the African-American Experience," in *Work, Family, and Religion in Contemporary Society,* ed. Nancy Tatom Ammerman and Wade Clark Roof (New York: Routledge, 1995), 190.

13. The structure and power of the Deaconess board varies throughout the Black Church. It can range from being the equivalent of a Mothers Board, made up of women elders with spiritual maturity, to being the domain of only those women who are married to deacons. In some cases, although visually distinct because of their uniforms, deaconess have the same duties as deacons and are referred to as the diaconate ministry/board.

14. The clergy surveyed by C. Eric Lincoln and Lawrence Mamiya, *The Black Church in the African American Experience* (Durham: Duke University Press, 1990), 289–301, who opposed females preaching legitimated their stance by use of the Bible. Sometimes they used it as a thin veil for roles they accepted as normative, for example, "They do not have any business preaching. She has no voice. If she has any questions, let her ask her husband at home"; "In order to pastor, one must be blameless and the husband of one wife, that's what the Bible says, and there is no way a woman can be the husband of one wife. I don't care what kind of operation she has"; "Women have been preaching for years but not identified as preachers. That role, pastor, has not been distinguished for her. As one within, I could not accept a woman pastor—a masculine role"; "The responsibility of the pastor is too strenuous for women. The pastor is on call twenty-four hours a day but there are certainly times when women are incapacitated, e.g., during pregnancy, during times of menstrual cycle. However, I feel a woman can be an evangelist. Deacons must do dirty work—How can you expect a woman to do such? She loses her femininity, and it diminishes her womanhood."

15. The less-than-full approval of women clergy among the women clergy in the study was an unexpected finding. One possible explanation for it is that the female clergy who took an oppositional stance accepted pastorates reluctantly after the death of their spouse. An alternate explanation is that their attitudes may reflect the official policies of their denominations against ordaining women as pastors. Lincoln and Mamiya, *The Black Church,* 290–291.

16. See chapter 10 for a further discussion of the views of clergy on the ordination of women. The Baptist and the Pentecostal clergy voiced the strongest disapproval, while the Methodist clerics expressed the strongest approval. Of the National Baptist USA, Inc., clergy, 73.6 percent disapproved of women preachers; of clergy in The Church of God in Christ, 73.4 percent approved. Lincoln and Mamiya, *The Black Church*, 292.

17. Cheryl Townsend Gilkes, "The Roles of Church and Community Mothers: Ambivalent American Sexism or Fragmented African Familyhood," *Journal of Feminist Studies in Religion* 2 (Spring 1986): 41–59, 55.

18. Ibid., 55.

NOTES TO CHAPTER 6

1. Gayraud Wilmore, *Black Religion and Black Radicalism: An Interpretation of the Religious History of Afro-American People*, 3rd ed. (Maryknoll, N.Y.: Orbis Books, 1998); John Hope Franklin, *From Slavery to Freedom* (New York: Knopf, 1994).

2. Patricia Gurin, Arthur H. Miller, and Gerald Gurin, "Stratum Identification and Consciousness," *Social Psychology Quarterly* 43(1) (1980): 30–47.

3. G. Christopher Ellison and Darren E. Sherkat, "The Semi-Involuntary Institution Revisited: Regional Variations in Church Participation among Black Americans," *Social Forces* 73 (1995): 1415–1437.

4. Dr. Maulana Karenga, professor and chair of the Department of Black Studies at California State University, Long Beach, created Kwanzaa in 1966. He is an author and scholar-activist who stresses the indispensable need to preserve, continually revitalize, and promote African American culture. Kwanzaa is a cultural holiday, not a religious one, observed by persons of African descent worldwide, during which African Americans celebrate and reaffirm their cultural roots and principles. The name comes from the Swahili word for "first fruits." Kwanzaa is observed from December 26 through January 1 and is based on seven guiding principles called the Nguzo Saba. A different principle is observed each day. See the website www.officialkwanzaawebsite/org.origins1.html

5. Peter Paris, *The Social Teaching of the Black Churches* (Philadelphia: Fortress Press, 1985), 10.

6. Elllison and Sherkat, "The Semi-Involuntary Institution Revisited"; G. Christopher Ellison and Darren Sherkat, "Identifying the Semi-Involuntary Institution: A Clarification," *Social Forces* 78(2) (December 1999): 793–800.

7. Ellison and Sherkat, "Identifying the Semi-Involuntary Institution: A Clarification," 794.

NOTES TO CHAPTER 7

1. Brenda E. Brasher, *Godly Women: Fundamentalism and Female Power* (New Brunswick, N.J.: Rutgers University Press, 1998); N. Lynne Westfield, *Dear Sisters: A Womanist Practice of Hospitality* (Cleveland: Pilgrim Press, 2001).

2. Kelly Brown Douglas, *Sexuality and the Black Church: A Womanist Perspective* (Maryknoll, N.Y.: Orbis Books, 1999).

3. Marla F. Frederick, *Between Sundays: Black Women and Everyday Struggles of Faith* (Berkeley: University of California Press, 2003), 197–198.

4. See chapter 3, note 2, for the complete definition of womanist by Alice Walker.

5. Evelyn Brooks Higginbotham, *Righteous Discontent: The Women's Movement in the Black Baptist Church, 1880–1920* (Cambridge, Mass.: Harvard University Press, 1993), 120–149.

6. JoAnne Marie Terrell, *Power in the Blood? The Cross in the African American Experience* (Maryknoll, N.Y.: Orbis Books, 1998), 144.

7. I have cited many of the seminal works in womanist thought in chapter 3, note 3. For a concise volume on womanist thought, see Stephanie Y. Mitchem, *Introducing Womanist Theology* (Maryknoll, N.Y.: Orbis Books, 2002).

8. Katie G. Cannon broke new ground by expanding the corpus of sources for constructive ethics to include the black women's literary canon. She argued that "the Black woman's literary tradition has not previously been used to interpret and explain the community's socio-cultural patterns from which ethical values can be gleaned. In doing so, I have found that this literary tradition is the nexus between the real-lived texture of Black life and the oral-aural cultural values implicitly passed on and received from one generation to the next." Katie G. Cannon, *Black Womanist Ethics* (Atlanta: American Academy of Religion, 1988), 5. Emilie M. Townes further develops this methodological shift by using black women's biographies and autobiographies as sources for ethical reflection. Emilie M. Townes, *Womanist Justice, Womanist Hope* (Atlanta: American Academy of Religion, 1993), 17–39; Theresa Frye, *God Don't Like Ugly: African American Women Handing on Spiritual Values* (Nashville: Abingdon Press, 2000), 65–79.

9. Jacquelyn Grant, *White Women's Christ, Black Women's Jesus: Feminist Christology and Womanist Response* (Atlanta: Scholars Press, 1989), 205.

10. Jacquelyn Grant, "Black Theology and the Black Woman," in *Black Theology: A Documentary History, 1966–1979*, ed. Gayraud S. Wilmore and James H. Cone (Maryknoll, N.Y.: Orbis Books, 1979), 423.

11. Frances E. Wood, "Take My Yoke upon You: The Role of the Church in the Oppression of African-American Women," in *A Troubling in My Soul:*

Womanist Perspectives on Evil and Suffering, ed. Emilie M. Townes (Maryknoll, N.Y.: Orbis Books, 1993), 37–47, 42.

12. Teresa Brown, *God Don't Like Ugly,* 170.

13. Ibid., 171.

14. My comments are based on the cassette version of this sermon. Tapes were available for purchase from the church. I was not present at the actual service, which was preached in 1998. The pastor of the church is the Reverend Zan Holmes. This was her second year as the revivalist for St. Luke's, according to the tape.

15. Katie G. Cannon, "Hitting a Straight Lick with a Crooked Stick: The Womanist Dilemma in the Development of a Black Liberation Ethic," in *Black Theology: A Documentary History, Vol. 2: 1890–1992,* ed. James H. Cone and Gayraud S. Wilmore (Maryknoll, N.Y.: Orbis Books, 1993), 305.

16. Anthony B. Pinn, *The Black Church in the Post–Civil Rights Era* (Maryknoll, N.Y.: Orbis Books, 2002), 121.

17. Brown, *God Don't Like Ugly,* 58.

18. Ibid., 177.

19. Mark Chaves found three interlocking dynamics that determine how denominations have responded to ordaining women. They are the disjuncture between the timing of organizational policy changes and trends in the numbers of women actually seeking clergy status; the historical and contemporary evidence that, in denominations with restrictive rules, women still perform many of the same functions as men; and evidence that, in denominations with formal gender equality, women face many obstacles that prevent the attainment of real parity with male clergy. The resulting phenomenon is what he calls "loose coupling." Mark Chaves, *Ordaining Women* (Cambridge, Mass.: Harvard University Press, 1997), 15.

NOTES TO APPENDIX I

1. Nancy Tatom Ammerman, *Congregation and Community* (New Brunswick, N.J.: Rutgers University Press, 1996).

2. Barbara Mostyn, "The Content Analysis of Qualitative Research Data: A Dynamic Approach," in *The Research Interview: Uses and Approaches,* ed. Michael Brenner, Jennifer Brown, and David Canter (Orlando: Academic Press, 1985), 115–145.

Bibliography

Bernstein, Adam. "Mamie Till-Mobley; Civil Rights Figure." *Washington Post,* January 8, 2003, B06.

Biema, David Van. "Spirit Raiser." *Time* 158, no. 11, September 17, 2001.

Blassingame, John S. *The Slave Community.* New York: Oxford University Press, 1972.

Brasher, Brenda E. *Godly Women: Fundamentalism and Female Power.* New Brunswick, N.J.: Rutgers University Press, 1998.

Brown, Teresa L. Fry. *God Don't Like Ugly: African American Women Handing on Spiritual Values.* Nashville: Abingdon Press, 2000.

Cannon, Katie Geneva. "Hitting a Straight Lick with a Crooked Stick: The Womanist Dilemma in the Development of a Black Liberation Ethic." In *Black Theology: A Documentary History, Vol. 2: 1890–1992.* Ed. James H. Cone and Gayraud S. Wilmore. Maryknoll, N.Y.: Orbis Books, 1993.

———. *Black Womanist Ethics.* Atlanta: Scholars Press, 1988.

———. *Katie's Canon: Womanism and the Soul of the Black Community.* New York: Continuum, 1995.

Chaves, Mark. *Ordaining Women.* Cambridge, Mass.: Harvard University Press, 1997.

De Vaus, David. "Workforce Participation and Sex Differences in Church Attendance." *Review of Religious Research* 25 (1984): 247–258.

De Vaus, David, and Ian McAllister. "Gender Differences in Religion: A Test of the Structural Location Theory." *American Sociological Review* 52 (August 1987): 472–484.

Dodson, Jualynne E. "Women's Ministries and the African Methodist Episcopal Tradition." In *Religious Institutions and Women's Leadership: New Roles inside the Mainstream.* Ed. Catherine Wessinger. Columbia: University of South Carolina Press, 1996, 124–138.

Douglas, Ann. *The Feminization of American Culture.* New York: Knopf, 1977.

Douglas, Kelly Brown. *The Black Christ.* Maryknoll, N.Y.: Orbis Books, 1993.

———. *Sexuality and the Black Church: A Womanist Perspective.* Maryknoll, N.Y.: Orbis Books, 1999.

Du Bois, W. E. B. *The Souls of Black Folk.* 1903. Reprint, New York: Fawcett, 1961.

———, ed. *The Negro Church.* Atlanta: Atlanta University Press, 1903.

Ellison, G. Christopher, and Darren Sherkat. "Identifying the Semi-Involuntary Institution: A Clarification." *Social Forces* 78 (1999): 793–800.

———. "'The Semi-Involuntary Institution' Revisited: Regional Variations in Church Participation among Black Americans." *Social Forces* 73 (1995): 1415–1437.

Felder, Cain Hope, ed. *Stony the Road We Trod: African American Biblical Interpretation.* Minneapolis: Fortress Press, 1991.

Franklin, Robert M. "The Safest Place on Earth: The Culture of Black Congregations." In *American Congregations: New Perspectives in the Study of Congregations,* ed. James P. Wind and James W. Lewis, vol. 2. Chicago: University of Chicago Press, 1994.

———. "Reclaiming the Souls of Black Men: The Mission of African American Religious Institutions." Unpublished paper presented at the One-Third of a Nation Conference, Howard University, Washington, D.C., April 1988.

Frederick, Marla L. *Between Sundays: Black Women and Everyday Struggles of Faith.* Berkeley: University of California Press, 2003.

Gilkes, Cheryl Townsend. *"If It Wasn't for the Women": Black Women's Experience and Womanist Culture in Church and Community.* Maryknoll, N.Y.: Orbis Books, 2001.

———. "The Storm and the Light: Church, Family, Work, and Social Crisis in the African-American Experience." In *Work, Family, and Religion in Contemporary Society.* Ed. Nancy Tatom Ammerman and Wade Clark Roof. New York: Routledge, 1995, 177–198.

———. "The Roles of Church and Community Mothers: Ambivalent American Sexism or Fragmented African Familyhood." *Journal of Feminist Studies in Religion* 2 (Spring 1986): 41–59.

———. "Together and in Harness: Women's Traditions in the Sanctified Church." *Signs* 10 (Summer 1985): 678–699.

———. "The Black Church as a Therapeutic Community: Suggested Areas for Research into the Black Religious Experience." *Journal of the Interdenominational Theological Center* 8, no. 1 (Fall 1980): 29–44.

Glaser, Barney G., and Anselem L. Straus. *The Discovery of Grounded Theory: Strategies for Qualitative Research.* Chicago: Aldine, 1967.

Grant, Jacquelyn. *White Women's Christ, Black Women's Jesus: Feminist Christology and Womanist Response.* Atlanta: Scholars Press, 1989.

———. "Black Theology and the Black Woman." In *Black Theology: A Documentary History, 1966–1979.* Ed. Gayraud S. Wilmore and James H. Cone. Maryknoll, N.Y.: Orbis Books, 1979, 418–433.

Gurin, Patricia, Arthur H. Miller, and Gerald Gurin. "Stratum Identification and Consciousness." *Social Psychology Quarterly* 4 (1980): 30–47.

Gusfield, Joseph R. *Community: A Critical Response.* New York: Harper and Row, 1975.

Hertel, Bradley R. "Work, Family, and Faith: Recent Trends." In *Work, Family, and Religion in Contemporary Society.* Ed. Nancy Tatom Ammerman and Wade Clark Roof. New York: Routledge 1999, 81–122.

Higginbotham, Evelyn Brooks. *Righteous Discontent: The Women's Movement in the Black Baptist Church, 1880–1920.* Cambridge, Mass.: Harvard University Press, 1993.

James, Janet Wilson. *Women in American Religion.* Philadelphia: University of Pennsylvania Press, 1980.

Janssen, Al, and Larry K. Weeden, eds., *Seven Promises of a Promise Keeper.* Colorado Springs, Colo.: Focus on the Family, 1994.

Kunjufu, Jawanza. *Adam! Where Are You? Why Most Black Men Don't Go to Church.* Chicago: African American Images, 1994.

Lincoln, C. Eric, and Lawrence Mamiya. *The Black Church in the African-American Experience.* Durham: Duke University Press, 1990.

McGolothen, Mattie, ed. *Women's Handbook, Newly Revised Edition of Organization and Procedure.* Memphis: Church of God in Christ Publishing House, 1980.

Mendieta, Ana. "Mamie Till Mobley, Mother of Lynched Teen." *Chicago Sun Times,* January 9, 2003; www.suntimes.com/output/obituaries/cst-nws-xmob 09.html.

Mitchem, Stephanie Y. *Introducing Womanist Theology.* Maryknoll, N.Y.: Orbis Books, 2002.

Moran, Gerald F. "Sisters in Christ." In *Women in American Religion.* Ed. Janet Wilson James. Philadelphia: University of Pennsylvania Press, 1976, 47–66.

Morris, Aldon D. *The Origins of the Civil Rights Movement: Black Communities Organizing for Change.* New York: Free Press, 1984.

Nelsen, Hart M. "Unchurched Black Americans: Patterns of Religiosity and Affiliation." *Review of Religious Research* 29 (June 1988): 398–412.

Paris, Peter. *The Social Teaching of the Black Churches.* Philadelphia: Fortress Press, 1985.

Pinn, Anthony B. *The Black Church in the Post–Civil Rights Era.* Maryknoll, N.Y.: Orbis Books, 2002.

Reinharz, Shulamit. *Feminist Methods in Social Research.* New York: Oxford University Press, 1992.

Remsen, Jim. "Women Take a Stand at Baptist Gathering." *Philadelphia Inquirer,* September 5, 2002; www.philly.com/mld/inquirer.

Riggs, Marcia. *Awake, Arise, and Act: A Womanist Call for Black Liberation.* Cleveland: Pilgrim Press, 1994.

Scott, Kesho Yvonne. *The Habit of Surviving: Black Women's Strategies for Life.* New York: Ballantine Books, 1991.

Sernett, Milton C., ed. *Afro-American Religious History: A Documentary Witness.* Durham: Duke University Press, 1985.

Smith, Wallace Charles. *The Church in the Life of the Black Family.* Valley Forge: Judson Press, 1985.

St. Petersburg Times, December 1, 2003, 1A.

Taylor, Robert J., and Linda M. Chatters. "Church-based Informal Support among Elderly Blacks." *Gerontologist* 26, no. 6 (1986): 637–642.

Townes, Emilie M. *In a Blaze of Glory: Womanist Spirituality as Social Witness.* Nashville: Abingdon Press, 1995.

———. *Womanist Justice, Womanist Hope.* Atlanta: American Academy of Religion, 1993.

Walker, Alice. *In Search of Our Mother's Gardens: Womanist Prose.* San Diego: Harcourt Brace Jovanovich, 1983.

Weems, Renita J. "Reading Her Way through the Struggle: African American Women and the Bible." In *Stony the Road We Trod: African American Biblical Interpretation.* Ed. Cain Hope Felder. Minneapolis: Fortress Press, 1991, 57–77.

Wessinger, Catherine, ed. *Religious Institutions and Women's Leadership: New Roles inside the Mainstream.* Columbia: University of South Carolina Press, 1996.

West, Cornel. *Race Matters.* New York: Vintage Books, 1994.

Westfield, N. Lynne. *Dear Sisters: A Womanist Practice of Hospitality.* Cleveland: Pilgrim Press, 2001.

Wiggins, Daphne C. "African Americans, Gender and Religiosity." In *Culture and Difference: Critical Perspectives on the Bicultural Experience in the United States.* Ed. Antonio Darder. Westport, Conn.: Bergin and Garvey, 1995, 169–184.

Williams, Delores. *Sisters in the Wilderness: The Challenge of Womanist God-Talk.* Maryknoll, N.Y.: Orbis Books, 1993.

Wilmore, Gayraud. *Black Religion and Black Radicalism: An Interpretation of the Religious History of Afro-American People.* 3rd ed. Maryknoll, N.Y.: Orbis Books, 1998.

Wilmore, Gayraud S., and James H. Cone, eds. *Black Theology: A Documentary History, 1966–1979.* Maryknoll, N.Y.: Orbis Books, 1979.

Wood, Frances E. "Take My Yoke upon You: The Role of the Church in the Oppression of African-American Women." In *A Troubling in My Soul: Womanist Perspectives on Evil and Suffering.* Ed. Emilie M. Townes. Maryknoll, N.Y.: Orbis Books, 1993, 37–47.

Wuthnow, Robert. *Acts of Compassion: Caring for Others and Helping Ourselves.* Princeton: Princeton University Press, 1991.

SUPPLEMENTAL BIBLIOGRAPHY

Ammerman, Nancy Tatom. *Congregation and Community.* New Brunswick, N.J.: Rutgers University Press, 1997.

Ammerman, Nancy Tatom, and Wade Clark Roof. *Work, Family, and Religion in Contemporary Society.* New York: Routledge, 1995.

Billingsley, Andrew. *Mighty like a River: The Black Church and Social Reform.* New York: Oxford University Press, 1999.

Carpenter, Delores. *A Time for Honor: A Portrait of African American Clergywomen.* St. Louis: Chalice Press, 2001.

Carroll, Jackson, Barbara Hargrove, and Adair T. Lummis. *Women of the Cloth: A New Opportunity for Churches.* San Francisco: Harper and Row, 1982.

Childs, John Brown. *The Political Black Minister: A Study in Afro-American Politics and Religion.* Boston: G. K. Hall, 1980.

Cornwall, Marie. "The Social Bases of Religion: A Study of Factors Influencing Religious Belief and Commitment." *Review of Religious Research* 29, no. 1 (September 1987): 44–56.

Darder, Antonio, ed. *Culture and Difference: Critical Perspectives on the Bicultural Experience in the United States.* Westport, Conn.: Bergin and Garvey, 1995.

Du Bois, W. E. B., and Monroe N. Work. "The Negro Ministry in the Middle West." In *The Negro Church.* Ed. W. E. B. Du Bois. Atlanta: Atlanta University Press, 1903.

Eugene, Toinette M. "Moral Values and Black Womanists." *Journal of Religious Thought* 44 (Winter–Fall 1988): 23–34.

Ellison, Christopher G. "Identification and Separatism: Religious Involvement and Racial Orientations among Black Americans," *Sociological Quarterly* 32 (1991): 477–494.

Felety, K., and M. Poloma, "From Sex Differences to Gender Role Beliefs: Exploring Effects on Six Dimensions of Religiosity," *Sex Roles* 25 (1991): 181–193.

Fitcher, Joseph H. *Social Relations in the Urban Parish.* Chicago: University of Chicago Press, 1954.

———. *Southern Parish.* Chicago: University of Chicago Press, 1951.

Franklin, John Hope. *From Slavery to Freedom: A History of African Americans.* New York: Knopf, 1994.

Gayles, Gloria Wade, ed. *My Soul Is a Witness: African-American Women's Spirituality.* Boston: Beacon Press, 1995.

Gee, Ellen M. "Gender Differences in Church Attendance in Canada." *Review of Religious Research* 32 (March 1991): 267–272.

Hill, Napoleon. *Think and Grow Rich.* Greenwich, Conn.: Fawcett, 1961.

Hoover, Theressa. "Black Women and the Churches: Triple Jeopardy." In *Black*

Theology: A Documentary History, 1966–1979. Ed. Gayraud Wilmore and James Cone. Maryknoll, N.Y.: Orbis Books, 1979.

Johnstone, Ronald L. "Negro Preachers Take Sides." *Review of Religious Research* 11 (Fall 1969): 81–89.

Kirk-Duggan, Cheryl. *Exorcising Evil: A Womanist Perspective on the Spirituals.* Maryknoll, N.Y.: Orbis Books, 1997.

Lawless, Elaine J. *Holy Women, Wholly Women: Sharing Ministries of Wholeness through Life Stories and Reciprocal Ethnography.* Philadelphia: University of Pennsylvania Press, 1993.

Lehman, Edward C. *Women Clergy: Breaking through Gender Barriers.* New Brunswick, N.J.: Transaction Books, 1985.

Marder, Janet R. "Are Women Changing the Rabbinate? A Reformed Perspective." In *Religious Institutions and Women's Leadership: New Rules inside the Mainstream.* Ed. Catherine Wessinger. Columbia: University of South Carolina Press, 1996, 271–290.

Marx, Gary. *Protest and Prejudice: A Study of Black Belief in the Black Community.* San Francisco: Harper, 1967.

Mays, Benjamin E., and Joseph W. Nicholson, "The Genius of the Negro Church." In *Afro-American Religious History: A Documentary Witness.* Ed. Milton Sernett. Durham: Duke University Press, 1985, 337–348.

Montgomery, William E. *Under Their Own Vine and Fig Tree: The African-American Church in the South, 1865–1900.* Baton Rouge: Louisiana State University Press, 1993.

Morris, Aldon. *The Origins of the Civil Rights Movement: Black Communities Organizing for Change.* New York: Free Press. 1984.

Mostyn, Barbara. "The Content Analysis of Qualitative Research Data: A Dynamic Approach." In *The Research Interview: Uses and Approaches.* Ed. Michael Brenner, Jennifer Brown, and David Canter. Orlando: Academic Press, 1985, 115–145.

Nelsen, Hart M., and Anne K. Nelsen, *The Black Church in the Sixties.* Lexington: University of Kentucky Press, 1975.

Nesbitt, Paula. *Feminization of the Clergy in America: Occupational and Organizational Perspectives.* New York: Oxford University Press, 1977.

Peale, Norman Vincent. *The Power of Positive Thinking.* New York: Prentice-Hall, 1952.

Price, Fred K. C. *Name It and Claim It: The Power of Positive Confession.* Tulsa: Harrison House, 1992.

Purvis, Sally B. *The Stained Glass Ceiling: Churches and Their Women Pastors.* Louisville: Westminster John Knox Press, 1995.

Sanders, Cheryl. *Saints in Exile: The Holiness-Pentecostal Experience in African American Religion and Culture.* New York: Oxford University Press, 1996.

Schmidt, Frederick W. *A Still Small Voice: Women, Ordination and the Church.* New York: Syracuse University Press, 1996.

Sherkat, Darren, and Christopher Ellison. "Identification and Separatism: Religious Involvement and Racial Orientations among Black Americans." *Sociological Quarterly* 32 (1991): 477–494.

Simon, Rita J., and Pamela S. Nadell. *Women Who Would Be Rabbis: A History of Women's Ordination, 1889–1985.* Boston: Beacon Press, 1998.

Stanton, Elizabeth Cady, et al. *The Woman's Bible.* Seattle: Coalition Task Force on Women and Religion, 1895. Reprint, New York: Arno Press, 1974.

Taylor, Clarence. *The Black Churches of Brooklyn.* New York: Columbia University Press, 1994.

Taylor, Robert J. "Correlates of Religious Non-Involvement among Black Americans." *Review of Religious Research* 29 (December 1988): 126–139.

———. "Structural Determinants of Religious Participation among Black Americans." *Review of Religious Research* 30 (December 1988): 114–125.

Terrell, JoAnne Marie. *Power in the Blood: The Cross in the African American Experience.* Maryknoll, N.Y.: Orbis Books, 1998.

Thompson, Edward H., Jr. "Beneath the Status Characteristic: Gender Variations in Religiousness." *Journal for the Scientific Study of Religion* 30 (1991): 381–394.

Townes, Emilie M. *A Troubling in My Soul: Womanist Perspectives on Evil and Suffering.* Maryknoll, N.Y.: Orbis Books, 1993.

Weisenfeld, Judith. *African American Women and Christian Activism: New York's Black YWCA, 1905–1945.* Cambridge, Mass.: Harvard University Press, 1997.

———. *This Far by Faith: Readings in African-American Women's Religious Biography.* New York: Routledge, 1996.

Wheeler, Edward L. *Uplifting the Race: The Black Minister in the New South, 1865–1902.* Lanham, Md.: University Press of America, 1986.

Zikmund, Barbara Brown, Adair T. Lummis, and Patricia M. Y. Chang. *Clergy Women: An Uphill Calling.* Louisville: Westminster John Knox Press, 1998.

Index

AIDS: need for response, 103; silence of the church, 68

Bible: in preaching, 48–51; regard for, 61–62, 178; womanist views of, 175; women's ability to interpret, 54

Black Church: characteristics of, 2–3; definition, 2, 203n. 1; distinctions from white Protestants, 1; as female enclave, 30; images of, 96–99; non-punitive, 88–89, 90; a political organ, 100–102; scholarship, 6, 204n. 8; semi-involuntary institution, 164–165; as surrogate family, 42–45, 63–64, 97; voices competing with, 64, 95, 182; and volunteerism, 107–109

Black Church in the African American Experience, The (Lincoln and Mamiya), 29

Black men: absent from church, 30–31; heightened interest in, 7; as role models, 27

Black women: acts of resistance, 114–115, 121–122; church loyalty, 165–167; community involvement, 108–111; description of sample, 3–4, 17, 194; disregard for, 6; in leadership roles 118; Mamie Till Mobley, 110; as role models, 27

Blassingame, John, 86

Brasher, Brenda, 172

Brown, Teresa L. Fry, 182–184; *God Don't Like Ugly*, 176; Sisters Working Encouraging Empowering Together (S.W.E.E.T), 179–180

Calvary Baptist Church: missionary efforts 109; profile, 32–35;

Cannon, Katie G., 176, 181, 217n. 8

Chatters, Linda M., 69–70

Clergy, female: building alliances with, 184; consciousness raising among women, 182–184; cultural obstacles, 133–136; exposure to, 119–121; Cheryl Gilkes, 112–113; interpretation of a "calling," 131–132, 136; loose coupling, 184; opposition by women, 126–130; opposition within the Black Church, 138; ordination, 218n. 2; recent scholarship, 112, 218n. 1, 218n. 3; support by lay women, 122–126

Community: definition, 16; detachment from, 45–47; norms of attendance, 27–29; outreach to, 104–106

About the Author

Daphne C. Wiggins, Ph.D., is the Associate Pastor and Coordinator of Congregational Ministries at Union Baptist Church, in Durham, North Carolina. Formerly she was Assistant Professor of Religion at Texas Christian University and Assistant Professor of Congregational Studies at the Divinity School at Duke University. Her present position is a fertile context for the integration of her scholarly interests with the tasks of congregational ministry.